SO-ACB-196

SONGS
OF THE CIVIL WAR

COMPILED AND EDITED BY
IRWIN SILBER

Music Arrangements by
Jerry Silverman

DOVER PUBLICATIONS, INC.
New York

In placing a copyright notice on this book and its contents, I want to make it abundantly clear that I am in no way attempting to claim ownership of any of the songs which appear on these pages. With the exception of a few songs bearing the copyright imprints of their publishers, the songs in this collection are in the public domain. In a few cases, I have made slight alterations either in the texts or in the tunes, or both, but these do not constitute the kind of major creative additions which would make a copyright claim morally justifiable. These songs are a priceless part of our national heritage and can no more be re-moved from the public domain than the flag, the Constitution, or any other symbol of our existence as a nation and a people. On the other hand, the piano and guitar arrangements made for these songs do constitute substantial creative work and, as such, are protected by the copyright on this book. Those who may want to use any of these arrangements will find no difficulty in receiving permission upon application to the editor, in care of Dover Publications, Inc. It is hoped that these arrangements will prove useful and rewarding.

I.S.

Bibliographical Note

This Dover edition, first published in 1995, is an unabridged and unaltered republication of the work first published by Columbia University Press, New York, 1960. Irwin Silber has written a new Preface to the Dover Edition.

Library of Congress Cataloging-in-Publication Data

Songs of the Civil War / compiled and edited by Irwin Silber ; music arrangements by Jerry Silverman.
    1 score.
    Piano acc.; includes chord symbols.
    Reprint. Originally published: New York : Columbia University Press, 1960.
    Includes bibliographical references and indexes.
    ISBN 0-486-28438-7
    1. United States—History—Civil War, 1861–1865—Songs and music. 2. War songs—United States. 3. Popular music—United States—To 1901. I. Silber, Irwin, 1925– . II. Silverman, Jerry.
M1637.S66 1995   94-23601
                                                              CIP
                                                                 M

Manufactured in the United States of America
Dover Publications, Inc., 31 East 2nd Street, Mineola, N.Y. 11501

To Sylvia

Acknowledgments

No book of this kind can possibly be the work of any single individual. Civil War America left us a heritage of song which, unfortunately, has been woefully neglected. Perhaps this work will help to give our present age an appreciation of the musical legacy left by such American composers and writers as George Frederick Root, Henry Clay Work, Daniel Decatur Emmett, Harry Macarthy, William Shakespeare Hays, Charles Carroll Sawyer, Henry Tucker, George Cooper, and John Hill Hewitt. It is to these men and the countless unknown and long-forgotten bards of city street and backwoods anonymity that I am most deeply indebted, for these are their songs, a priceless heritage from another age.

In the thirty-odd years immediately after the Civil War, many editors and writers set about collecting these songs for posterity. To these men and women, who valued our music and helped to preserve it for us, we should be extremely grateful.

In addition to my debt to history, however, I wish to express my thanks and appreciation to the many individuals and institutions who made my task much easier and aided me with songs, historical material, suggestions, and criticism. Much of the material in this collection comes from the archives of four fine libraries. The Library of Congress, Washington, D.C., undoubtedly has the finest collection of Civil War songs in the country. With the courteous and considerate help of Mr. William Lichtenwanger, Assistant Head of the Reference Section of the Music Division, I was able to spend many fruitful hours in the collection of Civil War sheet music and songsters. In addition, Mrs. Rae Korson of the Archive of American Folk Song and her staff were most cooperative in making material available to me.

In the New York Public Library, Mr. John Edmunds of the Americana Section, Music Division, was extremely helpful, as were all of the other librarians in that musical treasure house; my researches in the American History Division, the Rare Book Division, and the Manuscripts Division of the New York Public Library were also

most rewarding, and I wish to thank all of the librarians in these areas who were always cooperative and understanding of my needs.

Mrs. Bernice B. Larrabee, Head of the Music Department in the Free Library of Philadelphia proved both creative and patient in her efforts to make the material in the library's collection available to me. Librarians at the New York State Historical Society and at the Los Angeles Public Library likewise showed great interest in my researches and proved helpful in tracking down certain songs which appear here.

The illustrations which are used in this book are almost all from wood engravings by artists of the Civil War period. Most of these appeared originally in the pages of *Harper's Weekly, Frank Leslie's Illustrated Weekly,* and the *London Illustrated News.* The librarians in charge of the Picture Collection of the New York Public Library and Miss Eugenia Porter and members of her staff at Columbia University Press were particularly helpful in finding and selecting these illustrations.

Some of the songs in this collection are drawn from the library of *Sing Out!,* a folk-song magazine. To Pete Seeger, Alan Lomax and, especially, Waldemar Hille, whose tireless efforts and selfless contributions are largely responsible for this mammoth collection of folk and topical songs, my deepest thanks; to Waldemar Hille, also, I am indebted for songs learned from that wonderful folk singer and great repository of folk songs, Emma Dusenberry.

A special word of thanks to Moses Asch, of Folkways Records, who, as both scholar and friend, has given me encouragement, criticism, invaluable suggestions, and much specific information on both songs and history. His monumental record catalogue, from which I have been encouraged to draw freely, stands as a symbol of integrity in the world of letters.

For specific songs included in this collection, for criticism, encouragement, advice, and suggestions, I am grateful to Ben Botkin, Hermes Nye, Ellen Stekert, Frank Warner, Herbert Aptheker, Daryl

ACKNOWLEDGMENTS

Heymann, Albert Wood, Virginia B. Herbert, Paul Clayton, Walter Lowenfels, and many others. Appreciative acknowledgment is also made to Oxford University Press for permission to include in this collection "The Rebel Soldier" and "The Battle of Shiloh" from *English Folksongs from the Southern Appalachians,* edited by Cecil Sharp; to Shapiro, Bernstein & Co. for their kind permission to include the song "Two Brothers," by Irving Gordon, in this book, and to Folkways Music Publishers for permission to print their copyrighted arrangement of "Follow the Drinking Gourd."

I have been particularly fortunate in having as a coworker on this collection, a young man of rare musical talent and insight, Jerry Silverman. His arrangements for piano and guitar of the songs in this book testify to his musical sensitivity and his appreciation of the historical treasures which have been our subject matter. In addition to his musical abilities, however, Jerry Silverman brings to all of his work an intellectual honesty and depth which have made our partnership a stimulating and enriching experience for me.

Finally, a word of thanks to my wife Sylvia who somehow managed to live with this work in progress for two years, all the while managing two incredibly active small boys and taking just enough time to bring a daughter into the world. Her understanding, her devotion, and her own musical talents are indelibly inscribed on these pages.

New York, N.Y.
December, 1959

IRWIN SILBER

On the Music Arrangements

The reader will find in this volume songs which, it is hoped, he would like to sing for himself and for others. With that end in mind those songs have been selected which seemed to offer as much promise as possible of being musically valid and interesting. The piano arrangements themselves have been generally kept simple but stylistically in keeping with arrangements of that period of American history which saw the piano firmly entrenched as the central musical instrument of the home.

Whether the piano still retains this unchallenged position at home these days is open to some question. In recent years we have witnessed a tremendous upsurge in the popularity of the guitar and, to a lesser extent, the banjo.

Therefore, although the arrangements are "piano arrangements," the choice of keys—primarily from the "sharp side of the circle of keys"—has been dictated by the limitations of the guitar.

If in some instances the guitar chord symbols are at variance with the piano arrangement beneath them, it is because the customary folk-guitar techniques do not call for the rapid sequence of chord progressions found in the piano arrangement. The broad harmonic outline, however, is sufficiently taken care of by the chord symbols.

The practice of stemming together the notes in the vocal part (as is customary in instrumental parts) has been employed because of the greater ease of reading it affords to all.

New York, N.Y.
December, 1959

JERRY SILVERMAN

Preface to the Dover Edition

Much has changed since 1959. The typewriter on which that earlier manuscript was brought to life has long since been replaced by a computer, and the view from my office window is that of Lake Merritt in the heart of Oakland rather than the Williamsburg Bridge in downtown Manhattan. Likewise reflecting changes in culture and life style, I now have considerably more hair on my chin than on my head. The musical arranger of this volume, Jerry Silverman, has gone on to a successful career as a musician, teacher and editor. The "two incredibly active small boys" of 1959 (Joshua and Fred) are now two incredibly active adults pursuing lives of their own, while Nina, the infant daughter of yesteryear, is today a professor of American history whose particular area of expertise is the Civil War and its aftermath.

There have also been remarkable changes in the way in which historians and the public tend to view America's most profound military-political conflict. In 1960, when *Songs of the Civil War* was first published, the imminent centennial of that great conflict was undoubtedly the impetus for the decision by Columbia University Press to bring out a volume which at any other time would probably have been deemed far too esoteric. Thirty-five years later, however, there seems to be a heightened interest in what used to be considered the more ephemeral aspects of great historical events. Where the story of the Civil War was traditionally told principally by recounting the military exploits of its generals and the political considerations of its most prominent figures, there is a growing trend among today's historians to focus more on the human cultural experiences that were so central to that monumental sea change in our history.

Of course, earlier historians had not completely overlooked the cultural memorabilia—diaries, letters, songs, photographs, drawings—through which one glimpsed the human dimensions of that titanic struggle. But the approach generally taken to such expressions was largely antiquarian, more suited to the preservation of "precious memories" than to deepening our understanding of the main currents that shaped the lives of those who lived in such perilous times.

Today, our understanding of the past is immeasurably enriched by the work of new generations of historians exploring these topics not simply as amusing or sentimental artifacts of an earlier time but as a source of new insights into the lives of those who preceded us in the American saga. Here I can cite by way of example two books by Nina Silber: *The Romance of Reunion: Northerners and the South, 1865–1900* (University of North Carolina Press, 1993); and, with Catherine Clinton, *Divided Houses: Gender and the Civil War* (Oxford University Press, 1992).

In a deeper sense, I believe that this expansion of the historical agenda reflects two important shifts in public consciousness over the past thirty-five years. First, a series of seminal historical events—the moral-political crusade against state-endorsed white supremacy in the early sixties, the mass alienation from a brutal war waged by our government in Southeast Asia, and the political scandal that led to the first resignation of an elected United States President—have helped discredit the climate of jingoism that tended to distort our general view of history. Second, these same events have helped us understand that democracy is not simply the right to vote or to speak one's mind—important though such rights are—but is even more bound up with the actual empowerment of people to have a direct say in the decisions that affect their lives and their society. It is only natural, therefore, that the culture which furnishes the sinews of everyday existence should also now be looked at in a new way.

In introducing a new edition of *Songs of the Civil War*, I like to believe that its first publication was a harbinger of things to come.

Oakland, Cal.   IRWIN SILBER
September, 1994

Contents

The Union Forever
MARCHING AND INSPIRATIONAL SONGS OF THE UNION 5

In Dixie Land I'll Take My Stand
MARCHING AND INSPIRATIONAL SONGS OF THE CONFEDERACY 47

Old Abe Lincoln Came Out of the Wilderness
SONGS OF ABRAHAM LINCOLN 87

CONTENTS

Weeping Sad and Lonely
SENTIMENTAL WAR SONGS OF A SENTIMENTAL AGE 113

Tenting on the Old Camp Ground
SONGS THE SOLDIERS SANG 165

It's All About That Terrible Fight
SONGS OF BATTLES AND CAMPAIGNS 229

Let My People Go!
NEGRO SPIRITUALS, ABOLITIONIST SONGS, SONGS OF THE NEGRO SOLDIER 267

CONTENTS

Grafted into the Army
DIALECT, MINSTREL, AND COMIC SONGS 301

The Blue and the Gray
POST-WAR SONGS AND SONGS INSPIRED BY THE CIVIL WAR 347

Songs of the Civil War

The people, yes, the people,
Move eternally in the elements of surprise,
Changing from hammer to bayonet and back to hammer,
The hallelujah chorus forever shifting its star soloists.
Carl Sandburg, *The People Yes*

Introduction

The Civil War, that great fratricidal conflict which played such a decisive role in shaping our history and our national consciousness, exists no longer in the first-hand memories of living men. The aging, gray-haired veterans, whose grand reunions and garrulous recollections were, for so many decades, living reminders of the Civil War, have all crossed over into Jordan. The memories of the Civil War are now dependent on less fragile material—on histories and biographies, on the printed page and the time-worn photograph, on artists' sketches and such minute memorabilia as wartime maps, fading uniforms, medals (some tarnished, some still shining), bayonets, swords, battle flags, and other material objects, trifling and important, of an age gone by, which remain after human flesh has paid its inevitable price to mortality.

Among our less tangible but no less real keepsakes are the songs of Civil War America—the stirring marching songs and patriotic hymns, the unabashedly sentimental ballads and the comic ditties, the boasting songs and drinking songs and fighting songs and loving songs of America's bloodiest and most significant struggle. And through these songs, an age which is past is brought to life, and we live with the men and women who walked this land a century ago.

The music of the Civil War is more than a succession of lyrics and melodies bounded by Sumter and Appomattox. For nineteenth-century America was a youngster among nations, a brash adolescent emerging from the long shadow of European tradition and culture, the smoke from its newly sprung factories fashioning a soot-grimed image against the stars, the burgeoning music of steam whistles and pounding engines and slave cries giving birth to melodies and tunes and manners of speech which the world would soon call "American."

In 1861, in those fierce and turbulent months when the Union was falling apart, America's music was struggling to break through the thick crust of its European legacy. True, for the two decades preceding the Civil War, a few gifted tunesmiths had begun to write a new kind of music. It was a zestful, lively, tuneful, rhythmic music composed of plaintive plantation chants and energetic pioneer shouts, seasoned liberally with a healthy dash of Irish and Scottish melody, with traces of French and German song idioms occasionally audible. Such men as Stephen Collins Foster and Daniel Decatur Emmett had discovered the rich melodic and rhythmic patterns of the Southern Negro and had begun to fashion them into a music which the world had never heard before. On the minstrel stages in the big cities and in small meetinghouses on the frontier, an indigenous American music was growing.

But this new music was still only a small voice in the American consciousness. A country whose national songs were created in another land and age, whose composers and poets were, by and large, inheritors of musical and literary styles and idioms not of their own making, was only tentatively reaching for its own form of expression.

A process which might have lasted for generations was underway, and none could foresee its outcome. But the Civil War, with its military and political urgencies, with its grand mixing of backgrounds and cultures, with its need for songs of inspiration and sorrow and laughter, and with its focus on the inner meaning of the American Union, acted as a catalyst in the development of our music, and the hitherto slow process of Americanization was suddenly squeezed into a few short years. As the Civil War liberated the Negro slave, it also liberated American music from its hidebound, alien tradition.

It was with the Civil War that the music of the Negro began to penetrate fully the national consciousness and play the decisive role it eventually assumed in the emergence of a distinctively American musical idiom, combining with the Scotch-Irish–Anglo-Saxon tradition which had been, up until then, the main form of musical expression of white America. It was, by no means, an overnight development. Many songs of Civil

INTRODUCTION

War America continued to reflect the European heritage. But where America of 1812–1814 produced, as its most lasting musical memory, the patriotic verses written to the melody of an old English drinking song, which eventually became our national anthem, from the Civil War emerged such undeniably American works (in tune and lyric) as "John Brown's Body," "Dixie," "Battle Cry of Freedom," and "Marching Through Georgia."

The four years of the Civil War produced a startling upheaval in the American idiom, decisively affecting literature, music, and all other forms of creative expression. No other war in American history has produced such a great variety of songs, nor such a quantity. In searching through library and personal manuscript collections, through aged and yellowing songsters and old newspapers, through folksong collections and regimental histories, I have seen some 10,000 songs which would fall, roughly, within the scope of this book. Choosing some one hundred songs or so from this vast body of musical literature required, I confess, a certain presumptuousness on my part, as well as the realization that many good songs were undoubtedly left behind.

In selecting the songs which appear in this volume, I have employed a number of criteria. Among them were: (*a*) popularity; (*b*) musical worth; (*c*) historical significance; (*d*) representation of main trends; (*e*) musical pertinence today —or, stated more simply, whether or not people would still be interested in singing the songs today; (*f*) my personal taste.

This collection has been broken down into nine main sections, but I rush to admit that the categorization is often arbitrary and that some songs, which defy classification, are placed among their particular bedfellows for want of a better home.

With the exception of the last two songs in this collection, "Dance Me a Jig" and "Two Brothers," all of the songs presented here date from the period of the Civil War. In practically all cases, I have kept the original lyrics and melody intact—as matters of historical documentation. In the case of sheet music of the time, however, I have chosen to dispense with the original piano parts and harmonizations in favor of musical arrangements which, I hope, will make the songs more useful to our own day. At the same time, the music editor and I have endeavored to preserve the flavor of the period.

In a few cases, I have taken the liberty of making slight alterations in the original text—through minor word changes or by presenting composite versions of songs. In one case, we have made a slight abridgment in the original melody of a song. Wherever such changes have been made, I have indicated this fact together with the nature of the change. All told, there are no more than four or five such abridgments in the entire collection.

One more word to the reader by way of introduction and warning. I do not claim to be a historian. I have come to this work through the music, since the field of American song has been my main activity for the past dozen years or so. I have relied on a number of standard historical sources to document the circumstances which gave rise to the songs, but I have not endeavored, except in occasional cases, to use original historical sources for this purpose. My musical sources, on the other hand, are almost unanimously from the sheet music and the songsters of the period and other first-hand sources, both written and oral.

In addition, I must say that I am not "neutral" on the subject of the Civil War. I believe that the verdict of history was both necessary and just, that the destiny of America rested on the banners and fighting capacity of the Union Armies, and that a Confederate victory would have resulted in a national catastrophe which might have kept America from emerging in the front ranks of the nations of the world.

At the same time, I have endeavored to understand and represent, through the songs in this collection, the outlook of both Unionist and Rebel, of Northern Democrat and Southern slave. And despite my historical sympathies, I have come to a new respect and understanding for all the Billy Yanks and Johnny Rebs who took up arms in their respective causes and made these songs their expressions of hardship and love, of faith and sorrow, of hope and laughter.

In conjunction with this book, Folkways Records has produced a record album (two 12-inch long-playing records) containing over thirty songs which appear in this collection.*

The songs in this collection represent the spirit of a brave and terrible time. The relentless pages of history can never be unwritten, and so we sing the songs of war from the fearful conflict of a century ago. But let us hope that all songs of war will soon be but memories in the minds of men to be recalled and wondered at in an eternity of peace.

4

*Currently available [1995] as the two-cassette set "Songs of the Civil War" (Catalog No. 5717) through Smithsonian/Folkways Mail Order, 414 Hungerford Drive, Suite 444, Rockville, MD 20850.

The Union Forever

MARCHING AND INSPIRATIONAL SONGS OF THE UNION

The Union forever,
Hurrah, boys, hurrah!
Down with the traitor,
And up with the star.

In the early morning hours of April 12, 1861, shortly before dawn, Captain George S. James of the army of the recently formed Confederate States of America fired a ten-inch mortar which burst upon the cool night air some one hundred feet or so above the stone ramparts of Fort Sumter in Charleston Harbor, South Carolina. Almost 36 hours later, the Union troops, under the command of Major Robert Anderson, ran a white flag up the flagpole and surrendered the fort to Confederate troops.

The firing on Sumter stunned the nation. Despite the ominous war clouds which had hung over the country ever since South Carolina had seceded from the Union four months earlier, most Americans did not believe that war was inevitable. But the cannon fire which drew thousands of Charleston citizens down to the waterfront during the bombardment was heard and felt in every corner of the nation, and the country awoke to the realization that Civil War was a bloody and tragic fact.

Throughout the war, soldiers and civilians of the Union States were inspired and propagandized by a host of patriotic songs. An endless stream of compositions poured forth from the dedicated pens of scores of professional song writers and hundreds of eager amateurs. Many of these works were published only to languish and collect dust on the shelves of sheet music dealers in New York, Boston, and Philadelphia. But a few of these songs caught the tempo and the spirit of the age and swept across the country carried on the lips of millions of Americans.

Songs like George F. Root's "The Battle Cry of Freedom," "John Brown's Body," "The Battle Hymn of the Republic," and, at the end of the war, Henry C. Work's "Marching Through Georgia," were high on the "hit parade" of 1861–1865 and have, by now, become ingrained in our national consciousness.

When the political leaders of the slaveholding states led their respective governments out of the Union in the waning days of 1860 and the early part of 1861, they certainly did not anticipate that what was left of the United States of America could find sufficient an ideological meeting ground to stem the secession tide. Undoubtedly, Jefferson Davis, Alexander Stephens, and the other Confederate leaders did not believe that a minority president could forge any degree of national unity out of a badly divided nation.

It is paradoxical, of course, that while the South publicly proclaimed Lincoln as black an Abolitionist as William Lloyd Garrison or Frederick Douglass, secession would have had a greater chance of success if Lincoln had acted on the advice of some of the extreme Abolitionists who were happy to see the slaveholding states out of the Union. Scores of Northern Democrats, on the other hand, were clamoring for concessions to the Confederacy on every count—a policy of "peace and Union at any price."

At the outbreak of hostilities, the Union was indeed sorely divided. But unity of action and purpose were forged in the furnace of Civil War—the battlefields of Bull Run and Shiloh were drenched with the blood of Irish and German immigrants as well as the sons of old Yankee stock; the tears of sweethearts, wives, and mothers swept across party lines; Confederate shellfire did not distinguish Abolitionist, Free-Soiler, Republican, or Democrat.

The directly inspirational and propaganda songs of the Union reflect the way in which Northern unity developed. The first songs were statements of purpose and appeals for valor. George F. Root, who probably wrote more Civil War songs than any other composer, responded to the attack on Sumter with "The First Gun Is Fired," and copies were in print within three days of the action:

> We will bow no more to the tyrant few
> Who scorn our long forbearing,
> But with Columbia's stars and stripes,
> We'll quench their trait'rous daring.
>
> Arise! Arise! Arise!
> And gird ye for the fight....

For the arm of freedom is mighty still,
Its strength shall fail us never,
That strength we'll give to our righteous cause,
And our glorious land forever.

More direct was H. T. Merrill who, in the first flush of the war fever, wrote "Take Your Gun and Go, John." In later years there would be no wives to say:

Don't stop a moment to think, John,
Our country calls, then go.

Then the wives and sweethearts would ask, "When Will This Cruel War Be Over?" But in 1861 the war was young, the casualty lists were short, and the song writers could still ask:

Have you sharpened your swords for the war that's
begun?
. . .

Have you sharpened your swords for the red carnival?

The Union songs of 1861 relied on the standard symbols of righteousness—God and the Flag. The clash of arms was not yet ready to bring forth a battle cry of freedom. That would come in time. For now, George Root would write "God Bless Our Brave Young Volunteers," "Forward, Boys, Forward," and

Stand up for Uncle Sam, my boys,
For he has stood by you.

An unknown and undistinguished tunesmith by the name of E. T. Baldwin wrote:

Come forth to the conflict,
The stern bloody war.
. . .

Up yeomen, come freemen!
The call is for you;
Don't dally, but rally,
For Liberty true.

(In the South, the Confederacy's best and most popular songs were written in the first flush of secession and military victory, with "The Bonnie Blue Flag," "Maryland," and the most popular parodies to "Dixie" all being created in 1861.)

Undoubtedly, great inspirational songs in wartime can breathe the spirit of unity into the ranks of soldiers and civilians alike, but a song itself cannot create the conditions for a unified people. In the Civil War, it was the tide of battle, the bloody defeats and the equally bloody victories, and the eventual realization that the war was for *both* freedom and Union, and that without one there

could not be the other, which brought into being the national unity essential to win the conflict. And from that emerging unity, partially inspired by it and partially influencing it, came the great inspirational songs of the Union. For it was only with a determination born of sorrow that the people could finally sing:

Mine eyes have seen the glory of the coming of the Lord,
He is trampling out the vintage where the grapes of wrath
are stored,
He hath loosed the fateful lightning of His terrible swift
sword,
His truth is marching on.

Appropriately enough, literary critics of the immediate post-Civil War era dismissed many of the finest inspirational songs as "wartime doggerel." When George Cary Eggleston published his two-volume set of *American War Ballads* in 1889, a collection composed predominantly of Civil War songs, he begrudgingly consigned "John Brown's Body," "Battle Cry of Freedom," "Tramp, Tramp, Tramp," and "Marching Through Georgia" to the very last pages in his collection with the following remarks:

The strong hold which (these songs) had upon the favor of the Union soldiers during the war entitles them to insertion here in spite of their lack of poetic merit. The critics, from the time of Mr. Richard Grant White's collection until now, have condemned them as doggerel, but songs that were sung with enthusiasm by all the soldiers of the republic during the dark years of the Civil War cannot be denied the possession of merit, whether criticism is able to recognize it or not.

History, which consistently proves to be the literary pundit's worst enemy, has, of course, completely reversed the criticism—for it is precisely these lines of "doggerel" which have lasted beyond the circumstances which gave them birth to become a significant part of our national musical heritage.

THE BATTLE CRY OF FREEDOM (Rallying Song). The war was little more than one year old when George F. Root wrote "The Battle Cry of Freedom." According to the Chicago *Tribune,* the song was first introduced at a war rally in Chicago on July 24, 1862, by the Lumbard Brothers, a popular singing team of the time.

The folklore of the Civil War has created a legend about the song. Diaries, reminiscences, and newspaper stories are replete with anecdotes concerning the inspirational effect of "The Battle Cry of Freedom" in the ranks of the Union Army. A Union soldier, who had been stationed at a camp near Murfreesboro early in 1863 described, in later years, the low state of morale resulting from a recent costly "victory," together with the dissatisfaction of many Tennessee and Kentucky regiments with the just-issued Emancipation Proclamation. But suddenly the depressed atmosphere changed:

By a happy accident, the glee club which came down from Chicago a few days afterward, brought with them the brand-new song, "We'll Rally 'Round the Flag, Boys," and it ran through the camp like wildfire. The effect was little short of miraculous. It put as much spirit and cheer into the camp as a splendid victory. Day and night you could hear it by every camp fire and in every tent. Never shall I forget how those men rolled out the line: "And although he may be poor, he shall never be a slave." I do not know whether Mr. Root ever knew what good work his song did for us there, but I hope so.

A Confederate Major, in another post-war reminiscence, adds additional luster to the legend:

I shall never forget the first time that I heard "Rally 'Round the Flag." 'Twas a nasty night during the "Seven Days Fight," and, if I remember rightly, it was raining. I was on picket when, just before taps, some fellow on the other side struck up that song and others joined in the chorus until it seemed to me the whole Yankee Army was singing. Tom B——, who was with me, sung out: "Good Heavens, cap, what are those fellows made of, anyway? Here we've licked 'em six days running, and now on the eve of the seventh, they're singing 'Rally 'Round the Flag.' "

I am not naturally superstitious, but I tell you that song sounded to me like the "knell of doom," and my heart went down into my boots; and though I've tried to do my duty, it has been an uphill fight with me ever since that night.

Whether the stories are fact or fancy, there is no doubt of the song's popularity. The famous singing Hutchinsons introduced the song in the East, and by the end of the war, "The Battle Cry of Freedom" was on the lips of millions of Americans from New York to California, with various Confederate versions springing up below the Mason-Dixon line.

The firm of Root & Cady claimed a sheet music sale of more than 350,000 copies two years after the war, but even that substantial figure is an insufficient indication of the song's widespread popularity, for the tune was catchy and the words were direct and simple, and the lilting melody passed from mouth to mouth much faster than the printed copies could move.

Root, who saw no harm in a bit of musical nepotism, refers to the popularity of "The Battle Cry of Freedom" in a subsequent song "Just Before the Battle, Mother":

> Hear the "Battle Cry of Freedom,"
> How it swells upon the air,
> Oh, yes, we'll rally 'round the standard,
> Or we'll perish nobly there,

In the musical tradition of the times, other song writers tried to cash in on Root's success. William S. Bradbury, whose "Marching Along" was one of the more successful patriotic songs, wrote the music for "Rally 'Round the Flag," with lyrics by James C. Fields:

> Their flag is but a rag,
> Ours is the true one,
> Up with the Stars and Stripes,
> Down with the new one.
>
> Rally round the flag, boys,
> Give it to the breeze,
> That's the banner we love
> On the land and seas.

Root's song retained its popularity throughout the war, invariably being included in all wartime concerts and patriotic rallies. During the ceremonies at Fort Sumter on April 14, 1865, when Major Anderson helped raise the flag over the historic site of the first Union defeat, the strains of "The Battle Cry of Freedom" could be heard across the bay in the streets of Charleston as the Union band symbolized freedom's victory with freedom's most effective war cry.

THE BATTLE CRY OF FREEDOM, II (Battle Song). Since the first edition of "The Battle Cry of Freedom" does not contain the set of lyrics which George F. Root designated as the "Battle Song" version of the song, we must presume that this was written subsequently in response to the song's growing popularity.

SOUTHERN "BATTLE CRY OF FREEDOM." If imitation be the sincerest form of flattery, then in the domain of song, parody must surely be the most certain sign of popularity. At first glance, it would seem that no Union song would lend itself less to popularization in Confederate ranks than "The Battle Cry of Freedom"—except, possibly, for "Marching Through Georgia" or "John Brown's Body." But the Union had no monopoly on the word "Freedom," no matter what judgment history might render. To Southern political leaders and Southern song writers, "Freedom" represented the *freedom* of a state to secede or the *freedom* of a slaveowner to his bought-and-paid-for property.

And so, with the tremendous popularity of "Battle Cry of Freedom" in the North, the lilting melody had little difficulty infiltrating the Confederate lines. The Southern parody printed below is quite obviously very close to the "Battle Song" version, with just enough changes in the cast of characters to make it a Southern song.

Another Rebel adaptation was made by one of the most prolific of Confederate composers, Herman L. Schreiner, who changed Root's tune sufficiently to justifiably claim composition, and set it to new words by William H. Barnes:

Our flag is proudly floating
On the land and on the main,
Shout, shout the battle cry of freedom;
Beneath it oft we've conquered
And will conquer oft again,
Shout, shout the battle cry of freedom.

Our Dixie forever, she's never at a loss,
Down with the Eagle and up with the Cross,
We'll rally 'round the bonny flag, we'll rally once again,
Shouting the battle cry of freedom.

THE BATTLE HYMN OF THE REPUBLIC. To Julia Ward Howe, a distinguished light of nineteenth-century New England society, falls the distinction of having written the single most popular parody to the most-parodied melody in American music. "The Battle Hymn of the Republic" was the first great inspirational song of the Union produced during the Civil War.

While the origin of the famous melody is obscure and uncertain, the facts concerning the creation of this lasting American hymn have been well documented in many accounts. Mrs. Howe was in Washington in the late autumn of 1861, accompanying her husband, Dr. Samuel Gridley Howe, who was a member of a Military Sanitary Commission appointed by President Lincoln. One day, while visiting the army camps, Mrs. Howe and the others in her party began singing some of the

more popular war songs, including "John Brown's Body." Rev. James Freeman Clarke, one of the group, knowing Mrs. Howe's literary bent, suggested that she write new words to the "John Brown" tune. But let the author herself tell the rest of the story:

I replied that I had often wished to do so. In spite of the excitement of the day I went to bed and slept as usual, but awoke next morning in the gray of the early dawn, and to my astonishment found that the wished-for lines were arranging themselves in my brain. I lay quite still until the last verse had completed itself in my thoughts, then hastily arose, saying to myself, "I shall lose this if I don't write it down immediately." I searched for an old sheet of paper and an old stump of a pen which I had had the night before, and began to scrawl the lines almost without looking, as I had learned to do by often scratching down verses in the darkened room where my little children were sleeping. Having completed this, I lay down again and fell asleep, but not without feeling that something of importance had happened to me.

The first draft of this song is dated November, 1861. In February, 1862, it was published in the *Atlantic Monthly,* appearing on the first page of that venerable journal. Mrs. Howe was paid five dollars by the *Atlantic,* whose editor, James T. Fields, is supposed to have given the song its title.

Julia Ward Howe was born May 27, 1819, in New York City, the daughter of Samuel Ward, a wealthy New York banker. In 1843, she married Dr. Samuel Gridley Howe of Boston. In the following years, she and her husband became ever more embroiled in the Abolitionist cause. Her daughter, Florence Howe Hall, came to believe in later years that their home in South Boston might have been one of the numerous "stops" on the Underground Railroad which helped fleeing Negro slaves escape to Canada. It was during this period that Mrs. Howe met John Brown, whom her husband had described to her as a man who "seemed to intend to devote his life to the redemption of the colored race from slavery, even as Christ had willingly offered His life for the salvation of mankind."

Mrs. Howe assayed other literary efforts over the years, but none of these even remotely approached the artistic level or popularity of "The Battle Hymn of the Republic." One other Civil War lyric of hers, "Harvard Students' Song," is a thoroughly undistinguished effort. Written to an old German melody, the first verse reads:

SONGS OF THE UNION

Remember ye the fateful gun that sounded,
To Sumter's walls from Charleston's treacherous shores?
Remember ye how hearts indignant bounded,
When our first dead came back from Baltimore?
The banner fell that every breeze had flattered,
The hum of thrift was hushed with sudden woe;
We raised anew the emblems shamed and shattered,
And turned a front resolved to meet the foe.

In later years, Mrs. Howe would become an outstanding champion of the woman's suffrage movement and enjoy a successful career as a lecturer and woman of letters. But for the half century after she wrote her famous work, until her death at the age of 91 in 1910, and until this very day, Julia Ward Howe is best known as "the woman who wrote 'The Battle Hymn of the Republic.'"

JOHN BROWN'S BODY. On December 2, 1859, John Brown's body was hung from a gibbet in Charlestown, Virginia. Colonel Preston of the Virginia militia, who was in charge of the execution, turned to the assembled crowd (which included Robert E. Lee, Stonewall Jackson, and an aspiring young actor by the name of John Wilkes Booth) and proclaimed:

So perish all such enemies of Virginia! All such enemies of the Union! All such foes of the human race!

Less than six weeks earlier, the man hanging from the hastily erected gallows had thrown the nation into consternation with his daring, suicidal raid on Harpers Ferry in a vain attempt to touch off a general slave uprising. With unseemly dispatch, a terror-stricken South had tried, sentenced, executed, and martyred the fifty-nine-year-old Abolitionist to whom slavery was "the sum of all villainies."

John Brown went to his grave—and his soul went marching on. Within two years of his death, millions throughout the Union were chanting:

John Brown's body lies a-mouldering in the grave,
But his truth goes marching on.

By a strange quirk of history, together with the fact that there are few, if any, more common American names than John Brown, "John Brown's Body" was not composed originally about the fiery Abolitionist at all. The namesake for the song, it turns out, was Sergeant John Brown of Boston, a Scotsman, a member of the Second Battalion, Boston Light Infantry, Massachusetts Volunteer Militia. Sergeant John Brown, as luck would have it, also happened to be a singer, a second tenor in the battalion glee club.

Among the most popular airs sung by the choristers was an old Methodist tune which went:

Say, brothers, will you meet us,
Say, brothers, will you meet us,
Say, brothers, will you meet us,
On Canaan's happy shore?

It was to this melody that the soldiers of Sergeant John Brown's Company began to improvise verses. Of course, everyone in the company got a big kick out of the fact that most listeners assumed that the song was inspired by the martyr of Harpers Ferry. In time, of course, the song attained its tremendous popularity *precisely* because of the identification with "Old Osawatomie" —for as the war increasingly developed along anti-slavery lines, the vision and sacrifice of old John Brown became a shining symbol throughout the North.

In the summer of 1861, the troops of the Massachusetts Twelfth Regiment came marching down Broadway in New York City singing "John Brown's Body." The crowd was instantaneously so taken by the singing that the outfit was quickly dubbed "The Hallelujah Regiment" while the song took New York by storm. As the war proceeded, the song swept across the country. Hardly a month passed in which some amateur chronicler did not employ the tune to relate a particular battle or incident of the conflict.*

And yet, with all the changes in words, and despite the great impact of Julia Ward Howe's "The Battle Hymn of the Republic," the song—and soul —of John "Osawatomie" Brown are still marching on.

THE JOHN BROWN SONG. Here is one of the best of the later parodies inspired by the original "John Brown's Body."

THE PRESIDENT'S PROCLAMATION. Another highly singable "John Brown" parody is this creation by Edna Dean Proctor, inspired by and written for the Emancipation Proclamation which freed all slaves in Rebel territory as of January 1,

* In post-war years, no song was as frequently parodied, and every major, as well as minor, political movement in the United States has created at least one set of lyrics to the good old tune.

11

1863. Here indeed was John Brown's vision come true, only a little more than three years after he had mounted the scaffold.

MARCHING SONG OF THE FIRST ARKANSAS (NEGRO) REGIMENT.

The first Negro troops in the Union Army donned their uniforms of blue in the spring of 1862. Some authorities credit Major General Benjamin F. Butler, one of the more controversial figures in the Union command, with this historic step, in organizing three regiments of Negro "Louisiana Native Guards" in New Orleans in May of that year. Major General David Hunter is reported to have organized the First South Carolina Regiment composed of Negro troops at about the same time.

It was not until the war was quite advanced, however, that widespread recruiting of Negroes was undertaken. For despite the emerging struggle against slavery, the Union as a whole was bounded by mores and prejudices which were of long standing and not readily overcome. For a short period of time, Negro regiments had Negro officers. These, however, were soon replaced by whites.

Captain Lindley Miller, a white officer of the First Arkansas Colored Regiment, is credited with writing the words to this marching song and an examination of the lyrics would tend partially to confirm such a claim. It is hard to imagine a Negro soldier at the time of the Civil War employing the literary artifice of "de sable army of de African descent." On the other hand, many of the lines have a genuine folk feeling and seem to grow right out of Negro idiom, so that I would venture to guess that the song was more in the nature of a joint effort of white officer and Negro troops, with Captain Miller "improving" upon his soldiers' efforts and adding lines and stanzas of his own.

One other fact pointing in the direction of Captain Miller's authorship is the use of dialect in the written song. The representation of Negro speech in these stanzas seems much closer to the blackface minstrel interpretation of Negro dialect than the real thing. Of course, part of Captain Miller's "improvement" of the original might have been an attempt to write down the dialect he heard.

In any event, the song apparently was sung with enthusiasm by the men of the First Arkansas

and, once the policy of employing Negro troops had been formalized, the song was published in broadside form by the Supervisory Committee for Recruiting Colored Regiments.

FOR THE DEAR OLD FLAG I DIE.

Stephen Collins Foster, America's master tunesmith of the nineteenth century, spent the last few years of his life in Civil War New York. Along with the rest of the song-writing fraternity, Foster tried his hand at war songs; but the great melody-maker had passed his creative prime and his Civil War songs are among his minor works.

In 1862, Foster wrote "That's What's the Matter," a song which seemed to express some of his own song-writing difficulties:

> We live in hard and stirring times,
> Too sad for mirth, too rough for rhymes,
> For songs of peace have lost their chimes,
> And that's what's the matter.
>
> That's what's the matter,
> The Rebels have to scatter;
> We'll make them flee by land and sea,
> And that's what's the matter!

Among Foster's other Civil War efforts was a musical setting for "We Are Coming, Father Abraham" which was not nearly as successful as the one which appears elsewhere in this volume and "Willie Has Gone to the War." A lyricist by the name of George Cooper, who later wrote "Sweet Genevieve," was Foster's closest collaborator on war songs, penning the lyrics to "Willie" and "For the Dear Old Flag I Die."

This last-named song was written in 1863 and manages to cram into a few short bars of music almost every Civil War song cliché of the time. The title, claim the authors, comes from "the last words of a brave little drummer boy who was fatally wounded at the Battle of Gettysburg." This "last-words" gimmick was a favorite with Civil War song writers who were constantly stumbling across some dying testament which magically lent itself to song (see, for example, "Who Will Care for Mother Now?"). Drummer boys were also favorite victims in the songs (see "Drummer Boy of Shiloh"), and few Civil War songs were complete without a mother. Add to this the patriotic sentiments in the title and one would think that Foster and Cooper almost had the "perfect" song for the times. Perhaps it was too perfect, perhaps

SONGS OF THE UNION

it was too calculated and did not quite ring with the sincerity which sentimentality demands. In any event, the song never achieved any great success despite a typically good Foster tune, but it holds our interest as one of the wartime efforts of our finest nineteenth-century melodist.

MARCHING ALONG. William B. Bradbury's hymnlike marching song was one of the favorites in the Union Army. Its first verse and chorus were sung throughout the war in "zipper" fashion, with the names of other military leaders "zipped" in for "Little Mac" as the circumstances and commanders changed.

Quartermaster Bingham of the First South Carolina Volunteer Regiment (Colored) is reported to have taught the song to his troops, although the phrase "Gird on the armor" proved troublesome and was changed by his soldiers to "Guide on de army."

Bradbury was best known as a composer of Sunday school songs and as the editor of numerous Sunday school song books, including such collections as *Bright Jewels for the Sunday School,* *Chapel Melodies,* and *Bradbury's Fresh Laurels for the Sabbath School.*

THE ARMY OF THE FREE. Divisional, regimental, and company songs were composed and sung in both armies. In practically every case these were rough parodies to popular tunes, with "John Brown's Body" the favorite melody, closely followed by such folk-style airs as "Rosin the Beau" and "Benny Havens, Oh."

The Fifty-first Regiment of New York sang, to the tune of "John Brown's Body" but directly parodying the original hymn:

> Say, Rebels, will you meet us,
> Say, Rebels, will you meet us,
> Say, Rebels, will you meet us,
> On North Carolina shore?

The "Brave Boys of Company D" (Tenth Regiment, National Zouaves) used the old tune of "Rosin the Beau," one of the most popular melodies for political parody and the air employed for "Lincoln and Liberty," to sing the praises of their outfit:

> Come gather around, gallant soldiers,
> With hearts full of mirth and of glee;

> Joyfully join in the chorus,
> With the brave sons of Company D.

And in the tradition of such songs, J. C. Gobright who wrote the "Company D" lyrics, brought in their commanding officer:

> When forward we march on the Rebels,
> They will be in a terrible fix,
> They will think that the devil is coming,
> When they see Col. John E. Bendix.

A Dubuque, Iowa, volunteer is credited with the "Rallying Song of the Sixteenth Regiment Iowa Volunteers." He employed the old Hutchinson family tune, "The Old Granite State," for his lyrics:

> We have come from the prairies,
> We have come from the prairies,
> We have come from the prairies
> Of the young Hawkeye State.

> . . . the patriot must not falter,
> When his country's foes assault her,
> And profane her sacred altar,
> With their pestilential breath.

And while that last line might have been a mouthful for the Yanks, they could certainly sing the rousing chorus with gusto and rhythm.

"The Army of the Free" was written by an otherwise unidentified Frank H. Norton to the air of "The Wearing of the Green." The Civil War Army was much more likely to know that melody, however, as "Benny Havens, Oh," one of the most popular of the ante-bellum army songs and still sung by West Pointers today. A Civil War songster lists it as the "Division Song of Porter's Division, Army of the Potomac," and the internal evidence of the song would seem to point to Major General Fitz-John Porter as the commanding officer in question.

TRAMP! TRAMP! TRAMP! (The Prisoner's Hope). MacKinlay Cantor's monumental novel, *Andersonville,* has focused new attention on the status of prisoners of war during the Civil War. By far the most popular of all Civil War songs on this theme was George F. Root's "Tramp, Tramp, Tramp."

The horrors of prison life have been graphically related in a number of songs of the time, many of which seem to have been composed by the POW's themselves, rather than by professional

SONGS OF THE UNION

song writers. One present-day collector came across a song titled "Andersonville Prison" in Missouri in 1929:

> On western Georgia's sandy soil,
> Within a lonesome prison pen,
> Lay many a thousand shattered forms
> Who once was brave and loyal men.
>
> A creek of filth run through that pen,
> From which each one was forced to take
> What little water he could get,
> His paltry gill of meal to bake.

Libby Prison in Richmond was the subject of a Kentucky folk ballad which Jean Thomas found in 1938:

> Who is here that don't remember some dear, noble comrade true,
> Who at Pemberton or Libby bid this earth of care adieu.
>
> There are tales about the prisons, turn we now our tears to hide,
> When we think of rats feasting on the form of comrades died.

Union soldiers in Libby used the time-honored device of writing on prison walls to express their feelings:

> Oh, may that cuss, Jeff Davis, float,
>   Glory Hallelujah!
> On stormy sea, in open boat,
> In Iceland's cold without a coat,
>   Glory Hallelujah!

George F. Root wrote the words and music to "Tramp, Tramp, Tramp" in 1863, when many Northern families were wondering about the fate of a son or a brother or a husband incarcerated in some prisoner-of-war camp in Dixie. The song was an instantaneous success, sweeping across the country with amazing speed and quickly picked up by the troops themselves, with whom it became a favorite marching song.

The song proved so successful that Root subsequently brought out a post-war sequel, called "On, On, On, The Boys Came Marching," or "The Prisoner Free." The melody was different, but the lyrics and tune were both constructed along exactly the same lines as "Tramp, Tramp, Tramp," while the sentiments were designed to give hope to the families of the prisoners:

> Oh! the day it came at last,
> When the glorious tramp was heard,

And the boys came marching fifty thousand strong,
And we grasped each other's hands
Though we uttered not a word,
As the booming of our cannon rolled along.

> On, on, on, the boys came marching,
> Like a grand majestic sea,
> And they dashed away the guard
> From the heavy iron door,
> And we stood beneath the starry banner free.

In 1865, after the war was over, Root tried his hand at one more prison song, this time for those who had died in captivity and were not returning. It was aptly titled "Starved in Prison":

> Had they fallen in the battle
> With the old flag waving high,
> We should mourn but not in anguish,
> For the soldier thus would die;
> But the dear boys starved in prison,
> Helpless, friendless, and alone,
> While the haughty Rebel leaders
> Heard unmoved each dying groan.
>
> Yes, they starved in pens and prisons,
> Helpless, friendless, and alone!
> And their woe can ne'er be spoken,
> Nor their agony known.

None of these, however, were as successful as "Tramp, Tramp, Tramp," which has been sung by soldiers in every war since that time and, in various forms, has become a part of the mainstream of our music.*

The tune is one of the liveliest created by this unusually inventive composer, and, at the time of its writing, it touched a universal chord with deep

* The song was still so popular around 1910 that the famous song writer of the International Workers of the World (IWW), Joe Hill, used it for one of his most famous parodies, the ballad of the hobo who can't get a job and who is greeted by everyone he turns to, a housewife, a cop, a preacher, and even St. Peter, with the same refrain:

> Tramp, tramp, tramp and keep on tramping.
> Nothing doing here for you,
> If I catch you 'round again,
> You will wear the ball and chain,
> Keep on tramping, that's the best thing you can do.

Even before that, the song had been transported to Ireland where it was employed as early as 1867 for a ballad commemorating the Manchester Martyrs of that year who were executed by the British. The ballad "God Save Ireland" was, for many years, the unofficial anthem of that oppressed nation:

> "God save Ireland!" said the heroes,
> "God save Ireland!" said they all.
> "Whether on the scaffold high,
> Or the battlefield we die,
> Oh, what matter when for Ireland dear we fall!"

emotional overtones which had impressed it thoroughly into our national consciousness.

TRAMP! TRAMP! TRAMP!, II (Southern Version). George F. Root's song was so popular that it quickly swept across the battlelines and, as with so many other Union songs, was adapted by Confederate troops. This parody takes over the first stanza and chorus of Root's song almost intact, with just one or two minor word changes. The sense of Root's second stanza has been substantially changed, however, despite the obvious parody. The original has the Union soldiers captured and hearing their comrades' victory song as they are herded to the Confederate lines. The parody does not indicate how or when the prisoners were captured. The balance of the Rebel version is quite obviously new.

For another Confederate prisoner-of-war song, see "The Bonnie White Flag."

NINE MILES TO THE JUNCTION. I have not been able to discover the specific incident on which this song is based, but from the internal evidence I have managed to piece together the following: The incident took place early in the war, probably in 1861, since Governor Sprague of Rhode Island became a member of the United States Senate in 1861. The Regiment is the Seventy-first New York Militia. The junction referred to is, more than likely, a specific point called Relay House on the Baltimore and Ohio Railroad, seven miles from Baltimore, where a junction with the Washington branch takes place. The author of this regimental marching song was a private in the Seventy-first.

THE WHY AND THE WHEREFORE. Here is a frank propaganda song in the good old New England catechism tradition, designed, obviously, to encourage volunteers to enlist in the Union Army. The reference to "Washington's flag" in the third verse is quite typical of many Civil War songs which drew upon the Revolutionary War tradition to inspire their generation to defense of and devotion to the Union. In "Forward, Boys, Forward," George F. Root asked:

> Shall the altars of our heroes,
> Shall the grave of Washington,
> Shall the holy soil of freedom,
> Ever blush to meet the sun?

And many a Union soldier sang the popular "Sword of Bunker Hill," which was written a few years before the outbreak of the war but seemed appropriate to the Union cause.

Confederate songs also used the heritage of the Revolution (as well as the Jeffersonian "states rights" tradition) to justify secession:

> Rebels! 'Tis a holy name!
> The name our fathers bore. . .
> Rebels! 'Tis our family name!
> Our father, Washington,
> Was the arch-rebel in the fight,
> And gave the name to us—a right,
> Of father unto son.

MARCHING THROUGH GEORGIA. The most dramatic military campaign of the Civil War was General William T. Sherman's famous "March to the Sea" in late 1864. From a military point of view, Sherman's daring maneuver split the Confederacy in two, destroyed hundreds of miles of railroad and, thereby, increased Lee's supply problem tremendously. But the "March to the Sea" had other results, too. In Europe, the newspapers began to focus attention on "The Lost Army" which had severed all telegraph communications on November 15 and, leaving its base at Atlanta, plunged into the great unknown of Rebel Georgia. Only Grant, Lincoln, and the War Department knew that Sherman's immediate objective was Savannah, although the Confederate high command was not long in doubt as to his destination.

And then, for a period of six weeks, there was no news from Sherman's army. In England, the military experts of *The Army and Navy Gazette* wrote:

If Sherman has really left his army in the air and started off without a base to march from Georgia to South Carolina, he has done either one of the most brilliant or one of the most foolish things ever performed by a military leader.

In addition to the military gains, however, the historic campaign had other effects. For one thing, Sherman was bringing the war to the heart of the deep South, to a huge section of the Confederacy which had yet to be turned into a battleground. Since Sherman had started out from Atlanta with the intention of having his army live off the land, there was no doubt that Georgia would learn graphically the meaning of the General's famous remark that "War is Hell!"

And then, on the first day of winter, December 21, 1864, the world suddenly learned that Sherman had accomplished his miracle and that his army had forged through the heart of the Confederacy and captured Savannah. With a flair for the dramatic, Sherman sent Lincoln a telegram:

I beg to present you as a Christmas gift, the city of Savannah, with one hundred and fifty guns and plenty of ammunition, also about 25,000 bales of cotton.

Throughout the North, Sherman's victorious march produced unbounded elation. One did not have to be an armchair general to realize the military implications of Sherman's feat. The people knew that the war would soon be over. A number of songs were written to celebrate Sherman and his army. H. M. Higgins saluted "General Sher-

man and His Boys in Blue," while S. T. Gordon penned "Sherman's March to the Sea." Elsewhere in this collection is "When Sherman Marched Down to the Sea," written by a soldier of the Iowa Cavalry.

But the most popular and effective song inspired by Sherman's "March to the Sea" was Henry C. Work's "Marching Through Georgia," a song which has outlasted the immediate circumstances which produced it. The tune has gone on to become a favorite medium for parody; there have been woman's suffrage songs, Populist songs, and modern-day square dances to the tune of "Marching Through Georgia."

There is probably no Union song more thoroughly detested in the white South today than "Marching Through Georgia." Sherman's "scorched earth" campaign through the heart of Dixie has left a long and bitter scar in Southern memories.

The Battle Cry of Freedom (Rallying Song)

Words and music by George F. Root

17

SONGS OF THE UNION

Shout-ing the bat-tle cry of free - dom. The Un - ion for-ev - er, Hur -

rah, boys, hur-rah! Down with the trai-tor, Up with the star; While we

ral - ly 'round the flag, boys, ral - ly once a - gain,

Shout - ing the bat - tle cry of free - dom.

18

2. We are springing to the call of our brothers gone before,
     Shouting the battle cry of freedom,
   And we'll fill the vacant ranks with a million freemen more,
     Shouting the battle cry of freedom.   (Chorus)

3. We will welcome to our numbers the loyal, true, and brave,
     Shouting the battle cry of freedom,
   And although they may be poor not a man shall be a slave,
     Shouting the battle cry of freedom.   (Chorus)

4. So we're springing to the call from the East and from the West,
     Shouting the battle cry of freedom,
   And we'll hurl the Rebel crew from the land we love the best,
     Shouting the battle cry of freedom.   (Chorus)

The Battle Cry of Freedom, II (Battle Song)

Words and music by George F. Root

1. We are marching to the field, boys,
     We're going to the fight,
       Shouting the battle cry of freedom,
     And we bear the glorious stars
     For the Union and the right,
       Shouting the battle cry of freedom.

Chorus:
     The Union forever!
     Hurrah! Boys, hurrah!
     Down with the traitor,
     Up with the star.
     For we're marching to the field, boys,
     Going to the fight,
     Shouting the battle cry of freedom.

2. We will meet the Rebel host, boys,
     With fearless heart and true,
       Shouting the battle cry of freedom,
     And we'll show what Uncle Sam has
     For loyal men to do,
       Shouting the battle cry of freedom.   (Chorus)

3. If we fall amid the fray, boys,
     We'll face them to the last,
       Shouting the battle cry of freedom,
     And our comrades brave shall hear us
     As they go rushing past,
       Shouting the battle cry of freedom.   (Chorus)

4. Yes, for Liberty and Union
     We're springing to the fight,
       Shouting the battle cry of freedom,
     And the vict'ry shall be ours
     For we're rising in our might,
       Shouting the battle cry of freedom.   (Chorus)

Southern "Battle Cry of Freedom"

Words: anonymous
Music: "Battle Cry of Freedom" (by George F. Root)

1. We are marching to the field, boys,
   We're going to the fight,
      Shouting the battle cry of freedom.
   And we bear the Heavenly cross,
   For our cause is in the right,
      Shouting the battle cry of freedom.

Chorus:
   Our rights forever,
   Hurrah! Boys! Hurrah!
   Down with the tyrants,
   Raise the Southern star,
   And we'll rally 'round the flag, boys,
   We'll rally once again,
   Shouting the battle cry of freedom.

2. We'll meet the Yankee hosts, boys,
   With fearless hearts and true,
      Shouting the battle cry of freedom,
   And we'll show the dastard minions
   What Southern pluck can do,
      Shouting the battle cry of freedom.   (Chorus)

3. We'll fight them to the last, boys,
   If we fall in the strife,
      Shouting the battle cry of freedom,
   Our comrades—noble boys!
   Will avenge us, life for life,
      Shouting the battle cry of freedom.   (Chorus)

The Battle Hymn of the Republic

Words by Julia Ward Howe
Music: "John Brown's Body"

21

SONGS OF THE UNION

22

2. I have seen Him in the watch fires of a hundred circling camps;
   They have builded Him an altar in the evening dews and damps;
   I can read His righteous sentence by the dim and flaring lamps,
   His day is marching on.   (Chorus)

3. I have read a fiery gospel writ in burnished rows of steel:
   "As ye deal with My contemners, so with you My Grace shall deal;
   Let the Hero, born of woman, crush the serpent with his heel,
   Since God is marching on."   (Chorus)

4. He has sounded forth the trumpet that shall never call retreat;
   He is sifting out the hearts of men before His Judgment Seat;
   Oh! be swift, my soul, to answer Him, be jubilant, my feet!
   Our God is marching on.   (Chorus)

5. In the beauty of the lilies Christ was born across the sea,
   With a glory in his bosom that transfigures you and me;
   As He died to make men holy, let us die to make men free,
   While God is marching on.   (Chorus)

John Brown's Body

Words: anonymous
Music: "Say, Brothers, Will You Meet Us?" (ascribed to William Steffe)

1. John Brown's body lies a-mouldering in the grave,
   John Brown's body lies a-mouldering in the grave,
   John Brown's body lies a-mouldering in the grave,
   But his soul goes marching on.

Chorus:

   Glory, glory, hallelujah,
   Glory, glory, hallelujah,
   Glory, glory, hallelujah,
   His soul goes marching on.

2. He's gone to be a soldier in the Army of the Lord,
   His soul goes marching on.   (Chorus)

3. John Brown's knapsack is strapped upon his back,
   His soul goes marching on.   (Chorus)

4. John Brown died that the slaves might be free,
   But his soul goes marching on.   (Chorus)

5. The stars above in Heaven now are looking
      kindly down,
   On the grave of old John Brown.   (Chorus)

The John Brown Song

Words: anonymous
Music: "John Brown's Body"

1. Old John Brown's body lies a-mouldering in the grave,
   While weep the sons of bondage whom he ventured all to save;
   But though he lost his life in struggling for the slave,
   His truth is marching on.

Chorus:
   Glory, glory hallelujah!
   Glory, glory hallelujah!
   Glory, glory hallelujah!
   His truth is marching on!

2. John Brown was a hero, undaunted, true, and brave;
   Kansas knew his valor when he fought her rights to save;
   And now though the grass grows green above his grave,
   His truth is marching on.   (Chorus)

3. He captured Harper's Ferry with his nineteen men so few,
   And he frightened "Old Virginny" till she trembled through and through,
   They hung him for a traitor, themselves a traitor crew,
   But his truth is marching on.   (Chorus)

4. John Brown was John the Baptist for the Christ we are to see,
   Christ who of the bondsman shall the Liberator be;
   And soon throughout the sunny South the slaves shall all be free,
   For his truth is marching on.   (Chorus)

5. The conflict that he heralded, he looks from heaven to view,
   On the army of the Union with its flag, red, white, and blue,
   And heaven shall ring with anthems o'er the deeds they mean to do,
   For his truth is marching on.   (Chorus)

6. Oh, soldiers of freedom, then strike while strike you may
   The deathblow of oppression in a better time and way;
   For the dawn of old John Brown has brightened into day,
   And his truth is marching on.   (Chorus)

The President's Proclamation

Words by Edna Dean Proctor
Music: "John Brown's Body"

1. John Brown died on a scaffold for the slave;
   Dark was the hour when we dug his hallowed grave;
   Now God avenges the life he gladly gave,
   Freedom reigns today!

Chorus:
   Glory, glory hallelujah!
   Glory, glory hallelujah!
   Glory, glory hallelujah!
   Freedom reigns today!

2. John Brown sowed and his harvesters are we;
   Honor to him who has made the bondmen free!
   Loved evermore shall our noble Ruler be—
   Freedom reigns today!   (Chorus)

3. John Brown's body lies a-mouldering in the grave!
   Bright, o'er the sod, let the starry banner wave;
   Lo! for the millions he periled all to save—
   Freedom reigns today!   (Chorus)

4. John Brown lives—we are gaining on our foes;
   Right shall be victor whatever may oppose;
   Fresh, through the darkness, the wind of morning blows—
   Freedom reigns today!   (Chorus)

5. John Brown's soul through the world is march-
        ing on;
   Hail to the hour when oppression shall be gone!
   All men will sing in the better age's dawn,
   Freedom reigns today!   (Chorus)

6. John Brown dwells where the battle strife is o'er;
   Hate cannot harm him nor sorrow stir him more;
   Earth will remember the crown of thorns he wore—
   Freedom reigns today!   (Chorus)

7. John Brown's body lies a-mouldering in the grave;
   John Brown lives in the triumphs of the brave;
   John Brown's soul not a higher joy can crave—
   Freedom reigns today!   (Chorus)

Marching Song of the First Arkansas (Negro) Regiment

Words ascribed to Capt. Lindley Miller
Music: "John Brown's Body"

1. Oh, we're the bully soldiers of the "First of Arkansas,"
   We are fighting for the Union, we are fighting for the law,
   We can hit a Rebel further than a white man ever saw,
   As we go marching on.
   Chorus:
   Glory, glory hallelujah,
   Glory, glory hallelujah,
   Glory, glory hallelujah,
   As we go marching on.

2. See, there above the center, where the flag is waving bright,
   We are going out of slavery; we're bound for freedom's light;
   We mean to show Jeff Davis how the Africans can fight,
   As we go marching on!   (Chorus)

3. We have done with hoeing cotton, we have done with hoeing corn,
   We are colored Yankee soldiers, now, as sure as you are born;
   When the masters hear us yelling, they'll think it's Gabriel's horn,
   As we go marching on.   (Chorus)

4. They will have to pay us wages, the wages of their sin,
   They will have to bow their foreheads to their colored kith and kin,
   They will have to give us house-room, or the roof shall tumble in!
   As we go marching on.   (Chorus)

5. We heard the Proclamation, master hush it as he will,
   The bird he sing it to us, hoppin' on the cotton hill,
   And the possum up the gum tree, he couldn't keep it still,
   As he went climbing on.   (Chorus)

6. They said, "Now colored brethren, you shall be forever free,
   From the first of January, Eighteen hundred sixty-three."
   We heard it in the river going rushing to the sea,
   As it went sounding on.   (Chorus)

7. Father Abraham has spoken and the message has been sent,
   The prison doors he opened, and out the pris'ners went,
   To join the sable army of the "African descent,"
   As we go marching on.   (Chorus)

8. Then fall in, colored brethren, you'd better do it soon,
   Don't you hear the drum a-beating the Yankee Doodle tune?
   We are with you now this morning, we'll be far away at noon,
   As we go marching on.   (Chorus)

For the Dear Old Flag I Die

Words by George Cooper
Music by Stephen Collins Foster

SONGS OF THE UNION

face, Moth - er take me to your heart, Let me die in your em - brace. For the dear old Flag I die, Moth - er, dry your weep - ing eye; For the hon - or of our land And the dear old Flag I die."

Chorus

28

2. "Do not mourn, my mother, dear,
   Every pang will soon be o'er;
   For I hear the angel band
   Calling from their starry shore;
   Now I see their banners wave
   In the light of perfect day,
   Though 'tis hard to part with you,
   Yet I would not wish to stay."   (Chorus)

3. Farewell mother, Death's cold hand
   Weighs upon my spirit now,
   And I feel his blighting breath
   Fan my pallid cheek and brow.
   Closer! closer! to your heart,
   Let me feel that you are by,
   While my sight is growing dim,
   For the dear old Flag I die.   (Chorus)

Marching Along

Words and music by William B. Bradbury

SONGS OF THE UNION

Chorus

March - ing a - long, we are march - ing a - long, Gird on the ar - mor and be march - ing a - long; Mc - Clel - lan's our lead - er, he's gal - lant and strong; For God and for coun - try we are march - ing a - long.

2. The foe is before us in battle array,
But let us not waver or turn from the way;
The Lord is our strength and the Union's our
    song;
With courage and faith we are marching along.
    (Chorus)

3. Our wives and our children we leave in your care,
We feel you will help them with sorrow to bear;
'Tis hard thus to part, but we hope 'twon't be
    long,
We'll keep up our heart as we're marching
    along. (Chorus)

4. We sigh for our country, we mourn for our dead,
For them now our last drop of blood we will
    shed;
Our cause is the right one—our foe's in the
    wrong;
Then gladly we'll sing as we're marching along.
    (Chorus)

5. The flag of our country is floating on high,
We'll stand by that flag till we conquer or die;
McClellan's our leader, he's gallant and strong,
We'll gird on our armor and be marching along.
    (Chorus)

31

The Army of the Free

Words by Frank H. Norton
Music: "Wearing of the Green"

In the ar-my of the Un-ion we are march-ing in the van, And will
do the work be-fore us, if the brav-est sol-diers can; We will
drive the Reb-el forc-es from their strong-holds to the sea, And will

SONGS OF THE UNION

live and die to-geth-er in the Ar-my of the Free. The
Ar-my of the Free, the Ar-my of the Free, We will
live and die to-geth-er in the Ar-my of the Free.

33

2. We may rust beneath inaction, we may sink beneath disease,
   The summer sun may scorch us or the winter's blasts may freeze,
   But whatever may befall us, we will let the Rebels see,
   That unconquered we shall still remain the Army of the Free.
      The Army of the Free, the Army of the Free,
      Unconquered we shall still remain the Army of the Free.

3. We are the best division of a half a million souls,
   And only resting on our arms till the war cry onward rolls;
   When our gallant General Porter calls, why ready we shall be,
   To follow him forever with the Army of the Free.
      The Army of the Free, the Army of the Free,
      We will follow him forever with the Army of the Free.

4. We have Butterfield the daring and we've Martindale the cool,
   Where could we learn the art of war within a better school;
   Add Morell to the list of names, and we must all agree,
   We have the finest Generals in the Army of the Free.
      The Army of the Free, the Army of the Free,
      We have the finest Generals in the Army of the Free.

5. Though we live in winter quarters now, we're waiting but the hour,
   When Porter's brave division shall go forth in all its power,
   And when on the field of battle, fighting we shall be,
   We'll show that we cannot disgrace the Army of the Free.
      The Army of the Free, the Army of the Free,
      We'll show that we cannot disgrace the Army of the Free.

6. Then hurrah for our Division, may it soon be called to go,
   To add its strength to those who have advanced to meet the foe;
   God bless it, for we know right well, wherever it may be,
   'Twill never fail to honor our great Army of the Free.
      The Army of the Free, the Army of the Free,
      'Twill never fail to honor our great Army of the Free.

Tramp! Tramp! Tramp! (The Prisoner's Hope)

Words and music by George F. Root

SONGS OF THE UNION

2. In the battle front we stood,
   When their fiercest charge they made,
   And they swept us off a hundred men or more,
   But before we reached their lines,
   They were beaten back dismayed,
   And we heard the cry of vict'ry o'er and o'er.
   (Chorus)

3. So within the prison cell
   We are waiting for the day
   That shall come to open wide the iron door,
   And the hollow eye grows bright,
   And the poor heart almost gay,
   As we think of seeing home and friends once
   more.   (Chorus)

Tramp! Tramp! Tramp!, II (Southern Version)

Words: anonymous
Music by George F. Root

1. In my prison cell I sit,
   Thinking, mother, dear, of you,
   And my happy Southern home so far away;
   And my eyes they fill with tears
   'Spite of all that I can do,
   Though I try to cheer my comrades and be gay.

Chorus:
   Tramp! Tramp! Tramp!
   The boys are marching;
   Cheer up, comrades, they will come.
   And beneath the stars and bars
   We shall breathe the air again
   Of freemen in our own beloved home.

2. In the battle front we stood
   When their fiercest charge they made,
   And our soldiers by the thousands sank to die;
   But before they reached our lines,
   They were driven back dismayed,
   And the "Rebel yell" went upward to the sky.
   (Chorus)

3. Now our great commander Lee
   Crosses broad Potomac's stream,
   And his legions marching northward take their
   way.
   On Pennsylvania's roads
   Will their trusty muskets gleam,
   And her iron hills shall echo to the fray.
   (Chorus)

4. In the cruel stockade-pen
   Dying slowly day by day,
   For weary months we've waited all in vain;
   But if God will speed the way
   Of our gallant boys in gray,
   I shall see your face, dear mother, yet again.
   (Chorus)

5. When I close my eyes in sleep,
   All the dear ones 'round me come,
   At night my little sister to me calls;
   And mocking visions bring
   All the warm delights of home,
   While we freeze and starve in Northern prison
   walls.   (Chorus)

6. So the weary days go by,
   And we wonder as we sigh,
   If with sight of home we'll never more be
   blessed.
   Our hearts within us sink,
   And we murmur, though we try
   To leave it all with Him who knowest best.
   (Chorus)

Nine Miles to the Junction

Anonymous

The troops from Rhode Is - land were post - ed a - long, On the road from An - na - po - lis Sta - tion, As the Sev'n - ty First Reg - i -ment, one thou-sand strong, Went on in de - fense of the na - tion. We'd been

SONGS OF THE UNION

SONGS OF THE UNION

Junc-tion? We asked Gov-'nor Sprague to show us the way, And how man-y miles to the Junc - tion?

2. And Rhode Island boys cheered us on out of
    sight,
  After giving the following injunction:
  "Just keep up your courage, you'll get there to-
    night,
  For it's only nine miles to the Junction."
  They gave us hot coffee, a grasp of the hand,
  Which cheered and refreshed our exhaustion,
  And we reached in six hours the long promised
    land,
  For 'twas only nine miles to the Junction.
    Only nine miles, only nine miles,
    Only nine miles to the Junction.
    We reached in six hours the long promised
    land,
  For 'twas only nine miles to the Junction.

3. And now as we meet them in Washington's
    streets,
  They always do hail us with unction,
  And still the old cry someone surely repeats:
  "It's only nine miles to the Junction!"
  Three cheers for the warmhearted Rhode Is-
    land boys,
  May each one be true to his function,
  And whenever we meet, let us each other greet,
  With, "Only nine miles to the Junction!"
    Only nine miles, only nine miles,
    Only nine miles to the Junction,
    Whenever we meet, let us each other greet,
    With, "Only nine miles to the Junction!"

4. Nine cheers for the flag under which we will fight,
  If the traitors should dare to assail it,
  One cheer for each mile that we made on that
    night,
  When 'twas only nine miles to the Junction.
  With hearts thus united, our breasts to the foe,
  Once again with delight we will hail it,
  And if duty should call us, still onward we'll go,
  If even nine miles to the Junction.
    Even nine miles, even nine miles,
    Even nine miles to the Junction,
    If duty should call, still onward we'll go,
    If even nine miles to the Junction.

The Why and the Wherefore

Anonymous

41

speak my mind quite free - ly Now ree - ly."

2. "Why, why, why, and why,
And why to the war, young man?"
"Did a man ever fight for a holier cause,
Than Freedom and Flag and Equal Laws?
Just speak your mind quite freely—Now reely."

3. "Which, which, which, and which,
And which is the Flag of the free?"
"O Washington's Flag, with the stripes and the
stars,
Will you give such a name to the thing with the
bars?
I speak my mind quite freely—Now reely."

4. "Who, who, who, and who,
And who goes with you to the war?"
"Ten thousand brave lads, and if they should
stay here,
The girls would cry shame, and *they'd* volunteer!
They speak their mind quite freely—Now reely."

5. "When, when, when, and when,
And when do you mean to come back?"
"When Rebellion is crushed and the Union re-
stored,
And Freedom is safe—yes, then, please the Lord!
I speak my mind quite freely—Now reely."

6. "What, what, what, and what,
And what will you gain by that?"
"O I've gained enough whatever the cost,
If Freedom, the hope of the world, isn't lost.
I speak my mind quite freely—Now reely."

Marching Through Georgia

Words and music by Henry C. Work

SONGS OF THE UNION

fif - ty thou-sand strong, While we were march - ing through Geor - gia. Hur - rah! Hur - rah! We bring the ju - bi - lee! Hur - rah! Hur rah! The flag that makes you free! So we sang the cho - rus from At - lan - ta to the sea, While we were march - ing through Geor - gia.

2. How the darkeys shouted when they heard the joyful sound!
   How the turkeys gobbled which our commissary found!
   How the sweet potatoes even started from the ground,
      While we were marching through Georgia.   (Chorus)

3. Yes, and there were Union men who wept with joyful tears,
   When they saw the honored flag they had not seen for years;
   Hardly could they be restrained from breaking forth in cheers,
      While we were marching through Georgia.   (Chorus)

4. "Sherman's dashing Yankee boys will never reach the coast!"
   So the saucy Rebels said, and 'twas a handsome boast;
   Had they not forgot, alas! to reckon with the host,
      While we were marching through Georgia.   (Chorus)

5. So we made a thoroughfare for Freedom and her train,
   Sixty miles in latitude, three hundred to the main;
   Treason fled before us, for resistance was in vain,
      While we were marching through Georgia.   (Chorus)

In Dixie Land I'll Take My Stand!

MARCHING AND INSPIRATIONAL SONGS

OF THE CONFEDERACY

In Dixie Land,
I'll take my stand,
To live and die in Dixie.

Come all ye sons of freedom,
And join our Southern band;
We are going to fight the Yankees
And drive them from our land.

So sang Rebel troops in the first days of the war as the newly organized Confederacy inflicted bitter defeats on the badly demoralized Union armies and the sweet marching songs of victory filled the Southern air. To the ordinary Southerner, "Northern Abolition" appeared helpless before the united stand of the Confederate states, whose songs declared their purpose:

Secession is our watchword;
Our rights we all demand.

And in the first heady successes of the war, the future of the Confederacy indeed appeared bright and hopeful. It was in this period that the best of the Southern war songs were written, when songsmiths could salute their nation's newborn flag, singing:

Bright Banner of Freedom, with pride I unfold thee,
Fair flag of my country, with love I behold thee,
Gleaming above us in freshness and youth,
Emblem of Liberty, symbol of truth.

A favorite theme of the inspirational and propaganda songs of the Confederacy was the glory of the South and of the new nation. John H. Hewitt, the Confederacy's leading composer, wrote:

A nation has sprung into life
Beneath the bright Cross of the South;
. . .
Then, hail to the land of the pine!
The home of the noble and free.

And a poet by the name of Daniel E. Townsend wrote of "Freedom's New Banner" flying gloriously over

. . . the land that's richest in beauty,
The homestead of justice and right,
Whose sons are the foremost in duty,
Whose daughters are peerless and bright.

The great tradition of rebellion was another source of inspiration to Southern song writers. Confederate leaders identified themselves with all revolutionary movements in history. The French "Marseillaise" was extremely popular throughout the South and came to be so identified with the Southern cause that it fell into general disfavor throughout the North. Confederate lyrics were written to the old French Revolution anthem, and while they were overly literary, the song had the great advantage of a stirring and familiar melody:

Ye men of Southern hearts and feeling,
Arm! Arm! your struggling country calls!

In New Orleans, the song writer-publisher, A. E. Blackmar, wrote "The Southern Marseillaise":

Sons of the South awake to glory,
A thousand voices bid you rise.

Mostly, of course, the identification was with the American Revolution and the great Southerners who played a leading role in the nation's formative years. A "Southern War Cry" called on the "Countrymen of Washington, Countrymen of Jefferson" to live or fall for "Liberty," while others gloried in the appellation "Rebel":

Rebel is a sacred name;
Traitor, too, is glorious;
By such names our fathers fought—
By them were victorious.

Washington a rebel was,
Jefferson a traitor,
But their treason won success,
And made their glory greater.

Few songs undertook the defense of slavery. More often the delicate subject would be handled obliquely and with gentle euphemisms, as in "Bonnie Blue Flag," which hailed the Southern states "fighting for the property we gained by honest toil."

While slavery itself was but lightly touched upon in Southern song, not so the Northern Abolitionists, those

. . . jealous, blind fanatics [who] dare
To offer in their zeal unbounded,
Our happy slaves their tender care.

In the heat of wartime zeal, of course, any Unionist was considered an Abolitionist. In one fierce outburst of regional chauvinism directed at the North, the Southerners declared:

> You have no such blood as ours
> For the shedding:
> In the veins of cavaliers
> Was its heading!
> You have no such stately men
> In your "abolition den."

And while there was no fouler appellation in the Rebel lexicon than "Abolitionist," a special degree of venom was reserved for the New England variety:

> How peaceful and blest was America's soil,
> Till betrayed by the guile of the Puritan demon.

The character of the Confederate inspirational songs reveals the glaring poverty of the South. With a hopelessly outdated economic system, and with a concurrent cultural lag, the musical and literary output of the South was bounded by the genteel tradition (and literary style) of Europe, on the one side, and the lack of development of an indigenous musical idiom on the other. Southern composers were prevented by reason of class, history, and outlook from tapping the great wealth of Negro music which was springing up around them—a hurdle which Northern composers were beginning to overcome with results highly favorable to their musical output. Of all the significant Confederate inspirational songs, it was only the Northern-composed "Dixie" which drew on the Negro musical idiom in any manner, while the other two most popular Southern war songs, "The Bonnie Blue Flag" and "Maryland, My Maryland," drew upon European sources for their melodies.

As with supplies, ammunition, and human resources, the songs with which the Southerners fought could prove no match for the marching melodies of the North. In published songs alone, the musical output of the Union was some ten times larger than that of the Confederacy.

These patriotic and inspirational songs of the Confederacy are extremely important, however, for what they tell us of the American South in the middle of the nineteenth century, and for their reflection of the hopes and dreams and outlook of both the political leaders and the common people of "The Lost Cause."

DIXIE'S LAND. The Confederacy's most popular song, indeed the only Southern war song to become a part of the national musical stream, was written in 1859 by one of the first and greatest of America's black-face minstrels, Daniel Decatur Emmett. (For additional discussion on minstrel songs in the Civil War, see section ". . . Grafted into the Army.") Emmett, a leading light of Bryant's famed Minstrels, who were performing in New York during the winter of '59, was asked to write a new tune for the company to be used as a "walk-around" by the troupe. Emmett dashed off the words and music one rainy Sunday afternoon and the song was immediately added to the show where it proved an instantaneous hit. (Le-Roy Rice, *Monarchs of Minstrelsy*, gives September 12, 1859, as the date of the song's first performance.)

Other minstrel companies and individual variety performers began singing it as the song's popularity grew. A year later, in 1860, Mrs. John Wood introduced the song to New Orleans, from which city it quickly spread throughout the South.

At a different time and under other circumstances, the zestful melody would undoubtedly have gone the way of most other minstrel hits of the day, fading into musical oblivion after a meteoric career. But the year was 1860, the year of Lincoln's election and the onset of Secession—and it almost seemed that fate had arranged to give the South a national anthem at the very moment of crisis. (That it was an anthem composed by a "Yankee" and written to be performed in Negro black-face style did not seem to affect the song's popularity, although many among the South's literati tried their best to improve on the original with what they considered to be more appropriate words to the engaging melody.)

As state after state declared for Secession and as the Confederacy girded for war, the song swept across the Southern states from Virginia to Texas. "Dixie" retained its popularity throughout the war, being the favorite model for soldier parodies and various propaganda efforts. Most of these retained the original chorus, and possibly it is those two middle lines in the refrain which account for the song's endurance:

> In Dixie Land I'll take my stand,
> To lib and die in Dixie.

SONGS OF THE CONFEDERACY

A fairly common Confederate soldier's version retained the chorus and added the following stanzas:

> Away down South in the fields of cotton,
> Cinnamon seed and sandy bottom, etc.
>
> Way down South in the fields of cotton,
> Vinegar shoes and paper stockings, etc.
>
> Pork and cabbage in the pot,
> It goes in cold and comes out hot, etc.
>
> Vinegar put right on red beet,
> It makes them always fit to eat, etc.

Emmett, himself, was undoubtedly one of the most gifted tunesmiths of his day, that marvelous combination of composer and performer who is so close to the process of folk creation. In fact, many of Emmett's compositions so nearly approach folk song in mood and idiom that, in one form or another, they have become a part of the American folk tradition. Songs like "Blue Tail Fly," "Old Dan Tucker," "Boatman's Dance," "Jim Along Josey," and many others by old Uncle Dan, have, by now, entered the mainstream of our folk music where they have been revised, refashioned and parodied countless times.

Whether "Dixie" had such staying power on its own merits we will never know. But taken over and sung as the musical symbol of rebellion in our great fratricidal war, it remains today a living melodic memory of the fiercest conflict ever fought on American soil.

DIXIE. This parody to Dan Emmett's tune by Brigadier General Albert Pike of the Confederate Army was the most popular and widely known of all the efforts at "literary improvement" which were imposed on "Dixie's Land." The comical dialect verses from the original have been thrown out, the refrain has taken on a military timbre, but those two key middle lines of the chorus still remain with but a minor change:

> For Dixie's Land we take our stand,
> And live or die for Dixie.

Pike, himself, was a veteran of the Mexican War and a successful newspaperman, with a national reputation as writer, poet, and lawyer. His chief assignment for the Confederacy was to win the Indian Five Nations to the Rebel cause, which re-sulted in his leading a force of Indians at the Battle of Pea Ridge in 1862. Differences with the Confederate High Command led to his resignation later that year.

A "Dixie War Song" dedicated to "the boys in Virginia" was still another literary parody, this one written by H. S. Stanton, Esq. Stanton's refrain was a rousing plea to battle, but he neglected to keep the "take our stand" lines and perhaps this is one reason why his song never caught on:

> Oh, fly to arms in Dixie!
> To arms! To arms!
> From Dixie's Land we'll rout the band
> That comes to conquer Dixie,
> To arms! To arms!
> And rout the foe from Dixie!

THE OFFICERS OF DIXIE. The conflict between officers and men is one that is common to all armies, and recent wars have produced a good number of soldier songs which are as outspokenly anti-officer as any private could wish. While the Civil War undoubtedly had its share of such songs, early collectors and anthologists were extremely reluctant to include such material in their works, probably out of some mistaken notion of loyalty to their cause. One of the most popular of Civil War songs, "All Quiet Along the Potomac," given in another section, touches on the theme in a more oblique way.

"The Officers of Dixie," however, written to the South's most popular tune by a self-styled "Growler" (presumably a Confederate private or noncom), is a head-on attack directed against the undue glorification of officers. Possibly it was an ordinary soldier's reaction to the type of effusive Southern war poetry which commemorated "The Officer's Funeral" in such shadowy images as:

> Hark to the shrill trumpet calling,
> It pierceth the soft summer air.

(For another Confederate song on this theme, see "The Brass-Mounted Army.")

UNION DIXIE. Northern parodies to "Dixie's Land" were probably as numerous as Southern, but no amount of Yankee rhyme or reason could reclaim Dan Emmett's song for the North. It is doubtful that any Northern parody stood much chance of winning popular favor once the melody itself had become so identified with the Southern cause. Even before hostilities broke out, Unionists were employing the tune to rally against Secession:

> As our fathers crushed oppression,
> Deal with those who breathe secession,
> Then away, then away,
> Then away to the fight.

Many of the songs indulged in disparaging the oft-sung "land of cotton":

> Let others praise the land of cotton,
> Nigger-slaves, and treason rotten,

wrote one Union poet, while another, equally explicit, exclaimed:

> Den I'm glad I'm not in de land of treason,
> Where folks nebber hear to reason,
> Look away, etc.

Others echoed the Southerner's yearning to be in "Dixie," but for different reasons:

> Then I wish I was in Dixie,
> Away, away,
> In Dixie land I'll take my stand
> To flog Jeff Davis and his band,
> Away, away, away down South in Dixie.

Still others set out to appropriate the tune itself, forsaking the original lyrics completely in an effort to construct a patriotic ditty:

> Let all good Union men about,
> Come join us in a glorious shout,
> Hurrah, hurrah, hurrah, hurrah!
> For Union and our country dear,
> We'll raise aloft a hearty cheer,
> Hurrah, hurrah, hurrah, hurrah!
>
> Then for our Union we will stand,
> Hurrah! Hurrah!
> And all throughout this happy land,
> Will join together heart and hand;
> Hurrah, hurrah! Then hurrah for our Union!
> Hurrah, hurrah! Then hurrah for our Union!

"Union Dixie" is one of the best of these parodies, but there is no evidence to show that it ever caught public fancy to any appreciable degree. It is presented here more as an example of the many Union efforts to "capture" the song than as a reflection of popularity or public acceptance.

THE BONNIE BLUE FLAG. Harry Macarthy, an English-born vaudevillian and songster, wrote the words for this, the second most popular song of the Confederacy. The melody is a traditional Irish air, "The Irish Jaunting Car."

As with so many popular Civil War songs, the exact circumstances surrounding the creation of "The Bonnie Blue Flag" are not clear, and a variety of conflicting stories has done little to clear up the mystery. One rather dramatic account ascribes the song's origin to the Mississippi Secession Convention, where, on January 9, 1861, a Mr. C. R. Dickson came to the hall carrying a blue silk flag bearing a single white star which his wife had just finished making. According to this story, Macarthy witnessed this scene and was inspired by it to pen the words to the well-known anthem. Other sources point out that South Carolina, the first of the states to secede, adopted a blue flag with a single white star as its standard upon leaving the Union, and that this was the direct inspiration for the song.

Still others take a more prosaic view of the matter, claiming that Macarthy merely dashed it off as an encore piece for his vaudeville turn, cashing in on the developing martial spirit of his Southern audiences in early 1861.

In any event, this much seems certain: The song was written by Macarthy early in 1861, and the entertainer began introducing it on his programs in Jackson, Mississippi, in the Spring of that year. Its success was assured, however, when Macarthy sang it to a soldier audience in New Orleans in September of '61, winning an instantaneous response. Soon, with the catchy melody and the simple chorus on the lips of scores of marching Rebel troops, the song spread in popularity throughout the South.

Written as a "parade of secession," the song reflected the rising and falling tide of Confederate hopes. After "the single star . . . [had] grown to be eleven," Macarthy and other enthusiasts sang verses dedicated to other defections from the Union which were more wish than fact.

We cast our eyes far northward and lo! Missouri comes,
With roar of dread artillery and sound of martial drums.

(A few months later, Macarthy would write another of his popular songs, "Missouri, or A Voice from the South," a plea to the "bright land of the West" to "add your bright Star to our Flag of Eleven.")

In still another verse, the South was advised to

Make room upon the Bonnie Blue Flag,
Kentucky makes thirteen!

The "Bonnie Blue Flag" of the Confederacy, soon to become the "Stars and Bars," was a favorite theme for Southern song writers, who celebrated "Freedom's New Banner" in scores of lyrics:

When clouds of oppression o'ershaded
The banner that liberty bore,
Bright stars from the galaxy faded,
The day of its splendor was o'er;
Those stars, in a fresh constellation,
A sky in the South now adorn;
And blazon throughout all creation,
That freedom's new banner is born.

Many Confederate "flag" songs parodied traditional American patriotic airs, such as "Columbia, the Gem of the Ocean," and "The Star-Spangled Banner":

Let the bars and stars of our banner ever wave,
O'er the land of the South, the home of the brave.

Perhaps it seems anomalous to us today that a Southern song should proclaim the "Stars and Bars" as the

... Flag of the free!
Ere thy sons will be slaves, they will perish with thee.

But Southerners believed that they were fighting for the freedom of the States in the Union to govern themselves and for the freedom to own slaves. And so they saw no contradiction in singing:

Bright banner of freedom! with pride I unfold thee,
Fair flag of my country, with love I behold thee,
Gleaming above us in freshness and youth,
Emblem of Liberty, symbol of truth.

In general, the South was careful to avoid undue reference to its "peculiar institution," so that subsequent versions of "Bonnie Blue Flag" appear with the second line changed from:

Fighting for the property we gained by honest toil,

a delicate allusion to slavery, to:

Fighting for our Liberty, with treasure, blood, and toil.

Many parodies to "Bonnie Blue Flag" sprang up throughout the South, two of which, "The Homespun Dress" and "The Bonnie White Flag," appear in this volume and are discussed separately, immediately following. Perhaps some of the Southern literary elite were disappointed in the mundane lyrics to this extremely popular song, just as the literati had no use for the "common lyrics" of "Dixie." (In the North, many among the more "cultivated" had nothing but scorn for the literary qualifications of "John Brown's Body," "Battle Cry of Freedom," and other songs.)

One of the many "Bonnie Blue Flag" parodies which seems to be an effort at "literary improvement" was written by Annie Chambers Ketchum, who could look forward to the day when

The gazing world afar,
Shall greet with shouts the Bonnie Blue Flag
That bears the cross and star.

The song retained its popularity throughout the war, and its publisher, A. E. Blackmar of New Orleans, is reported to have been arrested and fined by General Benjamin F. Butler during the Union occupation of New Orleans for continuing to publish the song despite an official ban against it.

Macarthy himself is supposed to have written a post-war parody, entitled "Our Country's Flag," suggesting the wisdom of reconciliation:

We're still the "Band of Brothers" that proudly once unfurled
The Bonnie Blue Flag, whose "single star" was sung throughout the world.
But now that war no longer reigns, let the cry be heard afar,
Hurrah for our country's flag, yes each and every star.

As did so many other Civil War songs, "The Bonnie Blue Flag" seeped through the battlelines, inspiring a number of Union parodies and replies. One of the most interesting of these is "The Flag with the Thirty-four Stars":

The Rebels sing "The Bonnie Blue Flag,"
But we the "Stripes and Stars,"
Our Union flag we love so true,
Will conquer their stars and bars,
Their Secesh airs, their "Maryland,"
Their contrabands of war,
Our cause is right, the flag for the fight
Is the one with the thirty-four stars.

Hurrah! Hurrah!
For equal rights, hurrah!
Hurrah for the dear old flag,
With every stripe and star.

Another Union parody, "The Stars and Stripes," follows the pattern of the original, counting off the states of the North who sent troops to man the Union armies. Thomas Williams, who wrote the words, set out to copy the original as closely as possible. Here are the first two verses of his fourteen-stanza lyric:

Brothers of free descent were we, and native to the soil,
Knit soul to soul in one great whole, fruit of our father's
   toil:
But when that bond of love was rent, the cry rose near
   and far,
To arms! To arms! long live the stripes! We know no
   "single star."

Hurrah! Hurrah!
For the Union Flag, hurrah!
Hurrah for the Union Flag,
That knows no "single star."

So long as Southern arrogance forbore to touch that flag,
Full many a taunt we meekly bore, and many an idle
   brag:
But when on Sumter's battlements, the traitors did it
   mar,
We flung abroad that Union Flag, that ne'er shall lose a
   star.

THE HOMESPUN DRESS. This widely known parody to "The Bonnie Blue Flag" has become a part of Southern folklore, finding even greater currency in oral tradition than in the printed text. Sometimes known as "The Southern Girl's Song," it has been found by folklorists in a number of variant forms but with the same basic theme and story. Arthur Palmer Hudson, in *Folksongs of Mississippi,* writes:

"The Homespun Dress" was immensely popular in Mississippi. Almost every woman, and many of the men, who lived through the period of the Civil War or grew up with the generation after the war could sing it.

Most authorities agree in attributing authorship to Miss Carrie Bell Sinclair, of Augusta, Georgia, reportedly a literary protégé of Alexander Stephens, vice-president of the Confederacy. Other sources have credited a Lieutenant Harrington of Alabama with authorship of the words, citing as inspiration for the song a dance in Lexington, Kentucky, given in honor of Morgan's Cavalry and at which the women wore homespun dresses. But this tale seems to be composed more of romance than truth.

Miss Sinclair, who also wrote the lyrics to such songs as "The Soldier's Suit of Gray," "Strike for the South," and "Georgia, My Georgia," is supposed to have written the song in 1862 or 1863. Sheet music copies do not appear until after the war, although it appears in at least one Confederate songster as early as 1864.

Folk singer Frank Warner has collected an interesting version of the song in which a Southern girl refuses the hand of a Yankee soldier, saying:

I cannot listen to your words,
The land's too far and wide;
Go seek some happy Northern girl
To be your loving bride.
My brothers, they were soldiers,
The youngest of the three
Was slain while fighting by the side
Of General Fitzhugh Lee.

Hurrah! Hurrah!
For the sunny South, I say,
Three cheers for the Southern girl
And the boy that wore the gray.

THE BONNIE WHITE FLAG. This interesting prisoner-of-war parody to "The Bonnie Blue Flag" appeared in print in 1864 in the *Camp Chase Ventilator,* a prison-camp newspaper. Its author was a Confederate colonel and the frank expression for peace, even if it meant surrender ("the Bonnie White Flag that ends this cruel war") is revealing of the fast-fading hopes of the Confederacy at this stage of the conflict.

MARYLAND, MY MARYLAND. The electric success of "Maryland, My Maryland" in the early days of the war has more to do with history than with literature or music, successful as James R. Randall's work may be on both the latter counts. The lyric was written on April 23, 1861, at Poydras College, Pointe-Coupée, Louisiana, where the twenty-two-year-old Randall, a native of Maryland, was a professor of English literature. Strongly Southern in his political sentiments, Randall had just heard the news that Massachusetts troops marching through the streets of Baltimore had been fired upon by the local citizenry.

The news was particularly heartening to Randall who had begun to despair of his native state casting its lot with that of the Confederacy. This latest incident seemed to him an indication that

Maryland would soon join her sister states beneath the "Bonnie Blue Flag."

His poem, exulting over this display of solidarity with the Confederate cause, was a fervent plea for Maryland to take the complete step of Secession. So impassioned was Randall's song, and so sure was he that Maryland would secede ("She breathes! She burns! She'll come! She'll come!") that Southern readers were swept along in the tide of emotion and believed that Randall truly spoke for all of Maryland.

The day after writing his poem, Randall read it to his class at Poydras, where the students received it enthusiastically, urging their professor to submit it for publication. Randall sent his poem to the New Orleans *Delta* in whose pages it appeared April 26, 1861.

In this first printed version of the poem, as in all subsequent purely poetic printings, the structure follows this pattern.

> The despot's heel is on thy shore,
> Maryland!
> His torch is at thy temple door,
> Maryland!

Following publication in the *Delta,* other Southern papers reprinted the poem extensively. In Baltimore itself, *The South,* a pro-Confederate paper, was the first to carry the famous lyric.

Pro-Southern Baltimoreans, caught by the power of Randall's fervent poem, tried setting it to music. The first tune to which it was adapted was the traditional French air, "Ma Normandie." The real success of the song, however, dates to its adaptation to the melody of "Lauriger Horatius" (a popular Yale college song, in turn from the German "Tannenbaum") by Miss Jennie Cary of Baltimore. Randall himself, in an account written years later, tells us that Miss Cary and her sister sang the song to Confederate troops in Virginia on July 4, 1861, where its reception was overwhelmingly enthusiastic.

In adapting Randall's lyric to the "Tannenbaum" tune, Miss Cary was forced to add the words "My Maryland" to the second, fourth, and eighth lines in each stanza—an addition which, in my opinion, has given the song an added poetic dimension.

But despite Randall's urging and the immense popularity of the song, Maryland did not secede. Randall tried to reassure the South that Maryland yet would join the Confederacy in still another lyric, "There's Life in the Old Land Yet":

> We sleep, but we are not dead.
>
> . . .
>
> And we—though we smite not—are not thralls,
> We are piling a gory debt;
> While down by McHenry's dungeon walls,
> There's Life in the Old Land yet!

But when, after a year of war, Maryland was still in the Union, it was obvious that the Rebel cause was not strong enough to bring the Old Line State over to the Confederacy. This change in Southern outlook is reflected in an 1862 song called "We'll Be Free in Maryland":

> The boys down South in Dixie's land,
> The boys down South in Dixie's land,
> The boys down South in Dixie's land,
> Will come and rescue Maryland.
>
> . . .
>
> We'll drink this toast to one and all,
> Keep cocked and primed for the Southern call;
> The day will come, we'll make the stand,
> Then we'll be free in Maryland.

Randall, who was born in Baltimore, January 1, 1839, and was educated at Georgetown College in the District of Columbia, wrote many other poems for the Confederate cause, and continued his literary activities after the war as well, becoming one of the South's better-known minor poets. Among his other war efforts were "John Pelham (The Dead Cannoneer)," "The Lone Sentry," and "Battle Cry of the South." None of these, however, came anywhere near achieving the success and popularity of "Maryland, My Maryland."

ANSWER TO "MY MARYLAND." Union responses to "Maryland" were turned out by scores of Yankee song writers, most of them following the pattern and wording of the original. Sep Winner, of Philadelphia, one of the more successful Civil War song writers, wrote:

> The Rebel horde is on thy shore,
> Maryland, my Maryland!
> Arise and drive him from thy door,
> Maryland, my Maryland!

while an Ohio songster wrote:

> Should traitor bands invade thy shore,
> Maryland, my Maryland,
> Thy sons will rally as of yore,
> Maryland, my Maryland.

Since the original was penned by "A Balti-morean in New Orleans," "a Baltimorean in New York" assayed one reply:

> The traitor's foot is on thy soil,
> Maryland, my Maryland!
> Let not his touch thy honor spoil,
> Maryland, my Maryland!

One parody merely appropriated the tune to sing, upon the issuance of the Emancipation Proclamation:

> This is the year of Jubilee,
> Abraham, my Abraham,
> The Darkies now can all be free,
> Abraham, my Abraham!

Of all the Union parodies, which I have come across, however, this "Answer to 'My Maryland'" seems easily the best, its earthy satire providing a most effective response to the florid imagery of the original. From a literary standpoint, at least, James Randall's high-sounding couplet,

> I see the blush upon thy cheek,
> But thou wast ever bravely meek,

is completely demolished by

> I see no blush upon thy cheek,
> It's not been washed for many a week.

None of these parodies, however, seem to have had any noticeable effect on the popularity or inspirational value of Randall's passionate poem.

KENTUCKY! O KENTUCKY! In the spring of 1862, General John Hunt Morgan ("Morgan the Raider") led his band of Confederate night raiders on a series of daring forays into Union territory in Tennessee and Kentucky. Born in Alabama and raised in Kentucky, Morgan harassed both Union troops and the civilian population with great success. This song, another Union parody to "Maryland," is an anonymous warning to Kentucky not to lend Morgan support. For more on Morgan's career and a Confederate song on the famed Rebel raider, see "How Are You, Jack Morgan?"

WE CONQUER OR DIE. James Pierpont's rallying song is a good example of the great host of Southern propaganda efforts written in the literary (and musical) style so common to the Confederacy. What is most distinguished about this song is the fact that its composer wrote the words

and music to one of America's all-time favorites, "Jingle Bells," published in 1857, in Boston, Massachusetts, by Oliver Ditson Company. Shortly after the outbreak of hostilities, Pierpont left Boston to return to his native South, where he devoted himself to the Secessionist cause. Pierpont also wrote a musical setting for Carrie Bell Sinclair's "Strike for the South!"

THE YELLOW ROSE OF TEXAS. This popular Confederate marching song was, like "Dixie," a product of the Northern minstrel stage. Its earliest recorded publication date is 1853 and its author is identified only as J.K. "The Yellow Rose of Texas" seems to be one of a group of songs (probably written in response to each other) concerning various "state sweethearts." The opening verse of one makes the reference explicit:

> Oh, niggers dey hab all sung sweet,
> About dar lubs ob late,
> But dar am none dat can compete
> Wid my Arkansas Kate.
>
> Oh Kate, my sweet Arkansas Kate,
> Dar's something tells dis nigger's heart,
> He's bound to marry Kate.

Another such song, "Belle ob Tenisee," contained a refrain which seems to make it a direct predecessor to "The Yellow Rose of Texas":

> You may talk about Susanna,
> An' your pretty Susa Teil,
> De belle ob Louisiana,
> An' de charming Lucy Neal.
> . . .
> Rosa, dearest Rosa,
> My heart still beats for thee,
> You're de only yaller gal I love,
> De belle ob Tenisee.

Subsequently, Southern troops would sing in almost direct reply:

> You may talk about your dearest May,
> And sing of Rosa Lee,
> But the Yellow Rose of Texas
> Beats the belles of Tennessee.

Unlike its companion pieces, "The Yellow Rose of Texas" was not written in the standard burnt-cork dialect of the day, the only such reference being the word "darkey" where the present text reads "soldier." (I have made this editorial change, since it seems more likely that Southern troops sang it in such a fashion and since "soldier" is, if anything, more consistent with the style of the song.)

Confederate parodies made their inevitable appearance, and Mrs. J. D. Young contributed a rather literary "Song of the Texas Rangers" to the same tune:

> The morning star is paling,
> The campfires flicker low,
> Our steeds are madly neighing,
> For the bugle bids us go:
> So put the foot in stirrup
> And shake the bridle free,
> For today the Texas Rangers
> Must cross the Tennessee.

A soldier parody sung by the troops of General John B. Hood's command succinctly sums up the disastrous Tennessee campaign of 1864:

> And now I'm going Southward,
> For my heart is full of woe,
> I'm going back to Georgia
> To find my Uncle Joe.
> You may talk about your dearest May
> And sing of Rosalie,
> But the gallant Hood of Texas
> Played hell in Tennessee.

STONEWALL JACKSON'S WAY. Songs commemorating generals were composed by the score on both sides of the war. Lee, Jackson, and Beauregard were favorite Southern subjects, while Union tunesmiths, due to the constantly changing Northern high command, had a large and fruitful field to choose from.

General Thomas Jonathan "Stonewall" Jackson was, and continues to be, one of the great legendary figures of the Confederacy. His untimely death, when he was accidentally shot by his own men during the Battle of Chancellorsville, left a gaping hole in Confederate ranks.

A number of musical tributes to Jackson appeared shortly after his death, although the best of these, "Stonewall Jackson's Way," was written before the fatal engagement. The inscription on the sheet music claims that the lyric was "found on a Confederate sergeant of the *old* Stonewall brigade taken at Winchester, Virginia,"—an occurrence so frequent as to immediately raise the direst suspicions concerning the song's origin. Subsequent research has shown that the poem

was written by John Williamson Palmer, a Confederate war correspondent for some New York newspapers. The earliest sheet music print we have is dated 1862, and one source specifically dates the composition of the song to September 17, 1862, at Oakland, Maryland, during the course of the Battle of Antietam.

While the composer of the tune remains anonymous, Brander Matthews indicates that the song may have originally been sung to the tune of "Camptown Races," and indeed, the lyrics fit the melody, if not the mood, of Foster's classic minstrel tune.

RIDING A RAID. General James Ewell Brown Stuart, one of the daring Confederate cavalry leaders of the war, was considered by Lee to be "the eyes of my army." In his plumed hat, with an air of roguish gallantry and daring adventure, Stuart was the picture of the Southern cavalier, more frequent in fiction than fact.

This musical tribute to Stuart may relate to a period when the famed cavalryman had been assigned to work with Stonewall Jackson during the early Virginia campaigns in which the reputations of both were built.

The tune is the traditional Scottish air, "Bonnie Dundee." Some post-war collections omit the third verse with the reference to "a man in a white house with blood on his mouth!"

THE YOUNG VOLUNTEER. Here is one of the many wartime compositions of John Hill Hewitt, one of the South's most prolific composers and considered by many the most legitimate claimant to the title, "Bard of the Stars and Bars." Hewitt, whose melodies championed and inspired the Southern cause, was not a Southerner by birth; his native city was New York, where he was born into a musical family in 1801. In 1823 he settled in the South, beginning as a music teacher in Augusta. Hewitt remained in the South for the rest of his life, except for a brief period in Boston after his father's death.

His best-known song, "The Minstrel's Return from the War," was written in 1825. Thirty-five years later, Hewitt parodied his own early success for one of the first songs of the Confederacy, "Southern Song of Freedom":

Our flag, with its cluster of stars,
Firm fixed in a field of pure blue,
All shining through red and white bars,
Now gallantly flutters in view.

Among Hewitt's other compositions were "Flag of the Sunny South," "The Soldier's Farewell,"

"The Stonewall Quick-Step," "You Are Going to the Wars, Billy Boy," an extremely popular setting for "All Quiet Along the Potomac," and the music to another song in this collection, "Somebody's Darling."

Dixie's Land

Words and music by Daniel D. Emmett

SONGS OF THE CONFEDERACY

Dix - ie Land whar I was born in, Ear - ly on one frost - y morn-in', Look a -

way! Look a - way! Look a - way! Dix - ie Land. Den I

wish I was in Dix - ie, Hoo - ray! Hoo - ray! In

Dix - ie Land I'll take my stand, To lib and die in Dix - ie, A -

SONGS OF THE CONFEDERACY

2. Ole missus marry "Will de weaber,"
   Willium was a gay deceaber;
      Look away! Look away!
      Look away! Dixie Land.
   But when he put his arm around 'er,
   He smiled as fierce as a forty pounder,
      Look away! Look away!
      Look away! Dixie Land.　(Chorus)

3. His face was sharp as a butcher's cleaber,
   But dat did not seem to greab 'er;
      Look away, etc.
   Ole missus acted de foolish part,
   And died for a man dat broke her heart,
      Look away, etc.　(Chorus)

4. Now here's a health to the next old Missus,
   An' all de gals dat want to kiss us;
      Look away, etc.
   But if you want to drive 'way sorrow,
   Come and hear dis song tomorrow,
      Look away, etc.　(Chorus)

5. Dar's buckwheat cakes and Injun batter,
   Makes you fat or a little fatter;
      Look away, etc.
   Den hoe it down an' scratch your grabble,
   To Dixie's Land I'm bound to trabble,
      Look away, etc.　(Chorus)

Dixie

Words by Albert Pike
Music: "Dixie's Land" (by Daniel D. Emmett)

1. Southrons, hear your country call you!
   Up, lest worse than death befall you!
   To arms! To arms! To arms! In Dixie!
   Lo! all the beacon fires are lighted—
   Let all hearts be now united!
   To arms! To arms! To arms! In Dixie!

   Chorus:
   Advance the flag of Dixie!
   Hurrah! Hurrah!
   For Dixie's Land we take our stand,
   And live or die for Dixie!
   To arms! To arms!
   And conquer peace for Dixie!
   To arms! To arms!
   And conquer peace for Dixie!

2. Hear the Northern thunders mutter!
   Northern flags in South winds flutter!
   To arms! etc.
   Send them back your fierce defiance!
   Stamp upon the cursed alliance!
   To arms! etc.   (Chorus)

3. Fear no danger! Shun no labor!
   Lift up rifle, pike, and sabre!
   To arms! etc.
   Shoulder pressing close to shoulder,
   Let the odds make each heart bolder!
   To arms! etc.   (Chorus)

4. How the South's great heart rejoices
   At your cannon's ringing voices!
   To arms! etc.
   For faith betrayed and pledges broken,
   Wrongs inflicted, insults spoken,
   To arms! etc.   (Chorus)

5. Strong as lions, swift as eagles,
   Back to their kennels hunt these beagles!
   To arms! etc.
   Cut the unequal bond asunder!
   Let them hence each other plunder!
   To arms! etc.   (Chorus)

6. Swear upon your country's altar
   Never to submit or falter!
   To arms! etc.
   Till the spoilers are defeated,
   Till the Lord's work is completed,
   To arms! etc.   (Chorus)

7. Halt not till our Federation
   Secures among earth's powers its station!
   To arms! etc.
   Then at peace, and crowned with glory,
   Hear your children tell the story!
   To arms! etc.   (Chorus)

8. If the loved ones weep in sadness,
   Victory soon shall bring them gladness.
   To arms! etc.
   Exultant pride soon banish sorrow;
   Smiles chase tears away tomorrow.
   To arms! etc.   (Chorus)

The Officers of Dixie

Words by "A Growler"
Music: "Dixie's Land" (by Daniel D. Emmett)

1. Let me whisper in your ear, sir,
   Something that the South should hear, sir,
   Of the war, of the war, of the war in Dixie;
   A growing curse—a "burning shame," sir,
   In the chorus I will name, sir,
   Of the war, of the war, of the war in Dixie.

Chorus:
   The officers of Dixie, alone, alone!
   The honors share, the honors wear,
   Throughout the land of Dixie!
   'Tis so, 'tis so, throughout the land of Dixie.
   'Tis so, 'tis so, throughout the land in Dixie.

2. Swelling, 'round with gold lace plenty,
   See the gay "brass button" gentry,
   In the war, in the war, in the war in Dixie.
   Solomon in all his splendors
   Was scarce arrayed like these "defenders,"
   In the war, in the war, in the war in Dixie.
   (Chorus)

3. In cities, sir, it is alarming
   To see them 'round the hotel swarming,
   Such a war, such a war, such a war in Dixie.
   And at each little one-horse town, sir,
   See the "birds" how they fly 'round, sir,
   Such a war, such a war, such a war in Dixie.
   (Chorus)

4. On the steamboat, in the cars, sir,
   Deep respect is shown the "bars," sir,
   Of the war, of the war, of the war in Dixie.
   For with all sexes, sizes, ages,
   How the "gold lace fever" rages,
   Of the war, of the war, of the war in Dixie.
   (Chorus)

5. The ladies! Bless the darling creatures!
   Quite distort their pretty features,
   For the war, for the war, for the war in Dixie.
   And say (I know you've seen it done, sir),
   "They'll have an officer or none, sir,"
   For the war, for the war, for the war in Dixie.
   (Chorus)

6. And if when death shots 'round us rattle,
   An officer is killed in battle,
   In the war, in the war, in the war in Dixie.
   How the martyr is lamented!
   (This is right—we've not dissented.)
   In the war, in the war, in the war in Dixie.
   (Chorus)

7. But only speak of it to show, sir,
   Privates are not honored so, sir,
   In the war, in the war, in the war in Dixie.
   No muffled drum, no wreath of glory,
   If one dies, proclaims the story,
   In the war, in the war, in the war in Dixie.
   (Chorus)

8. List the moral of my song, sir,
   In Dixie there is something wrong, sir,
   With the war, with the war, with the war in
     Dixie.
   As all that glitters is not gold, sir,
   Read and ponder what I've told, sir,
   Of the war, of the war, of the war in Dixie.
   (Chorus)

Union Dixie

Words: anonymous
Music: "Dixie's Land" (by Daniel D. Emmett)

1. Away down South in the land of traitors,
   Rattlesnakes and alligators,
   Right away, come away, right away, come away.
   Where cotton's king and men are chattels,
   Union boys will win the battles,
   Right away, come away, right away, come away.

   Then we'll all go down to Dixie,
   Away, away,
   Each Dixie boy must understand,
   That he must mind his Uncle Sam,
   Away, away,
   And we'll all go down to Dixie.
   Away, away,
   And we'll all go down to Dixie.

2. I wish I was in Baltimore,
   I'd make Secession traitors roar,
   Right away, come away, right away, come away.
   We'll put the traitors all to rout,
   I'll bet my boots we'll whip them out,
   Right away, come away, right away, come away.

   Then they'll wish they were in Dixie,
   Away, away,
   Each Dixie boy must understand,
   That he must mind his Uncle Sam,
   Away, away,
   We'll all go down to Dixie.
   Away, away,
   We'll all go down to Dixie.

3. Oh, may our Stars and Stripes still wave
   Forever o'er the free and brave,
   Right away, come away, right away, come away.
   And let our motto ever be—
   "For Union and for Liberty!"
   Right away, come away, right away, come away.

   Then we'll all go down to Dixie, etc.

64

The Bonnie Blue Flag

Words by Harry McCarthy
Music: "The Irish Jaunting Car"

SONGS OF THE CONFEDERACY

toil; _____ And when our rights were threat - ened, the cry rose near and far: _____ "Hur - rah for the Bon - nie Blue Flag that bears a sin - gle star!"_____ Hur - rah! _____ Hur - rah! _____ For South - ern rights, hur - rah! _____ Hur -

SONGS OF THE CONFEDERACY

rah   for the   Bon- nie Blue Flag   that bears   a sin - gle star. ____

2. As long as the Union was faithful to her trust,
   Like friends and brethren, kind were we, and just;
   But now, when Northern treachery attempts our rights to mar,
   We hoist on high the Bonnie Blue Flag that bears a single star.   (Chorus)

3. First gallant South Carolina nobly made the stand,
   Then came Alabama and took her by the hand;
   Next, quickly, Mississippi, Georgia, and Florida,
   All raised on high the Bonnie Blue Flag that bears a single star.   (Chorus)

4. Ye men of valor gather round the banner of the right,
   Texas and fair Louisiana join us in the fight;
   Davis, our loved President, and Stephens statesmen are;
   Now rally round the Bonnie Blue Flag that bears a single star.   (Chorus)

5. And here's to brave Virginia, the Old Dominion State.
   With the young Confederacy at length has linked her fate.
   Impelled by her example, now other States prepare
   To hoist on high the Bonnie Blue Flag that bears a single star.   (Chorus)

6. Then here's to our Confederacy, strong we are and brave,
   Like patriots of old we'll fight, our heritage to save;
   And rather than submit to shame, to die we would prefer,
   So cheer for the Bonnie Blue Flag that bears a single star.   (Chorus)

7. Then cheer, boys, cheer, raise a joyous shout,
   For Arkansas and North Carolina now have both gone out;
   And let another rousing cheer for Tennessee be given,
   The single star of the Bonnie Blue Flag has grown to be eleven.   (Chorus)

The Homespun Dress

Words ascribed to Carrie Bell Sinclair
Music: "Bonnie Blue Flag" ("Irish Jaunting Car")

1. Oh, yes, I am a Southern girl,
   And glory in the name,
   And boast it with far greater pride
   Than glittering wealth or fame.
   We envy not the Northern girl,
   Her robes of beauty rare,
   Though diamonds grace her snowy neck,
   And pearls bedeck her hair.

   Chorus:

   Hurrah! Hurrah!
   For the sunny South so dear;
   Three cheers for the homespun dress
   The Southern ladies wear.

2. The homespun dress is plain, I know,
   My hat's palmetto, too;
   But then it shows what Southern girls
   For Southern rights will do.
   We have sent the bravest of our land
   To battle with the foe,
   And we will lend a helping hand;
   We love the South, you know.   (Chorus)

3. Now, Northern goods are out of date;
   And since old Abe's blockade,
   We Southern girls can be content
   With goods that's Southern made.
   We sent our sweethearts to the war,
   But dear girls, never mind,
   Your soldier-love will ne'er forget
   The girl he left behind.   (Chorus)

4. The soldier is the lad for me—
   A brave heart I adore;
   And when the sunny South is free,
   And fighting is no more,
   I'll choose me then a lover brave
   From out the gallant band,
   The soldier lad I love the best
   Shall have my heart and hand.   (Chorus)

5. The Southern land's a glorious land,
   And has a glorious cause;
   Then cheer three cheers for Southern rights,
   And for the Southern boys.
   We scorn to wear a bit of silk,
   A bit of Northern lace;
   But make our homespun dresses up,
   And wear them with such grace.   (Chorus)

6. And now, young man, a word to you;
   If you would win the fair,
   Go to the field where honor calls,
   And win your lady there.
   Remember that our brightest smiles
   Are for the true and brave,
   And that our tears are all for those
   Who fill a soldier's grave.   (Chorus)

The Bonnie White Flag

Words by Colonel W. S. Hawkins
Music: "Bonnie Blue Flag"

1. Though we're a band of prisoners,
   Let each be firm and true,
   For noble souls and hearts of oak,
   The foe can ne'er subdue.
   We then will turn us homeward,
   To those we love so dear;
   For peace and happiness, my boys,
   Oh, give a hearty cheer!

Chorus:
   Hurrah! Hurrah!
   For peace and home, hurrah!
   Hurrah for the Bonnie White Flag,
   That ends this cruel war!

2. The sword into the scabbard,
   The musket on the wall,
   The cannon from its blazing throat,
   No more shall hurl the ball;
   From wives and babes and sweethearts,
   No longer will we roam,
   For every gallant soldier boy
   Shall seek his cherished home.   (Chorus)

3. Our battle banners furled away,
   No more shall greet the eye,
   Nor beat of angry drums be heard,
   Nor bugle's hostile cry.
   The blade no more be raised aloft,
   In conflict fierce and wild,
   The bomb shall roll across the sward,
   The plaything of a child.   (Chorus)

4. No pale-faced captive then shall stand,
   Behind his rusted bars,
   Nor from the prison window bleak,
   Look sadly to the stars;
   But out amid the woodland's green,
   On pounding steed he'll be,
   And proudly from his heart shall rise,
   The anthem of the free.   (Chorus)

5. The plow into the furrow then,
   The fields shall wave with grain,
   And smiling children to their schools,
   All gladly go again.
   The church invites its grateful throng,
   And man's rude striving cease,
   While all across our noble land,
   Shall glow the light of peace.   (Chorus)

Maryland, My Maryland

Words by James R. Randall
Music: "Tannenbaum"

SONGS OF THE CONFEDERACY

flecked the streets of Bal - ti - more, And be the bat - tle queen of yore, Ma - ry-land, my Ma - ry-land!

2. Hark to an exiled son's appeal,
   Maryland, my Maryland!
   My Mother State, to thee I kneel,
   Maryland, my Maryland!
   For life or death, for woe or weal,
   Thy peerless chivalry reveal,
   And gird thy beauteous limbs with steel,
   Maryland, my Maryland!

3. Thou wilt not cower in the dust,
   Maryland, my Maryland!
   Thy beaming sword shall never rust,
   Maryland, my Maryland!
   Remember Carroll's sacred trust,
   Remember Howard's warlike thrust,
   And all thy slumberers with the just,
   Maryland, my Maryland!

4. Come! 'tis the red dawn of the day,
   Maryland, my Maryland!
   Come! with thy panoplied array,
   Maryland, my Maryland!
   With Ringgold's spirit for the fray,
   With Watson's blood at Monterey,
   With fearless Lowe and dashing May,
   Maryland, my Maryland!

5. Dear mother, burst the tyrant's chain,
   Maryland, my Maryland!
   Virginia should not call in vain,
   Maryland, my Maryland!
   She meets her sisters on the plain,
   "Sic temper!" 'tis the proud refrain
   That baffles minions back amain,
   Maryland, my Maryland!
   Arise in majesty again,
   Maryland, my Maryland!*

* The last two lines of verse 5 do not fit the music, but they appear in the original Randall poem.

71

6. Come! for thy shield is bright and strong,
    Maryland, my Maryland!
  Come! for thy dalliance does thee wrong,
    Maryland, my Maryland!
  Come to thine own heroic throng
  Stalking with liberty along,
  And chant thy dauntless slogan-song,
    Maryland, my Maryland!

7. I see the blush upon thy cheek,
    Maryland, my Maryland!
  But thou wast ever bravely meek,
    Maryland, my Maryland!
  But lo! there surges forth a shriek,
  From hill to hill, from creek to creek,
  Potomac calls to Chesapeake,
    Maryland, my Maryland!

8. Thou wilt not yield the vandal toll,
    Maryland, my Maryland!
  Thou wilt not crook to his control,
    Maryland, my Maryland!
  Better the fire upon thee roll,
  Better the shot, the blade, the bowl,
  Than crucifixion of the soul,
    Maryland, my Maryland!

9. I hear the distant thunder-hum,
    Maryland, my Maryland!
  The "Old Line's" bugle, fife, and drum,
    Maryland, my Maryland!
  She is not dead, nor deaf, nor dumb;
  Huzza! she spurns the northern scum—
  She breathes! She burns! She'll come! She'll
    come!
    Maryland, my Maryland!

Answer to "My Maryland"

Words: anonymous
Music: "Maryland, My Maryland"

1. The Rebel feet are on our shore,
    Maryland, my Maryland!
   I smell 'em half a mile or more,
    Maryland, my Maryland!
   Their shockless hordes are at my door,
   Their drunken generals on my floor,
   What now can sweeten Baltimore?
    Maryland, my Maryland!

2. Hark to our noses' dire appeal,
    Maryland, my Maryland!
   Oh unwashed Rebs, to you we kneel!
    Maryland, my Maryland!
   If you can't purchase soap, oh steal
   That precious article—I feel
   Like scratching from the head to heel,
    Maryland, my Maryland!

3. You're covered thick with mud and dust,
    Maryland, my Maryland!
   As though you'd been upon a bust,
    Maryland, my Maryland!
   Remember, it is scarcely just,
   To have a filthy fellow thrust
   Before us, till he's been scrubbed fust,
    Maryland, my Maryland!

4. I see no blush upon thy cheek,
    Maryland, my Maryland!
   It's not been washed for many a week,
    Maryland, my Maryland!
   To get thee clean—'tis truth I speak—
   Would dirty every stream and creek,
   From Potomac to Chesapeake,
    Maryland, my Maryland!

Kentucky! O Kentucky!

Words: anonymous
Music: "Maryland, My Maryland!"

1. John Morgan's foot is on thy shore,
    Kentucky! O Kentucky!
   His hand is on thy stable door,
    Kentucky! O Kentucky!
   You'll see your good gray mare no more,
   He'll ride her till her back is sore,
   And leave her at some stranger's door,
    Kentucky! O Kentucky!

2. For feeding John you're paying dear,
    Kentucky! O Kentucky!
   His very name now makes you fear,
    Kentucky! O Kentucky!
   In every valley, far and near,
   He's gobbled every horse and steer;
   You'll rue his raids for many a year,
    Kentucky! O Kentucky!

3. Yet you have many a traitorous fool,
    Kentucky! O Kentucky!
   Who still will be the Rebel's tool,
    Kentucky! O Kentucky!
   They'll learn to yield to Abra'm's rule,
   In none but Johnny's costly school,
   At cost of every "animule,"
    Kentucky! O Kentucky!

73

We Conquer or Die

Words and music by James Pierpont

SONGS OF THE CONFEDERACY

this be our watch-word, "We con-quer or die!" And

this be our watch-word, "We con-quer or die!"

2. The trumpet is sounding from mountain to shore,
   Your swords and your lances must slumber no
       more,
   Fling forth to the sunlight your banner on high,
   Inscribed with the watchword: "We conquer
       or die!"
   Inscribed with the watchword: "We conquer
       or die!"

3. March on to the battlefield, there to do or dare,
   With shoulder to shoulder all danger to share,
   And let your proud watchword ring up to the sky,
   Till the blue arch re-echoes, "We conquer or die!"
   Till the blue arch re-echoes, "We conquer or die!"

4. Press forward undaunted, nor think of retreat,
   The enemy's host on the threshold to meet,
   Strike firm, till the foeman before you shall fly,
   Appalled by the watchword, "We conquer or die!"
   Appalled by the watchword, "We conquer or die!"

5. Go forth in the pathway our forefathers trod,
   We too fight for Freedom, our Captain is God,
   Their blood in our veins, with their honors we vie,
   Their's, too, was the watchword, "We conquer
       or die!"
   Their's, too, was the watchword, "We conquer
       or die!"

6. We strike for the South—Mountain, Valley,
       and Plain,
   For the South we will conquer, again and again;
   Her day of salvation and triumph is nigh,
   Our's then be the watchword, "We conquer or
       die!"
   Our's then be the watchword, "We conquer or
       die!"

The Yellow Rose of Texas

Anonymous

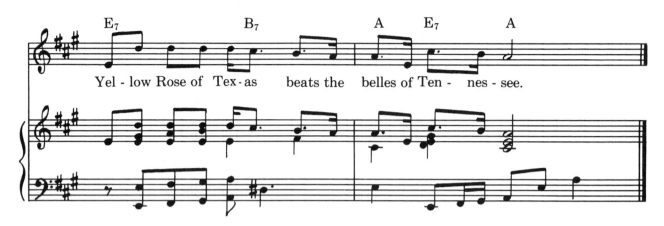

Yel - low Rose of Tex - as beats the belles of Ten - nes - see.

2. Where the Rio Grande is flowing and the starry skies are bright,
   She walks along the river in the quiet summer night;
   She thinks if I remember, when we parted long ago,
   I promised to come back again and not to leave her so.   (Chorus)

3. Oh, now I'm going to find her, for my heart is full of woe,
   And we'll sing the song together, that we sung so long ago;
   We'll play the banjo gaily, and we'll sing the songs of yore,
   And the Yellow Rose of Texas shall be mine forevermore.   (Chorus)

Stonewall Jackson's Way

Words by J. W. Palmer
Music: unknown

With spirit ♩. = 120

Come, stack arms, men, pile on the rails, Stir up the camp - fire bright; ___ No mat - ter if the can - teen fails, We'll make a roar - ing night. ___ Here Shen - an - do - ah brawls a - long, Here

bur - ly Blue Ridge ech - oes strong, To swell the Bri - gade's

rous - ing song of Stone - wall Jack - son's way. ———

2. We see him now—the old slouched hat
   Cocked o'er his eye askew.
   The shrewd, dry smile, the speech so pat,
   So calm, so blunt, so true;
   The "Blue Light Elder" knows 'em well:
   Says he, "That's Banks, he's fond of shell;
   Lord, save his soul! we'll give him"—well
   That's Stonewall Jackson's way.

3. Silence! Ground arms! Kneel all! Caps off!
   Old "Blue Light's" going to pray;
   Strangle the fool that dares to scoff!
   Attention! It's his way!
   Appealing from his native sod,
   "Hear us, Almighty God! *
   Lay bare Thine arm, stretch forth Thy rod,
   Amen!" That's Stonewall Jackson's way.

4. He's in the saddle now! Fall in!
   Steady! The whole brigade!
   Hill's at the ford, cut off—we'll win
   His way out, ball and blade!
   What matter if our shoes are worn?
   What matter if our feet are torn?
   "Quick-step! We're with him before dawn!"
   That's Stonewall Jackson's way.

5. The sun's bright lances rout the mists
   Of morning, and, by George!
   Here's Longstreet struggling in the lists,
   Hemmed in an ugly gorge.
   Pope and his Yankees, whipped before,
   "Bayonets and grape!" Hear Stonewall roar;
   "Charge, Stuart! Pay off Ashby's score!"
   Is Stonewall Jackson's way.

6. Ah, maiden, wait, and watch, and yearn
   For news of Stonewall's band!
   Ah, widow, read, with eyes that burn,
   That ring upon thy hand!
   Ah, wife, sew on, pray on, hope on!
   Thy life shall not be all forlorn.
   The foe had better ne'er been born
   That gets in Stonewall's way.

* Original reads: "In *forma pauperis* to God."

Riding a Raid

Words: anonymous
Music: "Bonnie Dundee"

Martial ♩. = 96

'Tis old Stone - wall, the Reb - el, that leans on his sword, And while we are mount-ing, prays low to the Lord: "Now each cav-a-lier that loves Hon- or and Right, Let him fol-low the feath-er of Stu-art to-night." Come

SONGS OF THE CONFEDERACY

tight - en your girth   and slack - en your rein;   Come buck - le your blan - ket and hol - ster a - gain;   Try the   click   of your   trig - ger and bal - ance your blade,   For   he must ride sure that goes   Rid - ing a Raid!

2. Now gallop, now gallop, to swim or to ford!
   Old Stonewall, still watching, prays low to the Lord:
   "Good-bye dear old Rebel! The river's not wide,
   And Maryland's lights in her window to guide."   (Chorus)

3. There's a man in a white house with blood on his mouth!
   If there's Knaves in the North, there are braves in the South.
   We are three thousand horses, and not one afraid;
   We are three thousand sabres and not a dull blade.   (Chorus)

4. Then gallop, then gallop, by ravines and rocks!
   Who would bar us the way take his toll in hard knocks;
   For with these points of steel, on the line of Penn,
   We have made some fine strokes—and we'll make 'em again.   (Chorus)

The Young Volunteer

Words and music by John Hill Hewitt

Our flag is un-furled and our arms flash bright, As the sun wades up the sky; But ere I join the doubt-ful fight, Love-ly maid, I would say, "Good-bye," I'm a

SONGS OF THE CONFEDERACY

falling on the ear; Should it so be de-creed that we
ne'er meet a-gain, Oh, re-mem-ber the Young Vol-un-teer.

2. When over the desert, through burning rays,
   With a heavy heart I tread;
   Or when I breast the cannon's blaze,
   And bemoan my comrades dead,
   Then, then I will think of my home and you,
   And our flag shall kiss the wind;
   With huzza for our cause and our country too,
   And the girls we leave behind.   (Chorus)

Old Abe Lincoln Came Out of the Wilderness

SONGS OF ABRAHAM LINCOLN

Old Abe Lincoln came out of the Wilderness,
Out of the Wilderness,
Out of the Wilderness,
Old Abe Lincoln came out of the Wilderness,
Many long years ago.

The great poet-biographer, Carl Sandburg, devoted four huge volumes of his monumental study of Abraham Lincoln to the last four years of Lincoln's life. With typical folk economy, some anonymous folk singer borrowed the tune of "When Johnny Comes Marching Home" to tell the same story in five verses:

In eighteen hundred and sixty-one,
For bales, for bales,
In eighteen hundred and sixty-one,
For bales, says I,
In eighteen hundred and sixty-one,
Abe Lincoln went to Washington,
And we'll all drink stone blind,
Johnny fill up the bowl.

In eighteen hundred and sixty-two,
Old Abe he put the Rebellion through.

In eighteen hundred and sixty-three,
Old Abe he set the niggers free.

In eighteen hundred and sixty-four,
Old Abe he called for a million more.

In eighteen hundred and sixty-five,
John Booth, he took Abe Lincoln's life.

Contrary to general belief, Lincoln was not a favorite subject for the professional songsmiths of his day. While the President received his share of "Grand Marches" and "Quick-Steps," the melody makers did far better by many others, particularly the Union generals—and especially General George B. McClellan. If the balloting in the election of 1864 had been restricted to song writers, "Little Mac" would have beaten "Old Abe" decisively.

The famous New York stage personality, Tony Pastor, summed up the judgments of many in the song-writing clan in a Civil War ditty called "One Hundred Years Hence." Pastor recounts the names of those who will be forgotten in a century, among them Secretary Chase, Gideon Welles, Jeff Davis, and Wendell Phillips,

. . . who crows it so loud,
He's head-abolitionist boss of the crowd;
And though for the nigger his love is intense,
Why, he will be forgotten a hundred years hence.

Pastor had little use for Lincoln, although he tempered his ridicule with respect for the Presidency:

Abe Lincoln is going it with a strong hand,
But still he's our ruler, and by him we'll stand;
Let us hope in the end he may prove he has sense,
For he'll be forgotten a hundred years hence.

With such distinguished company assigned to oblivion, who then will be remembered "a hundred years hence?"

There's little McClellan, of our army the boast,
He never complained when removed from his post—
The brave deeds he done bring their own recompense,
He *won't* be forgotten a hundred years hence.

At the same time, an image of Lincoln as the symbol of America was growing and taking root among the ordinary people. Songs like "We Are Coming, Father Abraham" and "Abraham's Daughter" confirmed and strengthened the identification. And no Confederate song addressed itself to "Fight for Uncle Jeff" as the Yankees did when they sang "We'll Fight for Uncle Abe." So that even though there was no great eruption of "Abraham Lincoln Grand Victory Marches" or "Sixteenth President Schottisches," the national musical idiom began to assume the rail splitter's coloring as Lincoln grew to the dimensions of his task and his responsibility.

This identification of Lincoln and the Union spread to the Confederacy as well, whose prime foe was "ABE-o-lition" and whose favorite quatrain was:

Jeff Davis rode a dapple gray,
Lincoln rode a mule,
Jeff Davis is a gentleman,
And Lincoln is a fool.

One Confederate song, refusing to be partisan in the Union's internecine quarrels, proclaimed:

McClellan is a humbug
And Lincoln is a fool,
All of them is liars
Of the highest greeting school.

Another Confederate ditty sympathized with Lincoln after the Battle of Bull Run:

King Abraham is very sick,
Old Scott has got the measles,
Manassas we have won at last,
Pop goes the weasel!

After Lincoln's assassination in 1865, the song writers finally decided that Lincoln songs were appropriate, and a raft of tributes, memoriams, dirges, and memorial grand marches flowed from the pens of the professional tunesmiths. By then, however, the folk had already claimed their own.

OLD ABE LINCOLN CAME OUT OF THE WILDERNESS. The tune to this, the best known of all the Lincoln songs, is familiar to everyone today as "The Old Gray Mare." Sigmund Spaeth traces the melody back to a song titled "Down in Alabam'," written by J. Warner in 1858—a song which concerned an "old hoss" that "came tearin' out de wilderness." Republicans in the election campaign of 1860 siezed upon the song and refashioned it as a campaign ditty for "Old Abe Lincoln" who "came tearing out the wilderness, down in Illinois." With the passage of time, the present words took shape.

A version of "Down in Alabam'" was collected as a play-party game in Western Nebraska in 1884, with such verses as:

Old gray horse came a-tearin' out the wilderness
Down in Alabama.

Great big sheep jumped over the meetin' house
Down in Alabama.

Johnny stole a ham and a piece of bacon
Down in Alabama.

LINCOLN AND LIBERTY. Hardly a Presidential candidate in nineteenth-century America survived the musical rigors of an election campaign without having his name melodically linked with "Liberty" at least once. Songs like "Adams and Liberty," "Jefferson and Liberty," "Jackson and Liberty," and scores of others have become a part of the musical literature of American elections.

In addition to this strong tradition, the election of 1860 had as its leading candidate a man whose stand for liberty was one of the key issues of the campaign, plus the added atttraction of a name which, coupled with the word "Liberty," made for a most euphonious alliteration. "Lincoln and Liberty" *had* to be written in 1860, and Jesse Hutchinson, of the famous singing family, supplied the words. The tune had also been used in many a campaign before, with supporters of William Henry Harrison ("Tippecanoe and Tyler, Too"), Henry Clay, and General Fremont, among others, chanting pleas for votes to its strains. The melody, Irish in origin, has led a varied and illuminating career on both sides of the Atlantic. It is best known as "Rosin the Beau."

In 1864, facing the challenge of George B. McClellan in the presidential contest, it seemed that Lincoln stood in great need of the tune which had helped sing him to victory four years earlier. McClellan's supporters waged a bitter and intensive campaign for the presidency. A typical "Little Mac" broadside, "It Reminds Him of a Story," reveals the depth of bitterness generated by the contest:

We're in Rebellion now, the greatest one in history!
And why it isn't settled, remains to us a mystery:
Five hundred thousand slain and the battlefield's all gory,
But Abe Lincoln takes it cool, it reminds him of a story.

Abe Lincoln is always joking, and widows are all weeping,
Oh husbands lost in battle, and under Southern soil now
   sleeping.

.   .   .

McClellan is our choice, the favorite of the nation,
One whom we choose to lead us to our former glorious
   station;
Our enemies they curse him; for they know he's hunkydory,
It's about time to tell Abe Lincoln: this reminds me of a
   story.

Lincoln supporters enjoyed their share of vitriol, as well, saving their deepest scorn for Northern "copperheads":

The snakes will all be buried this fall,
Abe is bruising them with his maul.

While one general battled Abe throughout the North, Lincoln had two generals who were winning the war and, thereby, winning the election for the Republicans. Sherman's capture of Atlanta and Grant's general offensive which finally seemed to be bearing fruit were Lincoln's greatest political assets—as the song writers could hail "Abraham the Great and General Grant His Mate," and sing that

Our boys in front of Richmond will drive old Jeff from town,
And cast their votes for Lincoln and put Rebellion down.

THE LIBERTY BALL. This antislavery song, popularized by the Hutchinson singers and attributed to Jesse Hutchinson, was an Abolitionist favorite for at least a decade prior to the Civil War. Many versions of the song are extant in various Abolitionist and Republican Party collections, with topical verses making their appearance dependent on the time and events.

One early verse, harking back to a favorite ante-bellum issue and, perhaps, anticipating future Republican Party platforms, forthrightly declared:

> Ye Whigs, forsake slavery's minions,
> And boldly step into the ranks,
> We care not for party opinion,
> But invite all the friends of the banks.

In the election of 1860, with an eye to the farm population and cognizant of the growing class consciousness among industrial laborers, Republicans abandoned the banks and rewrote the above:

> Ye fogies quit slavery's minions,
> And boldly renounce your old pranks,
> We care not for party opinions,
> But invite you all into our ranks.

The version of the song presented here is a composite taken from an antislavery songster of 1851, the Hutchinson Family rendition and a Republican Party campaign songster for 1860.

ABRAHAM'S DAUGHTER. While most Northern troops went to war in suits of "Union blue," many regiments and companies sported uniforms of a highly individual character. None was more unique, though, than the highly colorful "Zouave" uniforms worn by a number of Northern regiments. These were named for the Zouave corps in the French army. One such "Zouave" company was the One Hundred and Fourteenth Regiment Pennsylvania Volunteers organized in Philadelphia shortly after the beginning of the war.

It is most likely that this regiment was the direct inspiration for the song, "Abraham's Daughter," since its author, Septimus Winner, was himself a Philadelphian and undoubtedly saw the eye-catching red pantaloons, blue shirts, and white turbans in the streets of the Quaker City.

The song appears to have been extremely popular on the minstrel stage, with many printed versions appearing in the Negro "black-face" dialect of the times. Winner, who also wrote under the names Alice Hawthorne and Eastburn, was one of the best professional song writers of his day. Two of his most famous songs have become a part of our national musical literature—"Listen to the Mocking Bird" and "Der Deitcher's Dog,"—the latter a German-dialect piece better known today as "Where, Oh Where Has My Little Dog Gone?"

A loyal Unionist and an active song writer and music publisher, Winner was, by political persuasion, a Northern Democrat and a strong-minded supporter of McClellan. In 1863, shortly after Lincoln removed McClellan as Commander of the Union armies, Winner wrote his most controversial song. It was called "Give Us Back Our Old Commander: Little Mac, The People's Pride," and became so popular that it is reported to have sold 80,000 copies within a few days of publication. The general agitation concerning the removal of the extremely popular, albeit incredibly ineffectual, "Little Mac," was widespread, and Winner's song poured musical fuel on an extremely troubled sea. As a result, Union authorities arrested Winner on a charge of treason, an accusation which was eventually dropped when the song writer agreed to discontinue the sale of the song.

The reference to "Johnny Bull" in the fourth stanza of "Abraham's Daughter" reflects a recurring jingoistic theme in many of the songs of the day, as England appeared to be favoring and abetting the Confederate cause. Dan Bryant, the famous minstrel man, sang his own version of "Abraham's Daughter," with the following verse and chorus:

> Oh! Johnny Bull is gone to grass,
> To fatten up his calves, oh!
> He's talking of sending shilling-a-day
> Soldiers to the South, oh!
> But we licked them well, in 1812,
> And we can whip them weller: oh, oh, oh!

Whilst we're here, if they interfere,
Won't we give them a warmer!
Oh! I'm a-going down to Washington,
To fight for Abraham's daughter.

Parodies to "Abraham's Daughter" flourished throughout the country, with many minstrel troupes developing their own versions. "Abraham's Daughter, II" is one such, which was popular as far west as California, where Ben Cotton sang it nightly in San Francisco. A New York broadside parody, referring to the Battle of Bull Run, reveals how the song was kept up to date:

How are you and all my friends?
I've just come from the wars, Sirs!
For I've been at Bull Run, you know,
And fought for the Stars and Stripes, Sirs.
It's true enough we were repulsed,
But the Rebels' loss was great, Sirs;
And if you don't believe it's true:
Why read the Richmond papers!

WE ARE COMING, FATHER ABR'AM. In July, 1862, after a series of disheartening Union defeats, Lincoln issued a call for 300,000 Union volunteers to enlist for three years. This song, one of the most popular Northern inspirational songs, was written as a direct response to Lincoln's plea.

Its author, James Sloan Gibbons, was a Quaker and a well-known and outspoken New York Abolitionist, a long-time associate of Garrison, the Grimke Sisters, and many other antislavery figures. It first appeared as a poem in the New York *Evening Post* of July 16, 1862. The poem appeared anonymously and was generally thought to be the work of William Cullen Bryant, then the editor of the *Post*. It was reprinted in many other publications within a few weeks, and most credited Bryant with the lyric, so that the well-known poet finally had to issue a public disavowal of authorship in which he gave Gibbons proper credit.

The words were picked up and quickly set to music by a number of composers, among them the Hutchinson Family Singers and Stephen Foster. The music published here was composed by L. O. Emerson.

The song was performed for President Lincoln a number of times, a Baltimore official singing it for him on one occasion and eliciting the comment that the song "contained an excellent sentiment, and was sung in a manner worthy of the sentiment."

The most dramatic performance of the song occurred one night in Washington when young Tad Lincoln took his father to Grover's Theater to see a "spectacular extravaganza" titled "The Seven Sisters." During the performance, young Tad somehow managed to disappear from the Presidential box, and the next that Lincoln saw of him was on stage, where the youngster was dressed in an oversize army blouse and cap, waving an American flag, and leading the ensemble in singing:

We are coming, Father Abraham,
Three hundred thousand more.

Parodies, naturally, sprang up everywhere. One of the most virulently anti-Lincoln of these, "How Are You, Greenbacks?" lit into the President on a number of counts, from inflation to the removal of McClellan and the recruitment of Negro troops:

We're coming, Father Abram, three hundred thousand more,
Five hundred presses printing us from morn till night is o'er.

. . .

We're willing, Father Abram, one hundred thousand more
Should help our Uncle Samuel to prosecute the war;
But then we want a chieftain true, one who can lead the van,
Geo. B. McClellan, you all know, he is the very man.

. . .

We're coming, Father Abram, nine hundred thousand strong,
With nine hundred thousand darkies, sure the traitors can't last long,
With Corporal Cuff and Sergeant Pomp to lead us in the melee,
And at their head, without a red, our Brigadier General Greeley.

. . .

We're coming, Father Abram, nine hundred thousand more,
With the greatest fighting hero that lives upon our shore;
He fought in all the battles won, and shed his blood most freely,
But he's fought them with the *Tribune,* and his name is General Greeley.

Rebel soldiers picked up the song and fashioned their own version for Lincoln, stanzas which were subsequently printed in the Philadelphia *Evening Journal:*

We are coming, Abraham Lincoln,
From mountain, wood, and glen,
We are coming, Abraham Lincoln,
With the ghosts of murdered men.
Yes, we're coming, Abraham Lincoln,
With curses loud and deep,
That will haunt you in your waking
And disturb you in your sleep.

There's blood upon your garments,
There's guilt upon your soul,
For the host of ruthless soldiers
You let loose without control.
Your dark and wicked doings
A God of mercy sees,
And the wail of homeless children
Is heard on every breeze.

You may call your black battalions
To aid your stinking cause,
And substitute your vulgar jokes
For liberty and laws.

Ironically enough, Gibbons was one of the victims of the New York City draft riots of 1863, his luxurious home burned and ransacked by the mob while his daughters fled through a rear window and while Gibbons himself mingled with the crowd watching the destruction. Gibbons escaped with his life, however, and enjoyed a full and successful career until his death in 1892.

WE'LL FIGHT FOR UNCLE ABE. Here is another minstrel stage song for Lincoln, much in the style of "Abraham's Daughter." (It is interesting to see the growing popular personal identification with Lincoln in song titles which practically make Abe a member of the family—such as "Father Abraham," "Abraham's Daughter," and "Uncle Abe.") Typical of the minstrel songs of the period, which chose to comment on the events of the war, is the praise for McClellan and the attack on John Bull. Little is known of the lyricist, but the composer of this song, Frederick Buckley, was a member and leading spirit of one of the most famous minstrel troupes of the day, *The Buckley Serenaders*. Frederick Buckley, like his two brothers, was born in England, and the company was a favorite with audiences on both sides of the Atlantic.

BOOTH KILLED LINCOLN. This haunting folk ballad of the most dramatic and most tragic political assassination in American history comes from the family of the noted folksinger-collector, Bascom Lamar Lunsford of South Turkey Creek, North Carolina. Lunsford says:

The title of this ballad is "Booth," or "Booth Killed Lincoln." It's an old fiddle tune, and there are a few variants of the song. I heard my father hum it and sing a few of the stanzas when I was just a boy about six or ten years old.

In the fashion of true folk symmetry, reminiscent of the tragic note of irony so frequent in the old ballads, the last stanza has Lincoln's thoroughly unfactual dying words:

Of all the actors in this town,
I loved Wilkes Booth the best.

Old Abe Lincoln Came Out of the Wilderness

Words: anonymous
Music: "Down in Alabam" (by J. Warner)

Old Abe Lin-coln came out of the wil-der-ness, out of the wil-der-ness, out of the wil-der-ness, Old Abe Lin-coln came out of the wil-der-ness, Man-y long years a- go.

SONGS OF ABRAHAM LINCOLN

2. Old Jeff Davis tore down the government,
   tore down the government,
   tore down the government,
   Old Jeff Davis tore down the government,
   Many long years ago.   (Chorus)

3. But old Abe Lincoln built up a better one,
   built up a better one,
   built up a better one,
   Old Abe Lincoln built up a better one,
   Many long years ago.   (Chorus)

Lincoln and Liberty

Words by Jesse Hutchinson
Music: "Rosin the Beau"

SONGS OF ABRAHAM LINCOLN

too! _____ We'll go for the son of Ken - tuck - y The

he - ro of Hoo-sier-dom through, _____ The pride of the "Suck-ers" so

luck - y, For Lin-coln and Lib - er - ty, too! _____

2. They'll find what by felling and mauling,
   Our railmaker statesman can do;
   For the people are everywhere calling
   For Lincoln and Liberty too.
   Then up with the banner so glorious,
   The star-spangled red, white, and blue,
   We'll fight till our banner's victorious,
   For Lincoln and Liberty, too.

3. Our David's good sling is unerring,
   The Slavocrat's giant he slew,
   Then shout for the freedom preferring,
   For Lincoln and Liberty, too.
   We'll go for the son of Kentucky,
   The hero of Hoosierdom through,
   The pride of the "Suckers" so lucky,
   For Lincoln and Liberty, too.

The Liberty Ball

Words by Jesse Hutchinson
Music: "Rosin the Beau"

1. Come all ye true friends of the nation,
   Attend to humanity's call;
   Come aid in the slave's liberation,
   And roll on the Liberty Ball.

   And roll on the Liberty Ball,
   And roll on the Liberty Ball,
   Come aid in the slave's liberation,
   And roll on the Liberty Ball.

2. We're foes unto wrong and oppression,
   No matter which side of the sea,
   And ever intend to oppose them
   Till all of God's image are free.

   Till all of God's image are free,
   Till all of God's image are free,
   And ever intend to oppose them,
   Till all of God's image are free.

3. We'll finish the temple of freedom,
   And make it capacious within,
   That all who seek shelter may find it
   Whatever the hue of their skin.

   Whatever the hue of their skin,
   Whatever the hue of their skin,
   That all who seek shelter may find it,
   Whatever the hue of their skin.

4. Success to the old-fashioned doctrine,
   That men are created all free;
   And down with the power of the despot,
   Wherever his strongholds may be.

   Wherever his strongholds may be,
   Wherever his strongholds may be,
   And down with the power of the despot,
   Wherever his strongholds may be.

5. The liberty hosts are advancing,
   For freedom to all, they declare,
   The downtrodden millions are sighing,
   Come break up our gloom of despair.

   Come break up our gloom of despair,
   Come break up our gloom of despair,
   The downtrodden millions are sighing,
   Come break up our gloom of despair.

(Repeat first verse)

Abraham's Daughter

Words and music by Septimus Winner

SONGS OF ABRAHAM LINCOLN

I am right? For I am noth - ing short - er, And
I be - long to the Fire Zou - Zous, And don't you think I ought - er, I'm
go - in' down to Wash - ing - ton To fight for A - bra - ham's Daugh - ter.

2. Oh! should you ask me who she am,
   Columbia is her name, sir;
   She is the child of Abraham,
   Or Uncle Sam, the same, sir.
   Now if I fight, why ain't I right?
   And don't you think I oughter.
   The volunteers are a-pouring in
   From every loyal quarter,
   And I'm goin' down to Washington
   To fight for Abraham's Daughter.

3. They say we have no officers,
   But ah! they are mistaken;
   And soon you'll see the Rebels run,
   With all the fuss they're makin';
   For there is one who just sprung up,
   He'll show the foe no quarter,
   (McClellan is the man I mean)
   You know he hadn't oughter,
   For he's gone down to Washington
   To fight for Abraham's Daughter.

4. We'll have a spree with Johnny Bull,
   Perhaps some day or other,
   And won't he have his fingers full,
   If not a deal of bother;
   For Yankee boys are just the lads
   Upon the land or water;
   And won't we have a "bully" fight,
   And don't you think we oughter,
   If he is caught at any time
   Insulting Abraham's Daughter.

5. But let us lay all jokes aside,
   It is a sorry question;
   The man who would these states divide
   Should hang for his suggestion.
   One Country and one Flag, I say,
   Whoe'er the war may slaughter;
   So I'm goin' as a Fire Zou-Zou,
   And don't you think I oughter,
   I'm goin' down to Washington
   To fight for Abraham's Daughter.

Abraham's Daughter, II

SONGS OF ABRAHAM LINCOLN

if they call up-on this child, I'ze bound to die a mar- tyr. For
I be-long to the Fire Zou-Zous, And don't you think I ought- er? I'm
go- in' down to Wash-ing-ton To fight for A- bra-ham's Daugh- ter.

2. I am tired of a city life,
   And I will join the Zou-Zous;
   I'm going to try and make a hit
   Down among the Southern foo-foos;
   But if perchance I should get hit,
   I'll show them I'm a tartar;
   We are bound to save our Union yet,
   'Tis all that we are arter.

3. There is one thing more that I would state,
   Before I close my ditty,
   'Tis all about the volunteers
   That's left our good old city.
   They have gone to fight for the Stars and Stripes—
   Our Union, now or never!
   We will give three cheers for the volunteers,
   And Washington forever.

103

We Are Coming, Father Abr'am

Words by James Sloan Gibbons
Music by L. O. Emerson

SONGS OF ABRAHAM LINCOLN

SONGS OF ABRAHAM LINCOLN

2. If you look across the hilltops
   That meet the northern sky,
   Long moving lines of rising dust
   Your vision may descry;
   And now the wind, an instant,
   Tears the cloudy veil aside,
   And floats aloft our spangled flag
   In glory and in pride;
   And bayonets in the sunlight gleam,
   And bands brave music pour.
   We are coming, Father Abr'am,
   Three hundred thousand more!   (Chorus)

3. If you look all up our valleys
   Where the growing harvests shine,
   You may see our sturdy farmer boys
   Fast forming into line;
   And children from their mother's knees
   Are pulling at the weeds,
   And learning how to reap and sow
   Against their country's needs;
   And a farewell group stands weeping
   At every cottage door.
   We are coming, Father Abr'am,
   Three hundred thousand more!   (Chorus)

4. You have called us and we're coming
   By Richmond's bloody tide,
   To lay us down for Freedom's sake,
   Our brothers' bones beside;
   Or from foul treason's savage group,
   To wrench the murderous blade;
   And in the face of foreign foes
   Its fragments to parade;
   Six hundred thousand loyal men
   And true have gone before.
   We are coming, Father Abr'am,
   Three hundred thousand more!   (Chorus)

We'll Fight for Uncle Abe

Words by C. E. Pratt
Music by Frederick Buckley

SONGS OF ABRAHAM LINCOLN

Yan - kee boys are start - ing out The Un - ion for to save, And we're
go - ing down to Wash - ing ton To fight for Un - cle Abe.

Chorus

Rip, Rap, Flip, Flap, Strap your knap - sack on your back, For
we're goin' down to Wash - ing - ton to fight for Un - cle Abe.

2. There is General Grant at Vicksburg,
   Just see what he has done,
   He has taken sixty cannon
   And made the Rebels run,
   And next he will take Richmond,
   I'll bet you half a dollar,
   And if he catches General Johnson,
   Oh won't he make him holler.   (Chorus)

3. The season now is coming
   When the roads begin to dry;
   Soon the Army of the Potomac
   Will make the Rebels fly,
   For General McClellan, he's the man,
   The Union for to save;
   Oh! Hail Columbia's right side up,
   And so's your Uncle Abe.   (Chorus)

4. You may talk of Southern chivalry
   And cotton being king,
   But I guess before the war is done
   You'll think another thing;
   They say that recognition
   Will the Rebel country save,
   But Johnny Bull and Mister France
   Are 'fraid of Uncle Abe.   (Chorus)

Booth Killed Lincoln

Folk song
From the singing of Bascom Lamar Lunsford

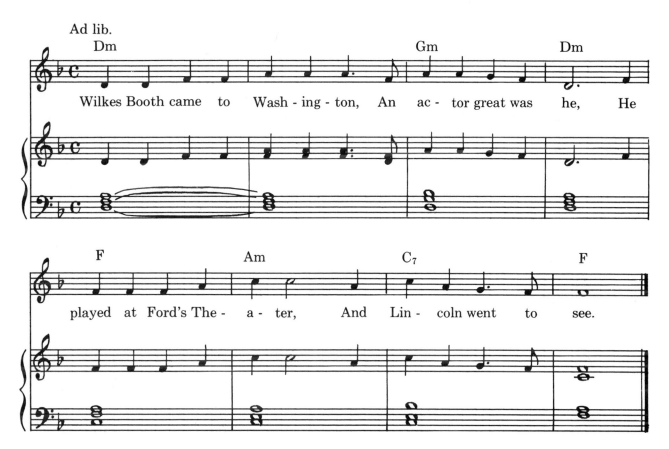

Wilkes Booth came to Wash-ing-ton, An ac-tor great was he, He played at Ford's The-a-ter, And Lin-coln went to see.

2. It was early in April,
   Not many weeks ago,
   The people of this fair city
   All gathered at the show.

3. The war it is all over,
   The people happy now,
   And Abraham Lincoln
   Arose to make his bow;

4. The people cheer him wildly,
   Arising to their feet,
   And Lincoln waving of his hand,
   He calmly takes his seat.

5. And while he sees the play go on,
   His thoughts are running deep,
   His darling wife, close by his side,
   Has fallen fast asleep.

6. From the box there hangs a flag,
   It is not the Stars and Bars,
   The flag that holds within its folds
   Bright gleaming Stripes and Stars.

7. J. Wilkes Booth he moves down the aisle,
   He had measured once before,
   He passes Lincoln's bodyguard
   A-nodding at the door.

111

8. He holds a dagger in his right hand,
   A pistol in his left,
   He shoots poor Lincoln in the temple,
   And sends his soul to rest.

9. The wife awakes from slumber,
   And screams in her rage,
   Booth jumps over the railing
   And lands him on the stage.

10. He'll rue the day, he'll rue the hour,
    As God him life shall give,
    When Booth stood in the center of the stage,
    Crying, "Tyrants shall not live!"

11. The people all excited then,
    Cried everyone, "A hand!"
    Cried all the people near,
    "For God's sake, save that man!"

12. Then Booth ran back with boot and spur
    Across the backstage floor,
    He mounts that trusty claybank mare,
    All saddled at the door.

13. J. Wilkes Booth, in his last play,
    All dressed in broadcloth deep,
    He gallops down the alleyway, ·
    I hear those horses feet.

14. Poor Lincoln then was heard to say,
    And all has gone to rest,
    "Of all the actors in this town,
    I loved Wilkes Booth the best."

Weeping Sad and Lonely

SENTIMENTAL WAR SONGS OF A SENTIMENTAL AGE

Weeping sad and lonely,
Hopes and fears how vain!
Yet praying,
When this cruel war is over,
Praying that we meet again!

Mid-nineteenth-century America was an age of unabashed sentiment—and the most popular songs of the Civil War were equally divided between stirring calls to martial valor and heart-rending appeals to such human sentiments as mother love, the tragedy of separation in wartime, the heroism of the young, and the bravery of the doomed.

The mood and idiom of both North and South were cast from the same mold, so that, almost without exception, these songs of sentiment were sung on both sides. Only in one or two cases did the partisanship or the locale of the songs necessitate changes when sung by the enemy.

The great majority of such songs were Northern in origin. Of the thirteen selected here, only two were composed in the South—"Somebody's Darling" and "Southern Soldier Boy."

Some of the songs in this section are actually pre-Civil War creations, but their popularity among the troops and on the home front was so great that it is logical to include them here. These earlier compositions are "Do They Miss Me at Home?" (1852), "Home Sweet Home" (1823), and "Lorena" (1857).

While sentimental songs covered a wide range of specific subjects, a few main themes emerge as reflections of the song writer's craft of the early sixties. A favorite jumping-off point for a good tear jerker of the times was to claim that the song was inspired by the last words of a dying soldier. The George Cooper-Stephen Foster song, "For the Dear Old Flag I Die," given elsewhere in this collection, claimed that its title was based upon "the last words of a brave little drummer boy who was fatally wounded at the Battle of Gettysburg." "Tell Mother I Die Happy" was, supposedly, "the last words of Lieutenant Crosby, who was killed in his battery at Salem Heights ... May 2, 1863," while the parting message of General James C. Rice was, "Then let me gaze through the cannon's blaze and die with my face to the foe." (How the unfortunate general managed a neat internal rhyme with his dying breath must be ascribed to that Providence which seems to have hovered over the song writers of that era.)

General Price's rhyming ability is an insignificant trifle, however, when compared to the talents of the author of "Oh Search Ye Well the Lists, Mother," the sheet music of which tells us:

A wounded soldier lying in a hospital who was told he could not recover ... wrote the words of this song as a dying farewell to his mother.

Perhaps the public was beginning to grow skeptical of these dying testaments, for one pair of tunesmiths hauled in a man of the cloth, Reverend M. P. Graddis, to testify to the accuracy of their "last words" which served to inspire the song, "I Loved That Dear Old Flag the Best." Graddis wrote:

A young soldier ... was dying from wounds received in battle; he requested me to get him the pictures of his mother and his sister from his knapsack. After kissing them tenderly, he raised his tear-dimmed eyes till they rested on a flag at the end of the hospital, when his eyes grew bright as he exclaimed: "Oh, Chaplain! I loved my dear old mother and sister, but I loved that dear old flag the best!"

Lonely and unsung death was another favorite theme of Civil War song writers, a sentiment expressed most typically in "All Quiet Along the Potomac Tonight" and "The Drummer Boy of Shiloh." "Minnie Minton" likewise bemoaned death in the midst of strangers:

> Minnie Minton, I am wounded,
> And I know that I must die;
> By a stranger host surrounded,
> And no loved one kneeling nigh;
> And I fain would hear you whisper
> In the twilight cold and gray,
> But I only hear the tramping
> As the armies march away.

A Confederate contribution to this bathos was "Richmond on the James," a parody to the extremely popular "Bingen on the Rhine":

A soldier boy from Bourbon lay, gasping on the field,
When battle's shock was over and the foe was forced to yield,

115

He fell, a youthful hero, before the foeman's aims,
On a blood-red field near Richmond, near Richmond on
the James.

Still another theme employed by the heart-break fraternity was the wounds of war, with various song writers staking out different parts of the human anatomy as their musical domain. Henry Badger wrote of the one-armed veteran in "The Empty Sleeve," while George Cooper penned a lyric with the brutally direct title of "Old Arm, Goodbye." A simple, pathetic cry, "I'm Blind," recounted the plight of a soldier who had lost his sight in battle. But the most heart-rending of the lot was George F. Root's "Will You Wed Me Now I'm Lame, Love?" Fortunately, Root answered the question in the affirmative:

> Oh, yes, your heart's the same, love,
> In all that we've passed through,
> You'll wed me though I'm lame, love,
> My beautiful, my true.

Although Civil War song writers doted on "last words" and lonely deaths, on wartime tragedies, and the wounds of war, the most important, the most popular, and the most sung about personage in all Civil War music was MOTHER. In the pre-Freudian era of 1863, song writers did not hesitate to employ this time-scarred symbol of the eternal verities, and scores of songs were written detailing the soldier's love for his mother and the mother's yearning for her son. Perhaps it is difficult for us in this sophisticated age to imagine the public emotional upheaval caused by songs like "Just Before the Battle, Mother" and "Who Will Care for Mother Now?"—each of which are reported to have sold more than one million sheet music copies.

Civil War "mother" songs included such melancholy items as "Tell Mother I Die Happy," "Mother Kissed Me in My Dream," "It Was My Mother's Voice," "Shall I Never See My Mother?" "Mother Would Comfort Me," "Oh, Will My Mother Never Come?" "Dear Mother, I'm Wounded," "Mother, When the War Is Over" ("and I'm home again with thee"), and scores of others. Frederick Buckley, represented in this collection by "We'll Fight for Uncle Abe," turned out a number of "mother" songs, including "Mother, I'll Come Home Tonight," "Break It Gently to My Mother," and "It's Growing Very Dark, Mother." Similarly, on the theme of dying

soldiers thinking of mother, were such songs as "Is It Mother's Gentle Touch?" and "Is That Mother?"

> . . . kneeling there in tears before me,
> Say! my sight is growing dim.
>
> Mother! Oh! we bravely battled,
> Battled till the day was done,
> While the leaden hail-storm rattled,
> Man to man and gun to gun.
>
> But we failed and I am dying. . . .
> Kiss me mother, ere I'm dead.

Others remembered mother in their dying moments in different ways, as in Frank Davis's "Bear It Gently to My Mother":

> . . . tell her that it came from me,
> 'Tis the little lock she cherished.

Obviously inspired by "Who Will Care for Mother Now?" was "Who'll Protect My Children Now?" But some mothers donned the mantle of heroism, as "The Conscript's Mother" showed:

Away with all sighing, away with all tears,
My boy shall behold not my grief, but my pride.
    .   .   .
I will arm him and bless him and send him away,
Tho' my heart break with grief when he goes from my
    sight.
    .   .   .
He's my all, he's my treasure,
But take him dear land.

Henry Tucker, whose "Weeping Sad and Lonely" was one of the genuine hits of the war, wrote the music to E. Bowers's lyric, "Dear Mother, I've Come Home to Die." So popular did this become that a "reply" under the title "My Boy, How Can I See You Die?" was written within a few months. A popular soldier parody made light of the thick sentimentality of the song, however:

> Dear mother, I remember well,
> The food we get from Uncle Sam:
> Hard tack, salt fish, and rusty pork,
> Sometimes a scanty piece of ham.
> When I a furlough did receive,
> I bade adieu to Brother Pete—
> Oh, mother, for a plate of hash,
> DEAR MOTHER, I'VE COME HOME TO EAT!

Occasionally, another member of the family circle would be allowed to weep over the dear departing, as in "Kiss Me, Father, Ere I Die" and "Tell Me Little Twinkling Star" ("Is my sister weeping now?") But for the most part, mother reigned supreme in the domain of the sentimental song. Southerners, by and large, sang the Northern songs, with Rebel music publishing companies issuing Confederate editions of the most popular ones. Occasionally, a Southern song writer would try his hand at a similar piece, coming up with such titles as "Let Me Kiss Him for His Mother" and "Kiss Me Before I Die, Mother."

One final theme which was a natural for the purveyors of sentimentality was "Brother Fighting Against Brother." Most typical of this theme was "Write a Letter to My Mother," one of those compositions which had everything, from a true story with "last words" to the "aged mother" waiting at home. The incident on which the song is supposedly based, is told in the accompanying sheet music:

An officer captured at the Battle of Bull Run relates the following incident: After our capture I observed a Federal prisoner tenderly cared for by a Rebel soldier. I gleaned from their conversation that they were brothers. The brave boy, while battling for the Union, received his death wound from his own brother, at that time a private in the Rebel ranks: never shall I forget the look of utter despair depicted upon that Rebel's face. The dying boy, with a smile of holy resignation, clasped his brother's hand, spoke of their father who was then fighting for the dear old Flag, of mother, of home, of childhood, then requesting his brother to "Write a letter to Mother," and imploring him never to divulge the secret of his death, the young boy yielded up his life.

And then the refrain:

> Write a letter to my mother,
> Send it when her boy is dead;
> That he perished by his brother,
> Not a word of that be said.

From the vantage point of time and sophistication, these overly dramatic, tearful songs, each shedding rays of glory in a glowing halo of noble sentiment, appear to us as ridiculously naive. But if the stylized lyrics and saccharine melodies strike us as clichés today, let us remember that these were new and fresh when they were written, and that constant imitation and parody over the years have dulled the creative sparkle of this music.

Even more important, however, is what these songs tell us of the mood and ethic and idiom of the people of Civil War America. For if we approach these songs only with laughter, we laugh at ourselves and our history and the American character which developed from the fierceness of the struggle. And if these songs take death and family ties in earnest, let us remember that the Civil War claimed the lives of some 700,000 Americans, a sum figure larger than the total of all American deaths in all other wars in our history combined. And these were the songs of the men who fought and suffered and died. As these songs live again today, so the memory of another America also comes to life once more.

WEEPING SAD AND LONELY (When This Cruel War Is Over). The widespread popularity of this song in both the North and South attests to the strong yearnings for peace which accompanied the mounting casualty lists. The lyric is by Charles Carroll Sawyer, one of the most prolific and successful of the Civil War song writers with a particular bent for popular sentimentality. The success of this song is rivalled only by Sawyer's other famous composition, "Who Will Care for Mother Now?" Henry Tucker, who wrote the tune, was a gifted melodist whose best-known work is the music for "Sweet Genevieve."

The "critics" of Civil War poetry never accepted "Weeping Sad and Lonely" as a good song, and, in fact, its popularity perplexed them. One wrote with revealing candor:

There is nothing in this sentimental song that enables one to read the riddle of its remarkable popularity during the Civil War. It has no poetic merit; its rhythm is commonplace, and the tune to which it was sung was of the flimsiest musical structure, without even a trick of melody to commend it. Yet the song was more frequently sung, on both sides, than any other.... The thing was heard in every camp every day and many times every day. Men chanted it on the march, and women sang it to piano accompaniment in all houses. A song which so strongly appealed to two great armies and to an entire people is worthy of a place in all collections of war poetry, even though criticism is baffled in the attempt to discover the reason of its popularity.

The bafflement of criticism aside, there is no question of the song's popularity. The Cleveland *Leader* called it the "greatest musical success ever known in this country," explaining that the "melody catches the popular ear and the words touch the popular heart." It was published in numerous editions throughout the North and in at least four editions in the South. Musical replies, those certain symbols of melodic popularity, sprang up everywhere. The indefatigable Sep Winner, writing under the pen name Alice Hawthorne, wrote "Yes, I Would the War Were Over," describing it as an "Answer to 'When This Cruel War Is Over.'"

Others frankly labeled as answers, replies, or companion pieces were "I Remember the Hour When Sadly We Parted" (Rossiter and Walters), "When This War Is Over, I Will Come Back to Thee" (Geuville-Mayer), "The War Is Nearly Over" (anonymous), "Yes, Darling, Sadly I Remember" (Grieg), and "When the Lonely Watch I'm Keeping" (Hastings). J. H. Hewitt and H. L. Schreiner composed a Confederate "reply," the chorus to which went:

> Weep no longer, dearest,
> Tears are now in vain,
> When this cruel war is over,
> We may meet again.

Other songs obviously inspired by the popularity of "Weeping Sad and Lonely" were "When the War Is Over, Mary" (Cooper and Thomas), "Mother, When the War Is Over" (Turner), and the Confederate "Wait Till the War, Love, Is Over" (Andrews and Burton).

Southern versions of the song changed the second part of the first stanza to read:

> Oh, how proud you stood before me,
> In your suit of gray,
> When you vowed from me and country
> Ne'er to go astray.

The fourth stanza was also altered to change "nation's sons" to "Southern boys" and "starry banner" to "Southern banner." It is an interesting commentary on the popular mood that so little had to be changed in one of the best-known songs of the Civil War to have it sung with equal intensity by both North and South.

The inevitable satirical parodies were also written. The irrepressible Tony Pastor sang in New York:

> Weeping sad and lonely,
> Laws, how bad I feel,
> When this cruel war is over,
> Praying for a good square meal.

In the course of time, "Weeping Sad and Lonely" has entered into the stream of our folk music, living through oral tradition and continuity in many parts of the United States today.

DOWN IN CHARLESTON JAIL. This parody to "Weeping Sad and Lonely" was written by a Negro soldier held in Charleston Jail as a prisoner of war, presumably Sergeant Robert Johnson of the Fifty-fourth Massachusetts (Colored) Regiment. This regiment took part in the costly raid on Fort Wagner in 1863, losing a large number of soldiers, including twenty-nine who were captured.

Confederate treatment of prisoners of war was not distinguished for its humaneness, and the treatment of Negro prisoners was particularly harsh, with many Northern Negroes forced to stand trial for "abandoning their masters" despite the fact that they were freeborn. Naturally enough, those found guilty were usually sold into slavery.

One white prisoner wrote, after the war, of his Negro fellow prisoners:

Often I was awakened at night by the singing of the colored prisoners. At such times, their voices coming down from the upper floors of the jail sounded very sweet, and there was a certain weird, indescribable sadness in the minor-key melodies. . . .

The Fifty-fourth Massachusetts Regiment was one of the best-known Negro outfits in the war. For more on this first Northern Negro Regiment, plus a song specifically dedicated to them, see "Give Us a Flag."

ALL QUIET ALONG THE POTOMAC. During the first days of the war, a familiar War Department announcement as it appeared in the nation's newspapers was: "All quiet along the Potomac." One day, in September, 1861, to the above announcement was appended the words, "A picket shot."

This brief newspaper report was, supposedly, the inspiration for this song which was written by Mrs. Ethel Lynn Beers of Goshen, New York. It was printed in *Harper's Weekly,* November 30, 1861, under the title of "The Picket Guard"; within a short time it had been set to music by a number of different composers, all of whom had been singularly struck by the song's direct appeal.

The song also proved immensely popular throughout the South (in a musical setting by

118

John H. Hewitt), and for many years it was believed to be of Confederate origin, with Major Lamar Fontaine of Mississippi the leading Rebel claimant to authorship. However, subsequent research by both Northern and Southern historians has substantiated Mrs. Beer's claim to the song. (See Harwell, Richard B., *Confederate Music,* page 81, for a discussion of the authorship controversy as well as an interesting literary critique of the song.)

An occasional "super-patriotic" editor undoubtedly took offense at the lines, "not an officer shot, only one of the men," and at least one edition completely eliminates the bitter lines—which probably proves that the mentality of censorship rarely changes, and that art and truth inevitably suffer when the political censor steps in.

But the song has outlived its "patriotic" critics and its rival claimants and remains one of the genuine lasting literary-musical efforts of the war.

DO THEY MISS ME AT HOME? This lush, sentimental period piece predates the Civil War by some nine years, but the lyric was so appropriate to the times when millions were uprooted from their homes, that the song was popular throughout the conflict and was sung extensively by both sides.

Answers, replies, and companion pieces were written by both Rebels and Yankees. In the North, H. H. Hawley wrote "Oh We Miss You at Home" and W. O. Fiske penned the lines to "Do They Pray for Me at Home?" In Georgia, John Hill Hewitt and E. Clarke Isley teamed up for "Yes, We Think of Thee at Home."

The original lyric was written by Caroline Atherton Mason, a minor mid-century poet in the genteel tradition. The music was composed by S. M. Grannis, whose other works included such typical period titles as "Sparking Sunday Night" and "Your Mission," the latter reputedly one of Lincoln's favorite hymns.

DO THEY MISS ME IN THE TRENCHES? A typically irreverent soldier parody to "Do They Miss Me at Home?" is this creation of a Rebel soldier of the Third Louisiana Regiment, J. W. Naff, who composed it during the siege of Vicksburg. Ironically, Naff was reportedly killed the day after penning these lines.

LORENA. Another pre-Civil War song which achieved wide popularity during the conflict was this composition by the Reverend H. D. L. Webster and J. P. Webster, who were, incidentally, not related to each other. For some reason, the song became a particular favorite of the Confederacy and, in time, came to be identified with the Southern cause. Hundreds of Southern girls were named for the song's heroine, while several pioneer settlements and even a steamship proudly bore the name. One Confederate veteran claimed to have "heard it more during the war than any other song."

J. P. Webster, creator of the melody, was a close collaborator of S. Fillmore Bennett, with whom he wrote several Civil War songs, including "The Irish Volunteer" and "The Negro Emancipation Song." Their best-known work, however, was one of the most popular hymns of all time, "Sweet By and By."

THE VACANT CHAIR. Written at Thanksgiving time in 1861, this maudlin piece of melancholia undoubtedly struck a responsive note in many a home, both North and South, where the family gathered for the annual celebration and found themselves staring at "the vacant chair."

Soldier and civilian alike responded to the unabashedly emotional pleading of the composition and made it one of the most widely sung songs of the war. The poem first appeared in the Worcester *Spy,* and was written in commemoration of the death of Lieutenant John William Grout, Fifteenth Massachusetts Volunteer Infantry.

Apparently some other composer had set Henry J. Washburn's poem to music without success, and the song did not achieve its popular acclaim until George F. Root tried his hand at setting a tune.

The song won many admirers on both sides of the lines, with at least three Southern editions reported.

THE DRUMMER BOY OF SHILOH. If we are to judge by the song literature of the Civil War, fully one third of the casualties on both sides were ill-fated drummer boys who marched into battle unarmed except for their instruments of doom. Of course, the image of a beardless youth of twelve marching bravely into battle, his drumsticks sounding a martial tattoo, defenseless, and, undoubtedly, the pride of a mourning family, was designed to appeal to a generation which thrived on sentimentality.

The most famous of these fictional drummer boys was "The Drummer Boy of Shiloh," the creation of a gifted and prolific Kentucky song writer with the effusive name of William Shakespeare Hays. Hays was a clerk in the music store of D. P. Faulds in Louisville, Kentucky, and it was Faulds who first published the song. The success of "The Drummer Boy of Shiloh" was so great that the song-writing fraternity could hardly allow a major battle to take place without producing at least one dead, heroic, drum-beating youngster.

George Cooper and Stephen Foster found such a lad in the Battle of Gettysburg (see "For the Dear Old Flag I Die"), while

> The drummer of Antietam
> Lays, dead and alone,
> Upon the cold battlefield
> Where his blood hath flown.

Vicksburg brought forth De Geer's "Drummer Boy of Vicksburg" (or "Let Him Sleep"), while "The Drummer Boy of Nashville"

> ... went to the war with a heart full of glee,
> There was no drummer boy so merry as he;
> And he left the log cabin with mother behind,
> The rest of the babies and sissies to mind.
> · · ·
> Onward he marched, not dreading that foe,
> Until death sent a bullet that laid him full low.

"Little Harry the Drummer Boy" (S. Wesley Martin) and "The Dying Drummer Boy" (Koch-Grube) were other doomed youngsters sent to early musical graves, while Henry C. Work, who had, until then, pretty much shied away from the purely maudlin, showed indications of such future melancholia as "Father, Dear Father, Come Home with Me Now," with his "Little Major," who lay dying on the battlefield yearning for a last drink of water, when some soldiers,

> God forgive them! They refuse his dying prayer,
> "Nothing but a wounded drummer,"
> So they say, and leave him there.

Hays was a border Unionist whose mixed feelings about the war were reflected in his songs. Unlike Root and Work who could match their sentimentality with martial airs, Hays could whip up no enthusiasm for the Northern cause, writing songs like "Oh! I Wish This War Was Over" and "My Southern Sunny Home." His political philosophy, so typical of Northern Democrats, was summed up in a McClellan campaign song which he wrote in 1864, "The Constitution as It Is—The Union as It Was":

> The North and South have acted wrong,
> And they will wrong remain,
> Till honest old-line Democrats
> Will make them right again.
> · · ·
> Let Abolition find its graves,
> Secession sleep beside—
> And give our "Little Mac" the helm.

Hays is credited with well over 300 songs in his song-writing career, with a reported sale of more than twenty million pieces of sheet music. Most of Hays's compositions are forgotten today, but one, "Little Old Log Cabin in the Lane," has entered into the folk stream (particularly through the parody "Little Old Sod Shanty on My Claim"), and "The Drummer Boy of Shiloh" lives as a memory and a symbol of the deep wellsprings of sympathy and sentimentality engendered by the Civil War.

HOME, SWEET HOME. One clear, starlit night along the banks of the Potomac River, while two mighty armies faced each other in the darkness from opposite sides of the river, the loneliness and heartaches and suffering of men at war overflowed into song. There were martial songs and patriotic songs and sentimental songs, first from one side and then the other. And then, one of the armies took up the yearning refrain of "Home, Sweet Home," and suddenly the sweet strains of the melody familiar to all Americans came drifting through the air from both sides of the Potomac. The two armies, locked in fierce and mortal combat, had stopped their killing for the length of a song, to share a common emotion.

It was only proper and appropriate that this musical unity should be achieved with one of the most popular songs ever written. The lyrics were by John Howard Payne, an American, who had written it as part of the libretto of an opera, "Clari," or "The Maid of Milan," in collaboration with the English composer, Sir Henry Bishop.

The opera was first produced in London in 1823. "Home, Sweet Home" quickly became the first genuine American "hit"—American despite its British composer because of the widespread popularity and commercial success which it enjoyed in the United States.

At the time of the Civil War, it was still one of the most popular American songs and was a natural favorite of soldiers on both sides of the conflict who, displaced and lonely in a bloody, brutal war, could sigh and say, "Be it ever so humble, there's no place like home."

SOMEBODY'S DARLING. Here is one of the best of the Southern-produced sentimental songs of the war and one of the few created in the Confederacy to become popular in the North. A musician in the band of the Third New Hampshire Volunteers lists "Somebody's Darling" as one of the songs sung by the troops in his outfit during the conflict. Various editions of sheet music appeared, each with a different author and composer. None of these editions, for some reason, used the refrain, and it seems likely that the original lyric appeared in print as an anonymous poem without a musical setting and without a refrain.

John Hill Hewitt, the gifted Southern composer, apparently added the refrain which helped make a distinguished song out of an ordinary poem. According to newspaper clippings in Hewitt scrapbooks, the lyric was written by a young woman of Savannah, Marie Ravenal de La Coste, who brought her poem to Herman L. Schreiner's publishing house in that city. Schreiner was impressed with the piece and sent it off to Hewitt to see if he cared to write a setting for it. Hewitt did, and the resulting song became so popular that Schreiner & Son had difficulty in meeting public demand for the sheet music. (For some reason, these editions of the music do not give the identity of the lyricist.)

In more recent years, the song was utilized in Margaret Mitchell's immensely popular Confederate view of the Civil War, *Gone with the Wind.*

THE SOUTHERN SOLDIER BOY. Wartime Richmond, the capital of the Confederacy, had a lively theatrical life, and even though the sound effects on stage frequently were forced to compete with the sound of artillery in the distance, the lights at the Richmond New Theater burned brightly throughout the war. One of the great hits staged at the Theater was "The Virginia Cavalier," a wartime musical featuring Miss Sallie Partington, "the prima donna of the Confederacy." The hit of the show was this song, "The Southern Soldier Boy," which was nightly greeted with cheers by the largely gray-uniformed audience. The words, according to the sheet music, are by an otherwise unidentified Captain G. W. Alexander, who set it to the familiar tune of "The Boy with the Auburn Hair." In time, the song was brought back to the Ozark hills by Confederate veterans, where it has passed into the folk tradition. In comparatively recent years, various collectors have come across the song under the title "Barbro Buck" and "Barbara Buck" after the hero of the song, Bob Roebuck. The original contains a rather outrageous refrain largely based on the repetition of "Yo! ho! yo! ho!, etc." The folk, wisely, have dropped this refrain in the versions collected, and the editor has seen fit to follow their lead and has adapted the song accordingly.

JUST BEFORE THE BATTLE, MOTHER. No man made a greater contribution to the music of the Civil War than George Frederick Root. With songs like "Battle Cry of Freedom" and "Tramp, Tramp, Tramp," he caught the fervor of the Union cause and created stirring, martial music which men could sing as they marched into battle.

Even in his songs of sentiment, and Root could be as maudlin as any song writer of the sixties, he directed his work to aiding the war effort. In "Just Before the Battle, Mother," one of the most widely sung songs of the war, Root takes the opportunity to inveigh against Northern Copperheads:

> Tell the traitors all around you,
> That their cruel words we know,
> In every battle kill our soldiers,
> By the help they give the foe.

Root, apparently, had also been reading his press notices when he wrote "Just Before the Battle" in 1862, for his reference to "Battle Cry of Freedom" came as a result of numerous reports to the effect that the song was actually sung by troops marching into battle.

Surprisingly enough, the song was also popular

in the South, where it was sung as written, including the reference to "The Battle Cry of Freedom." Early in the war, Christy's Minstrels brought the song to England where it became immensely popular; so popular, in fact, that the English could not believe that a "foreigner" had written it. In time, the English came to believe that *they* had written it, and that the war in question was the Crimean War. The melody even became a part of children's street literature, and just a few years ago was recorded by the Irish writer-folk singer, Dominic Behan as a street rhyme from his childhood, with the following words:

> Holy Moses, I am dying,
> Send for the doctor before I die,
> The cat is sitting in the lavvy,
> Turn her out before she cries for
> Holy Moses all the time.

Perhaps to us today the song is just another musical relic of a long dead era. But to the ordinary people of Civil War America, it reached out and touched a responsive nerve ending which was attached to the nation's heart.

FAREWELL, MOTHER. No song with the straight-faced sentimentality which typifies Root's composition could hope to escape the ravages of enemy parody. This is a devastating Confederate satire on "Just Before the Battle," and it is a tribute to Root's creative impulse that the original survived the parody. Soldier parodies persisted as late as the First World War which produced "Just Behind the Battle, Mother":

> Mother, don't you hear the hissing
> Of the bulletses so plain?
> I may be counted with the missing,
> But never, never with the slain!
> · · ·
> When I'm safely back, dear mother,
> From thy side I'll never roam,
> I will fight my younger brother
> In tranquility at home.

JUST AFTER THE BATTLE. It is doubtful that the Civil War era produced any more commercial-minded song writers than George F. Root—and this was surely an age which cherished the dollar. But where most song writers were content to create a "hit" and go on to other fields while lesser luminaries assayed imitations and sequels, Root was never one to let a good song go unrepeated. As he wrote "On, On, On" to sequel "Tramp,

Tramp, Tramp," so he tried to repeat his success with "Just Before the Battle, Mother" by composing "On the Field of Battle, Mother" (1863) and "Just After the Battle" (1863). While neither approached the success of the original, "Just After the Battle" possessed some worthwhile qualities on its own and achieved a small measure of popular approbation. One reason for Root writing the song was the fact that many people felt that "Just Before the Battle" was too sad, and the sequel was an attempt to show that there could be a silver lining, since the soldier in this one survives, albeit wounded.

Another "sequel" to "Just Before the Battle," this one by E. Bowers, also attempted to ease the aching hearts at home:

> Yonder comes a weary soldier,
> With faltering steps across the moor;
> Mem'ries of the past steal o'er me,
> He totters to the cottage door.
> Look! My heart cannot deceive me,
> 'Tis one we deemed on earth no more;
> Call mother, haste, do not tarry,
> For Brother's fainting at the door.

The song goes on to reveal that brother was in prison all the while the family had him "numbered with the slain." Another "answer" was Wesley Martin's "No, I'll Not Forget You Darling," while other songs which utilized the same word scheme were "Brother, Tell Me of the Battle" and "Mother, Is the Battle Over?" (this latter calling forth a reply, "Yes, My Boy, the Battle's Over").

WHO WILL CARE FOR MOTHER NOW? It is hard today to imagine the tremendous popularity of this incredibly maudlin song during the Civil War. Unlike many other extremely popular Civil War songs, there is little trace of this Charles Sawyer composition in modern song collections and recordings. But there can be little doubt of its wartime favor in the hearts of Americans both Northern and Southern.

Sawyer, who was no amateur at this sort of thing, used every trick in the book and a few that weren't in any book in the creation of this milestone of melodic melancholia. As with so many of the best sentimental songs of the time, the title was in the form of a question. ("Do They Miss Me at Home?" "What Is Home Without Mother?" "Can the Soldier Forget?" "Will You Wed Me Now I'm Lame, Love?" etc.)

Sawyer next came up with a "true story" on which the song was based, an inscription which surely stands as a classic example of its genre:

During one of our late battles, among many other noble fellows that fell, was a young man who had been the only support of an aged and sick mother for years. Hearing the surgeon tell those who were near him that he *could not live,* he placed his hand across his forehead, and with a trembling voice said, while burning tears ran down his fevered cheeks: *"Who will care for mother now?"*

With such a preface, the song itself might well have turned out to be an anticlimax. But Sawyer's eye-moistening lyric and saccharine melody lived up to the promise of both title and inscription, and the song which must be rated as the most woefully depressing air of the war was created.

No Civil War song garnered more musical "replies," each answer striving to reassure the "marching angel" that mother would be cared for in one way or another. Some writers relied on God in the hour of emergency:

> Weep no more, Oh nobly fallen!
> Let not sorrow cloud thy brow;
> Holy Angels round thee whisper,
> "God Will Care for Mother now."

"He's Watching o'er Thy Mother," wrote two well-known song writers, while an anonymous pair came up with the comforting thought that "Christ Will Care for Mother Now":

> He that is the God of battle
> Looks upon your anxious brow;
> He will comfort her in sorrow,
> He will care for mother now.

Others relied on neighbors and friends to pick up the dead soldier's cares, replying "Loyal Hearts Will Gather 'Round Her" and

> Friends will be near her,
> Angels will come
> To guard and cheer her,
> When you are gone.

Still others were willing to assume the burden themselves:

> While thou art an angel . . .
> Let thy spirit calmly slumber,
> I will care for mother now.

And some tried to reassure the dear departed:

> Comrade, I will guard thy mother,
> She will be my fondest care,
> I will be to thee a brother,
> While thou art an angel there.

Finally, C. G. Streval made a similar offer, at the same time voicing what was undoubtedly a growing and fervent wish:

> I will try to bear up nobly,
> To God's decree humbly bow,
> If you'll only cease your asking,
> "Who will care for mother now?"

WHO WILL CARE FOR MICKY NOW? Next to the Negro, the newly arrived Irishman was the favorite butt of song writers' satire in an era which reveled in national chauvinism and racial stereotypes. Needless to say, the Irish in the Civil War fought as valiantly and courageously as any other group, with many of the Irish Brigades of New York and other cities winning a measure of fame for their battlefield heroism. (For a more extensive discussion of stereotypes, chauvinism, dialect, etc., in Civil War song, see the section ". . . Grafted into the Army.")

This parody to "Who Will Care for Mother Now?" is an interesting reflection of Civil War humor and another instance of that wonderful American trait of satirizing the overly serious and the depressingly sentimental. Published as a broadside sheet in New York City, the song bears an inscription which is carefully and hilariously patterned after the original:

Amongst the many heroic fellows who drew a prize in the U.S. lottery, was a distinguished Frenchman from Limerick, the only support of himself. On being told by the surgeon he would "pass," he placed his hand on his empty stomach, and while a big tear of bravery rolled down his cheek, exclaimed in accents that would have touched the heart of a wheelbarrow, *"Who will care for Micky now?"*

THE FADED COAT OF BLUE. Written in the waning days of the war, this mournful dirge undoubtedly expressed the feelings of tens of thousands of families throughout the war-torn land. Sometimes known as "The Nameless Grave," the song passed into folk tradition at the war's end and was "collected" as a folksong in Mississippi in the 1930's. The Mississippi version is almost identical with the original, except that the more "literary" fourth stanza has been omitted (including the startling use of the word "startling") and the first two lines of the last stanza have been altered to read:

No dear one was by him to close his sweet blue eyes,
And no gentle one was by him to give him sweet replies.

Weeping Sad and Lonely (When This Cruel War Is Over)

Words by Charles C. Sawyer
Music by Henry Tucker

SENTIMENTAL WAR SONGS

125

SENTIMENTAL WAR SONGS

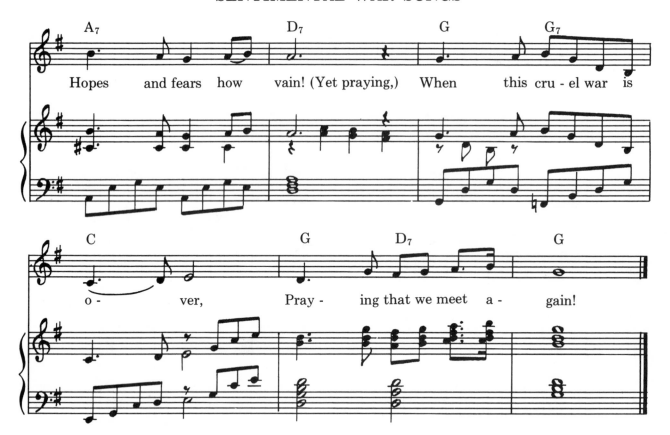

Hopes and fears how vain! (Yet praying,) When this cru - el war is o - ver, Pray - ing that we meet a - gain!

2. When the summer breeze is sighing
   Mournfully along;
   Or when autumn leaves are falling,
   Sadly breathes the song.
   Oft in dreams I see thee lying
   On the battle plain,
   Lonely, wounded, even dying,
   Calling but in vain.   (Chorus)

3. If amid the din of battle,
   Nobly you should fall,
   Far away from those who love you,
   None to hear you call,
   Who would whisper words of comfort,
   Who would soothe your pain?
   Ah! the many cruel fancies
   Ever in my brain.   (Chorus)

4. But our country called you, darling,
   Angels cheer your way;
   While our nation's sons are fighting,
   We can only pray.
   Nobly strike for God and liberty,
   Let all nations see,
   How we love the starry banner,
   Emblem of the free.   (Chorus)

Down in Charleston Jail

Words by Sergeant Johnson of the Fifty-Fourth Massachusetts Infantry
Music: "When This Cruel War Is Over"

1. When I enlisted in the army,
   Then I thought 'twas grand,
   Marching through the streets of Boston
   Behind a regimental band.
   When at Wagner I was captured,
   Then my courage failed;
   Now I'm dirty, hungry, naked,
   Here in Charleston Jail.

Chorus:
   Weeping, sad and lonely,
   Oh, how bad I feel!
   Down in Charleston, South Carolina,
   Praying for a good square meal.

2. If Jeff Davis will release me,
   Oh, how glad I'll be!
   When I get to Morris Island,
   Then I shall be free.
   Then I'll tell those conscript soldiers
   How they use us here;
   Giving us an old corn-dodger,
   They call it prisoners' fare.   (Chorus)

3. We are longing, watching, praying,
   But will not repine,
   Till Jeff Davis does release us,
   And send us in our lines.
   Then with words of kind affection
   How they'll greet us there!
   Wondering how we could live so long
   Upon the dodger fare.

Final Chorus:
   Then we will laugh, long and loudly,
   Oh, how glad we'll feel,
   When we arrive on Morris Island
   And eat a good square meal!

All Quiet Along the Potomac (The Picket Guard)

Words by Mrs. Ethel Lynn Beers
Music by W. H. Goodwin

SENTIMENTAL WAR SONGS

fro, By a ri - fle-man hid in the thick-et. 'Tis noth-ing, a pri - vate or two now and then Will not count in the news of the bat - tle; Not an of - fi - cer lost, on - ly one of the men, Moan-ing out all a - lone the death rat - tle.

2. All quiet along the Potomac tonight,
   Where the soldiers lie peacefully dreaming,
   Their tents in the rays of the clear autumn moon,
   O'er the light of the watch fires, are gleaming;
   A tremulous sign, as the gentle night wind,
   Through the forest leaves softly is creeping,
   While stars up above, with their glittering eyes,
   Keep guard for the army is sleeping.

3. There's only the sound of the lone sentry's tread,
   As he tramps from the rock to the fountain,
   And thinks of the two in the low trundle bed,
   Far away in the cot on the mountain.
   His musket falls slack, and his face, dark and grim,
   Grows gentle with memories tender,
   As he mutters a prayer for the children asleep,
   For their mother, may Heaven defend her.

4. The moon seems to shine just as brightly as then,
   That night when the love yet unspoken
   Leaped up to his lips when low-murmured vows
   Were pledged to be ever unbroken.
   Then drawing his sleeve roughly over his eyes,
   He dashes off tears that are welling,
   And gathers his gun closer up to its place
   As if to keep down the heart-swelling.

5. He passes the fountain, the blasted pine tree,
   The footstep is lagging and weary;
   Yet onward he goes, through the broad belt of
   light,
   Toward the shades of the forest so dreary.
   Hark! Was it the night wind that rustled the
   leaves?
   Was it moonlight so wondrously flashing?
   It looks like a rifle—"Ah! Mary, good-bye!"
   And the lifeblood is ebbing and splashing.

6. All quiet along the Potomac tonight,
   No sound save the rush of the river;
   While soft falls the dew on the face of the dead—
   [*Skip to last beat of fourth from last measure*]
   The picket's off duty forever.

Do They Miss Me at Home?

Words by Caroline A. Mason
Music by S. M. Grannis

Do they miss me at home, do they miss me? 'Twould be an as - sur - ance most dear, _____ To know that this mo - ment some loved one Were say - ing, "I wish he were here"; _____ To feel that the group at the

SENTIMENTAL WAR SONGS

2. When twilight approaches, the season
   That ever is sacred to song;
   Does someone repeat my name over,
   And sigh that I tarry so long?
   And is there a chord in the music,
   That's missed when my voice is away,
   And a chord in each heart that awaketh
   Regret at my wearisome stay?
   Regret at my wearisome stay?

3. Do they set me a chair near the table
   When evening's home pleasures are nigh,
   When the candles are lit in the parlor,
   And the stars in the calm azure sky?
   And when the "good nights" are repeated,
   And all lay them down to their sleep,
   Do they think of the absent, and waft me
   A whispered "good night" while they weep?
   A whispered "good night" while they weep?

4. Do they miss me at home—do they miss me,
   At morning, at noon, or at night?
   And lingers one gloomy shade round them
   That only my presence can light?
   Are joys less invitingly welcome,
   And pleasures less hale than before,
   Because one is missed from the circle,
   Because I am with them no more?
   Because I am with them no more?

Do They Miss Me in the Trenches?

Words by J. W. Naff
Music: "Do They Miss Me at Home?"

1. Do they miss me in the trench, do they miss me?
   When the shells fly so thickly around?
   Do they know that I've run down the hillside
   To look for my hole in the ground?
   But the shells exploded so near me,
   It seemed best for me to run;
   And though some laughed as I crawfished,
   I could not discover the fun,
   I could not discover the fun.

2. I often get up in the trenches,
   When some Yankee is near out of sight,
   And fire a round or two at him,
   To make the boys think that I'll fight.
   But when the Yanks commence shelling,
   I run to my home down the hill;
   I swear my legs never will stay there,
   Though all may stay there who will,
   Though all may stay there who will.

3. I'll save myself through the dread struggle,
   And when the great battle is o'er,
   I'll claim my full rations of laurels,
   As always I've done heretofore.
   I'll say that I've fought them as bravely
   As the best of my comrades who fell,
   And swear most roundly to all others
   That I never had fears of a shell,
   That I never had fears of a shell.

Lorena

Words by Rev. H. D. L. Webster
Music by J. P. Webster

SENTIMENTAL WAR SONGS

been. But the heart throbs on as warm-ly now, As

when the sum- mer days were nigh; Oh! — the sun can nev-er dip so

low, ——— A - down af -fec- tion's cloud-less sky.

2. A hundred months have passed, Lorena,
   Since last I held that hand in mine,
   And felt the pulse beat fast, Lorena,
   Though mine beat faster far than thine.
   A hundred months, 'twas flowery May,
   When up the hilly slope we climbed,
   To watch the dying of the day,
   And hear the distant church bells chime.

3. We loved each other then, Lorena,
   More than we ever dared to tell;
   And what we might have been, Lorena,
   Had but our lovings prospered well—
   But then, 'tis past, the years are gone,
   I'll not call up their shadowy forms;
   I'll say to them, "Lost years, sleep on!
   Sleep on! nor heed life's pelting storms."

4. The story of that past, Lorena,
   Alas! I care not to repeat,
   The hopes that could not last, Lorena,
   They lived, but only lived to cheat.
   I would not cause e'en one regret
   To rankle in your bosom now;
   For "if we *try,* we may forget,"
   Were words of thine long years ago.

5. Yes, these were words of thine, Lorena,
   They burn within my memory yet;
   They touched some tender chords, Lorena,
   Which thrill and tremble with regret.
   'Twas not thy woman's heart that spoke;
   Thy heart was always true to me:
   A duty, stern and pressing, broke
   The tie which linked my soul with thee.

6. It matters little now, Lorena,
   The past is in the eternal past;
   Our heads will soon lie low, Lorena,
   Life's tide is ebbing out so fast.
   There is a Future! O, thank God!
   Of life this is so small a part!
   'Tis dust to dust beneath the sod;
   But there, *up there,* 'tis heart to heart.

The Vacant Chair (We Shall Meet but We Shall Miss Him)

Words by Henry S. Washburn
Music by George F. Root

We shall meet but we shall miss him, There will be one va- cant chair; We shall lin- ger to ca- ress him, While we breathe our ev- 'ning pray'r; When a year a- go we

SENTIMENTAL WAR SONGS

SENTIMENTAL WAR SONGS

2. At our fireside, sad and lonely,
   Often will the bosom swell
   At remembrance of the story,
   How our noble Willie fell;
   How he strove to bear our banner
   Through the thickest of the fight,
   And uphold our country's honor,
   In the strength of manhood's night.   (Chorus)

3. True, they tell us wreaths of glory
   Ever more will deck his brow,
   But this soothes the anguish only,
   Sweeping o'er our heartstrings now.
   Sleep today, Oh early fallen,
   In thy green and narrow bed,
   Dirges from the pine and cypress
   Mingle with the tears we shed.   (Chorus)

The Drummer Boy of Shiloh

Words and music by Will S. Hays

SENTIMENTAL WAR SONGS

day. A wound-ed sol-dier held him up, His drum was by his

Chorus

side. He clasped his hands, then raised his eyes, And

prayed be - fore he died, — He clasped his hands, then raised his

eyes, And prayed be - fore he died.

2. Look down upon the battle field,
Oh, Thou our Heavenly Friend!
Have mercy on our sinful souls!
The soldiers cried, "Amen!"
For gathered 'round a little group,
Each brave man knelt and cried.
They listened to the drummer boy
Who prayed before he died.
They listened to the drummer boy
Who prayed before he died.

3. "Oh, mother," said the dying boy,
"Look down from Heaven on me,
Receive me to thy fond embrace—
Oh, take me home to thee.
I've loved my country as my God;
To serve them both I've tried."
He smiled, shook hands—death seized the boy
Who prayed before he died;
He smiled, shook hands—death seized the boy
Who prayed before he died.

4. Each soldier wept, then, like a child—
Stout hearts were they, and brave;
The flag his winding sheet—God's Book
The key unto his grave.
They wrote upon a simple board
These words: "This is a guide
To those who'd mourn the drummer boy
Who prayed before he died;
To those who'd mourn the drummer boy
Who prayed before he died."

5. Ye angels 'round the Throne of Grace,
Look down upon the braves
Who fought and died on Shiloh's plain,
Now slumb'ring in their graves!
How many homes made desolate—
How many hearts have sighed—
How many, like that drummer boy,
Who prayed before they died;
How many, like that drummer boy,
Who prayed before they died!

Home, Sweet Home

Words by John Howard Payne
Music by Henry Rowley Bishop

SENTIMENTAL WAR SONGS

2. An exile from home, splendor dazzles in vain,
   Oh, give me my lowly thatched cottage again;
   The birds singing gaily, that come at my call;
   Give me them, with that peace of mind, dearer
      than all.   (Chorus)

3. To thee, I'll return, overburdened with care,
   The heart's dearest solace will smile on me there.
   No more from that cottage again will I roam,
   Be it ever so humble, there's no place like home.
   (Chorus)

Somebody's Darling

Words by Marie Ravenal de la Coste
Music by John Hill Hewitt

SENTIMENTAL WAR SONGS

2. Matted and damp are his tresses of gold,
   Kissing the snow of that fair young brow;
   Pale are the lips of most delicate mould,
   Somebody's darling is dying now.
   Back from his beautiful purple-veined brow,
   Brush off the wandering waves of gold;
   Cross his white hands on his broad bosom now,
   Somebody's darling is still and cold.
   (Chorus)

3. Give him a kiss, but for Somebody's sake,
   Murmur a prayer for him, soft and low;
   One little curl from his golden mates take,
   Somebody's pride they were once, you know;
   Somebody's warm hand has oft rested there,
   Was it a mother's so soft and white?
   Or have the lips of a sister, so fair,
   Ever been bathed in their waves of light?
   (Chorus)

4. Somebody's watching and waiting for him,
   Yearning to hold him again to her breast;
   Yet, there he lies with his blue eyes so dim,
   And purple, child-like lips half apart.
   Tenderly bury the fair, unknown dead,
   Pausing to drop on his grave a tear;
   Carve on the wooden slab over his head,
   "Somebody's darling is slumbering here."
   (Chorus)

The Southern Soldier Boy

Words by Captain G. W. Alexander
Music: "The Boy with the Auburn Hair"

Bob Roe- buck is my sweet-heart's name, He's off to the wars and gone; He's fight - ing for his Nan - nie dear, His sword is buck- led on; He's fight - ing

SENTIMENTAL WAR SONGS

for _____ his own true love, His foes he does de - fy, He is the dar - ling of my heart, My South - ern Sol - dier Boy. He Boy.

149

2. When Bob comes home from war's alarms,
   We'll start anew in life,
   I'll give myself right up to him,
   A dutiful, loving wife.
   I'll try my best to please my dear,
   For he is my only joy;
   He is the darling of my heart,
   My Southern Soldier Boy.
   He is the darling of my heart,
   My Southern Soldier Boy.

3. Oh! if in battle he was slain,
   I am sure that I should die;
   But I am sure he'll come again
   And cheer my weeping eye;
   But should he fall in this our glorious cause,
   He still would be my joy,
   For many a sweetheart mourns the loss
   Of a Southern Soldier Boy.
   For many a sweetheart mourns the loss
   Of a Southern Soldier Boy.

4. I hope for the best, and so do all
   Whose hopes are in the field;
   I know that we shall win the day,
   For Southrons never yield.
   And when we think of those that are away,
   We'll look above for joy,
   And I'm mighty glad that my Bobby is
   A Southern Soldier Boy.
   He is the darling of my heart,
   My Southern Soldier Boy.

Just Before the Battle, Mother

Words and music by George F. Root

SENTIMENTAL WAR SONGS

view.   Com - rades brave are 'round me ly -ing,

Filled   with thoughts of home and God;   For   well   they know that on the

mor - row,   Some   will sleep be-neath the   sod.

Chorus

Fare - well, Moth-er, you may nev- er   Press   me to your breast a -

gain; But, Oh, you'll not for-get me, Moth-er,

If I'm num-bered with the slain.

2. Oh, I long to see you, Mother,
   And the loving ones at home,
   But I'll never leave our banner,
   Till in honor I can come.
   Tell the traitors all around you
   That their cruel words we know,
   In every battle kill our soldiers
   By the help they give the foe.   (Chorus)

3. Hark! I hear the bugles sounding,
   'Tis the signal for the fight,
   Now, may God protect us, Mother,
   As He ever does the right.
   Hear the "Battle Cry of Freedom,"
   How it swells upon the air,
   Oh, yes, we'll rally 'round the standard,
   Or we'll perish nobly there.   (Chorus)

Farewell, Mother

Words: anonymous
Music: "Just Before the Battle, Mother"

1. Just before the battle, mother,
   I was drinking mountain dew,
   When I saw the "Rebels" marching,
   To the rear I quickly flew;
   Where the stragglers were flying,
   Thinking of their homes and wives;
   'Twas not the "Reb" we feared, dear mother,
   But our own dear precious lives.

2. I hear the bugle sounding, mother,
   My soul is eager for the fray.
   I guess I'll hide behind some cover,
   And then I shall be O.K.
   Discretion's the better part of valor,
   At least I've often heard you say;
   And he who loves his life, dear mother,
   Won't fight if he can run away.   (Chorus)

Chorus: Farewell, mother! for you'll never
       See my name among the slain.
       For if I only can skedaddle,
       Dear mother, I'll come home again.

Just After the Battle

Words and music by George F. Root

SENTIMENTAL WAR SONGS

Man - y sleep to wak - en nev - er, In this world of strife and death, And man - y more are faint -ly call - ing, With their fee - ble dy - ing breath.

Chorus

Moth - er, dear, your boy is wound - ed, And the night is drear with pain, But

still   I feel that I shall see   you,   And   the dear old home a-   gain.

2. Oh, the first great charge was fearful,
   And a thousand brave men fell,
   Still amid the dreadful carnage,
   I was safe from shot and shell.
   So amid the fatal shower,
   I had nearly passed the day,
   When here the dreaded "minnie" struck me,
   And I sunk amid the fray.   (Chorus)

3. Oh, the glorious cheer of triumph,
   When the foeman turned and fled,
   Leaving us the field of battle,
   Strewn with dying and with dead.
   Oh the torture and the anguish,
   That I could not follow on,
   But here amid my fallen comrades,
   I must wait till morning's dawn.   (Chorus)

Who Will Care for Mother Now?

Words and music by Charles C. Sawyer

SENTIMENTAL WAR SONGS

com-rades, is this death? _____ Ah! how well I know your an - swer; To my fate I meek-ly bow, _____ If you'll on-ly tell me tru-ly, Who will care for moth - er now? _____

SENTIMENTAL WAR SONGS

2. Who will comfort her in sorrow?
   Who will dry the falling tear?
   Gently smooth her wrinkled forehead?
   Who will whisper words of cheer?
   Even now I think I see her
   Kneeling, praying for me! How
   Can I leave her in anguish?
   Who will care for mother now?   (Chorus)

3. Let this knapsack be my pillow,
   And my mantle be the sky;
   Hasten, comrades, to the battle,
   I will like a soldier die.
   Soon with angels I'll be marching,
   With bright laurels on my brow;
   I have for my country fallen,
   Who will care for mother now?   (Chorus)

Who Will Care for Micky Now?

Words by Eugene T. Johnston
Music: "Who Will Care for Mother Now"

1. Arrah! Molly darlin', I am drafted,
   Sure I must for a soger go,
   An' lave you all alone behind me—
   For to fight the Rebel foe;
   But be the powers, me pluck is failin',
   Big drops of swate rowl down me brow,
   Och, millia murther! I am drafted,
   Who will care for Micky now?

Chorus:

   Soon 'gainst Rebels I'll be marching,
   Wid the swate upon me brow—
   Och, blud an' nons, I'm kilt entirely,
   Who will care for Micky now?

2. Arrah! Who will comfort me in sorrow,
   Wid a drop of gin or beer?
   Wash me dirty shirts an' stockin's,
   Faith, there is no one I fear;
   Me fect are blistered wid the marchin',
   Me knapsack makes me shoulders bow,
   Pork an' crackers are me rations,
   Who will care for Micky now?

3. Indade, I miss me feather pillow
   An' bed on which I used to lie;
   The pine planks make me feel uneasy,
   If I had wings, och! Wudn't I fly?
   But one of me legs is stiff, dear,
   Since I was kicked by Murphy's cow,
   I'm afeard I niver can skedaddle,
   Who will care for Micky now?

The Faded Coat of Blue

Words and music by J. H. McNaughton

My — brave lad he sleeps in his fad - ed coat of blue, In a lone - ly grave un - known lies the heart that beat so true; He — sank faint and hun - gry a -

SENTIMENTAL WAR SONGS

mong the fam - ished brave, And they laid him sad and lone - ly with -

in his name-less grave.

Chorus

No more the bu - gle calls the wea - ry one,

Rest no - ble spir - it, in thy grave un-known! I'll _ find you and know you a -

mong the good and true, When a robe of white is giv'n for the fad-ed coat of blue.

SENTIMENTAL WAR SONGS

2. He cried, "Give me water and just a little crumb,
   And my mother she will bless you through all the years to come;
   Oh! tell my sweet sister, so gentle, good and true,
   That I'll meet her up in heav'n in my faded coat of blue."   (Chorus)

3. He said, "My dear comrades, you cannot take me home,
   But you'll mark my grave for mother, she'll find me if she'll come;
   I fear she'll not know me, among the good and true,
   When I meet her up in heav'n in my faded coat of blue."   (Chorus)

4. Long, long years have vanished, and though he comes no more,
   Yet my heart with startling beats with each footfall at my door;
   I gaze o'er the hill where he waved a last adieu,
   But no gallant lad I see in his faded coat of blue.   (Chorus)

5. No sweet voice was there, breathing soft a mother's prayer,
   But there's One who takes the brave and the true in tender care.
   No stone marks the sod o'er my lad so brave and true,
   In his lonely grave he sleeps in his faded coat of blue.   (Chorus)

Tenting on the Old Camp Ground

SONGS THE SOLDIERS SANG

We're tenting tonight on the old camp ground,
Give us a song to cheer
Our weary hearts, a song of home,
And friends we love so dear.

What did Johnny Reb and Billy Yank sing during the Civil War? Naturally, the most popular songs within the ranks were, by and large, the same songs which were being sung at home—the martial airs, the sentimental ballads, the comic ditties. Only a "professional" army enjoys a musical fare that is at variance with popular taste, and both of the Civil War armies were accurate cross sections of the people they represented.

But in addition to the songs which everyone sang, there was also a music which was almost exclusively the soldiers', spilling over into civilian life occasionally, and, in one or two cases, equally popular at home and camp. These include the traditional songs of complaint without which no army could survive, songs objecting to the food, the officers, the lack of feminine companionship, and the abundance of insect companionship; songs of soldiers, of raw recruits and rare exploits, of battles and of home, of practical jokes and politics and good things to eat and drink.

The songs in this section are, therefore, a miscellany, an unassorted collection of folk songs and sentimental songs, of narrative ballads and comic reliefs, of boasts and threats and promises and longings; they have in common only their popularity with the boys in blue and the boys in gray. Many of these songs were known only to a few, although some rank with the best and most lasting of the war.

TENTING ON THE OLD CAMP GROUND. Walter Kittredge, the author-composer of this hauntingly plaintive Civil War song, never did become a Union soldier, although it was his draft notice that was most responsible for "Tenting on the Old Camp Ground." A childhood bout with rheumatic fever kept Kittredge out of the army, but it was while preparing to answer the draft call he had received in 1863 that the inspiration came for this moving plea for peace. He wrote it, in a sense, as his farewell to civilian life, only to find himself exempt from service.

Having escaped the draft, Kittredge set out to sell the song, but the first Boston publisher to whom it was submitted turned it down. The publisher was looking for something a little more militant and patriotic than:

> Many are the hearts that are weary tonight,
> Wishing for the war to cease.

Kittredge, at one time a member of one of the many Hutchinson Family singing groups, then brought his song to the Hutchinsons. The famous singers were enthusiastic about it and decided to introduce it in a series of concerts which they were presenting at High Rock, near Lynn, Massachusetts. The song's success was instantaneous and Asa Hutchinson immediately interested the Oliver Ditson Company in Boston in publishing it. (Kittredge and Hutchinson worked out a 50 percent split on the royalties and, according to one Hutchinson biographer, Asa netted more income from "Tenting on the Old Camp Ground" than from any other song in the long career of the singing Hutchinsons.)

Civilian and soldier alike responded to Kittredge's song and, as the war continued and the casualty lists lengthened, it gained in mass appeal as a popular expression of the yearning for peace. The song retained its hold on the public for many years after the war and became one of the most popular songs of reminiscence at GAR reunions.

After the war, Kittredge tried his hand at many other songs, some of which enjoyed a limited appeal, but he never again approached the tremendous success of "Tenting on the Old Camp Ground."

J. W. Turner, attempting to cash in on Kittredge's success, and also in a reaction against the "gloominess" of the original, plagiarized Kittredge's lyric and wrote the closest thing to a "pirate" version possible. He called it "We're Tenting on the Old Camp Ground," but his "joyous" lyric sounded phony to his listeners, and the song was never very popular:

> We're tenting today on the old camp ground,
> Our hearts are light and joyous ever;

We think of home, we talk of friends,
And happy times we've had together.

TENTING ON THE OLD CAMP GROUND, II.

Walter Kittredge's song, like so many other popular songs of the Union, penetrated the front lines and was sung with equal depth of feeling by Southern soldiers as well as Yankees. Surprisingly enough, however, no Southern publisher seems to have bothered to print it, despite its evident popular appeal. One reason for this could be that the song came so late in the war that by the time a music publisher in Georgia or Louisiana could consider its publication, conditions of actual combat made such a venture impossible. The relatively late popularity of the song would seem to be confirmed by the note accompanying its publication (in considerably altered form) in an anthology of Southern war songs:

This song was very popular about the close of and immediately after the war. The air is sad and affecting, and chimed in well with the feelings of those who had laid down their arms, or who, just before its close, felt that the fight was hopeless and mourned lost comrades and wasted effort.

GOOBER PEAS.

The "goober peas" of this extremely popular Confederate camp song are plain, old-fashioned peanuts. In the waning days of the war, Johnny Reb subsisted on increasingly short rations. For long stretches of time, his diet might consist solely of "goobers"—which wasn't very good for the digestion but helped produce one of the best songs of the Civil War.

There is no record of the song having been published during the war, the first editions appearing in 1866, crediting the words to "A. Pindar, Esq." and the music to "P. Nutt, Esq." Every Southerner immediately recognized the names as obvious pseudonyms for "goobers."

An Alabama woman who learned the song in childhood from her mother reports that the Georgia soldiers in the Civil War were always known as "goober grabbers." The Alabama version consists only of one verse and chorus, the verse close to but still somewhat different from the third verse of the original:

'Twas just before the battle,
Before the fight begun,
The general looked around him

And swore he heard a gun,
And what did he see before him
Underneath the trees?
But the Georgia militia
Cracking goober peas.
Crack, crack, crack, crack,
Cracking goober peas, etc.

A similar Confederate soldier song, dealing with the same theme but never achieving the popularity of "Goober Peas" was "Short Rations," dedicated to "The Corn-Fed Army of Tennessee." The words were "concocted by Ye Tragic" and the music was "gotten up by Ye Comic." The song was written in response to an order reducing the already limited rations allowed the hard-pressed Rebel troops:

Reduce our rations at all?
It was difficult, yet it was done—
We had one meal a day—it was small—
Are we now, oh ye gods, to have none?
Oh, ye gentlemen issuing rations,
Give at least half her own to the State,
Put a curb on your maddening passions,
And commissaries—commiserate!

THE NEW YORK VOLUNTEER.

In the early days of the war, volunteers from every state in the North flocked to the colors with spirits and hopes high, their eagerness matched only by their inexperience. Undoubtedly, the North, by and large, underestimated the military task confronting it. Many, such as the "New York Volunteer," believed that the job of suppressing Rebellion would be relatively simple. (Two experienced fighting men, Ulysses S. Grant and William T. Sherman, vainly warned their countrymen that the job would be hard and bloody.)

This anonymous song of a New York volunteer was obviously written in the first days of the war before the bitterness of defeat and retreat had awakened the Union to the enormity of its undertaking.

DRINK IT DOWN.

If one were to judge solely by the songs of the Civil War, it would seem that both Confederate and Union troops were among the most temperate, strait-laced, soft-speaking soldiers known in the history of warfare. Only occasional drinking songs are found in collections of war airs, while melodic musings on the fair sex were confined to only the most proper of sentiments.

History, of course, contradicts this picture, leading one to believe that the songs were probably there. The collectors and anthologists, in the spirit of their times, probably passed them over with typical Puritan disdain.

Bell Irvin Wiley, in his excellent studies of the common soldier in the Civil War, reports on the prevalence of swearing, gambling, drinking, and other vices in the ranks of both armies. Wiley also mentions the existence of various types of soldier "erotic literature," including the usual off-color ditties and verses which the anthologists of later wars have seen fit to preserve, but which the Civil War collectors shunned as Satan himself.

Some of the songsters, especially those containing actual soldier material, published an occasional drinking song, such as this one, which we can imagine being sung with gusto around the evening campfire as the bottle passed from hand to hand.

FAREWELL TO GROG. One of the saddest (and soberest) days in the history of the United States Navy was September 1, 1862. For on that day, the tars of Uncle Sam, who had fought valiantly in every American war and who were maintaining an effective blockade of Southern ports, went down in bitter defeat before a merciless foe—Prohibition.

Up until that time, grog (a mixture of rum and water) had been served as a regular ration throughout the United States Navy. But mid-century America was an age of reform, and this official sanction (and aid) to the demon rum drew the wrath of every self-appointed reformer in the Union. A law abolishing the grog ration was, therefore, enacted under pressure from these forces of Puritanism.

Needless to say, the seamen who were being "protected" from the perils of alcohol were not appreciative of their benefactors nor overly enthusiastic about the new law. On the night of August 31, on the eve of the law's going into effect, sailors on the U.S.S. *Portsmouth* held a wake for their departing bottles. From all reports, the sailors laid in quite a supply of drink against the long, dry days ahead. In the course of the festivities, a seaman by the name of Caspar Schenck wrote, and then sang, a parody to a famous old English drinking song, "Landlord Fill the Flowing Bowl."

The end result was "Farewell to Grog," which holds an honored place in American naval history.

WAIT FOR THE WAGON. The lyric to this pre-Civil War song is, at best, undistinguished. But the song is blessed with a catchy chorus and a gay, completely irresistible melody. The song enjoyed the favor of both Union and Confederate troops and was a great campfire favorite.

One of the earliest sheet music editions credits the song to a J. P. Knauff, but later anthologists believe that the composer was R. Bishop Buckley, one of the outstanding figures of The Buckley Serenaders, a popular mid-century minstrel group. The company was organized by one of the earliest minstrels extant, English-born James Buckley. James brought his three sons, R. Bishop, G. Swayne, and Fred into his group and they all emigrated to America.

From the very beginning, song writers and propagandists realized that the tune was an excellent one for parodies. Both Republicans and Democrats used the song in the bitterly fought election of 1856. The Republican parody, "We'll Give 'em Jessie" (a reference to the newly organized party's candidate, J. C. Fremont and his wife, Jessie), was one of the most effective songs of the campaign:

Ye friends of freedom, rally now,
And push the cause along;
We have a glorious candidate,
A platform broad and strong.
"Free Speech, Free Press, Free Soil, Free Men,
Fremont," we have no fears,
With such a battle cry, but that
We'll beat the Buchaniers.

We'll give 'em Jessie,
We'll give 'em Jessie,
We'll give 'em Jessie,
When we rally at the polls.

Undaunted by Republican punning and preaching, the Democrats of 1856 replied in kind:

Will you come with me, good Democrats,
And rally round our flag,
To fight the black Republicans
Who play the game of brag?
. . .
There's Fremont with his wooly horse,
With Greeley on his back,
And Seward with the monster bank,
With all the Federal pack;

And King from old St. Lawrence,
With Giddings by his side,
We'll give those Negro worshippers
A good November ride.

Wait for the Wagon,
The old Democratic Wagon,
Wait for the Wagon,
And you'll all take a ride.

In the heated wartime election of 1864, both McClellan and Lincoln supporters tried to enlist the voters to their respective "wagons" with the popular air. Democrats had some pungent advice for Abe:

Good morning, Master Lincoln!
How do you feel today?
I think the joke is over now,
You'll move before next May.
We've got another tenant,
They call him Little Mac,
You'll find your house in Springfield, yet,
And better you go back!

Please take your wagon,
Please take your wagon,
Please take your wagon,
For the last little ride.

James D. Gay, a self-styled "celebrated Army song publisher and vocalist" of Philadelphia, took up the cudgels for Lincoln and against "Little Mac":

The traitors boast of treason,
And blow about the war,
And say if Abe's elected,
He'll fight them four years more.
But we'll show them in November
That McClellan's not the man,
So hold your horses, Jersey,
While we all go in for Sam.

Stick to the Wagon,
The Old Union Wagon,
The triumphant Wagon,
Abe Lincoln's bound to ride;
Hurrah boys for Lincoln,
Hurrah boys for Lincoln,
Hurrah boys for Lincoln,
Little Mac is played.

Other wartime parodies were sung by both Unionists and Confederates, and some examples appear on the next pages. By the end of the war, R. B. Buckley's delightful little melody had seen service in election campaigns, around army camp-

fires, and by troops on the march. It was a long road to travel for charming Phillis who had never expected so many to jump on the wagon and go for a ride.

THE OLD UNION WAGON. Union parodies to "Wait for the Wagon" were plentiful, but John Hogarth Lozier's "The Old Union Wagon" seems to have been the best known and best written. Lozier's song is a striking presentation of some of the outstanding issues of the Civil War and a notable defense of the Emancipation Proclamation, which Northern Democrats had strongly opposed:

Of all the Generals, high or low,
That help to save the nation,
There's none that strikes a harder blow
Than General Emancipation.

An 1861 rallying song used the "Wait for the Wagon" tune, but nothing else from the original:

Our flag shall be respected,
Not trampled in the dust,
The Stars and Stripes shall not come down,
Though traitors say they must;
Thank God, we have a captain,
To his country ever true,
We'll stand by Winfield Scott,
And the Red, White, and Blue.

Then hurrah for the Union!
Hurrah for the Union!
Hurrah for the Union!
And the Red, White, and Blue!

An interesting commentary on McClellan's oft-repeated claim that he could not pursue the Rebels because of lack of supplies is provided by this anonymous "Wait for the Wagon" parody:

A hundred thousand Northmen
In glittering war array,
Shout, "Onward now to Richmond!"
We'll brook no more delay.

Why give the traitors time and means
To fortify the way,
With stolen guns and ambuscades?
Oh, answer us, we pray.

You must wait for the wagons,
The real Army wagons,
The fat contract wagons,
Bought in the red-tape way.

Now, if for Army wagons,
Not for compromise you wait,

170

SONGS THE SOLDIERS SANG

Just ask them of the farmers
Of any Union State.

. . .

No growling, fat contractors
Shall block the proper way,
Nor real compromisers,
'Tis treason's reckoning day.

THE SOUTHERN WAGON.

THE SOUTHERN WAGON. "Wait for the Wagon" seems to have been equally popular in the South as a vehicle for Rebel sentiments. "The Southern Wagon" was known throughout the Confederacy and verses were constantly being added and deleted as the political and military situation changed.

In the style of "The Bonnie Blue Flag," many topical verses dealt with the "parade of Secession," saluting the States as they left the Union. One verse, obviously written in the first days after Sumter, complained of the slowness with which some of the Southern states were proceeding:

Missouri, North Carolina, and Arkansas are slow;
They must hurry, or we'll leave them, and then what will
    they do?
There's old Kentucky and Maryland won't make up their
    mind;
So I reckon, after all, we'll take them up behind.

Another verse celebrated General Beauregard and two Confederate martyrs:

Brave Beauregard, God bless him!
Led legions in his stead,
While Johnson seized the colors,
And waved them o'er his head.
So rising generations,
With pleasure we will tell,
How bravely our Fisher,
And gallant Johnson fell.

Some versions substitute "Secession" for "Dissolution" in the chorus, sacrificing musical cadence for political clarity, while others have the line: "The new Jeff Davis wagon."

A Stonewall Jackson "wagon" song gloated over Yankee defeats in the first year of the war:

We had a fight at Royal,
Where the Yankees took a stand,
And when we opened on them,
They retreated man to man.

. . .

Dick Taylor was our General,
But Jackson chief command,

We drove them down the valley,
And into Maryland;

But Banks, we couldn't catch him,
For all our generals tried,
He went to tell old Lincoln
How fast he had to ride.

Wait for the wagon,
We've an iron wagon;
Jackson is the wagon,
And we'll all take a ride.

A Yankee reply to "The Southern Wagon" was recalled by an Iowa Civil War veteran. The Yankee answer first satirized the "Secession parade of States" and then recounted the Union line-up:

New York and Pennsylvania,
With a host of Yankee boys,
Got up into the wagon,
And called for Illinois;
And old Ohio, she jumped in,
Missouri tried her luck,
And Indiana threw her arms
Around old Kentuck.

Bully for the wagon,
The old Union wagon!
Oh! Grant holds the horses in
While we all take a ride.

THE BRASS-MOUNTED ARMY.

THE BRASS-MOUNTED ARMY. Here is one of the most unusual and interesting Confederate soldier songs of the war. Written by an anonymous soldier in Colonel A. Buchel's Regiment, this detailing of foot-soldier gripes against the "brass" and the wealthy Southern slaveholders and property-owners provides us with a revealing insight into the attitudes and outlook of many Southern soldiers.

Indications are that the song was popular among "Western" regiments of the Confederate Army, where up-country, non-slaveholding mountain folk were more likely to be found in Rebel ranks. An Arkansas version of the song, in fact, mentions "old Kerby's army" rather than "our noble army," and this seems an obvious reference to General Kirby-Smith, commander of all Confederate forces west of the Mississippi from March 7, 1863, through the end of the war.

The tune is quite apparently a reworking of "Wait for the Wagon," but different enough to warrant printing separately.

THE VALIANT CONSCRIPT. The rigors of "basic training" for the raw recruit, particularly the draftee, have always been a subject for army humor. This Confederate camp song also mocks the "heroism" of the conscript, although one can detect a glimmer of sympathetic identification on the part of the anonymous author with the Civil War "sad sack" in the last stanza.

Songs complaining of army life were sung in both Union and Confederate camps. Another Southern soldier song directs its fire against that traditional army bugaboo, The Bugler:

> In nice log huts he saw the light,
> Of cabin fires, warm and bright,
> The sight afforded him no heat,
> And so he sounded the "Retreat."
>
> Upon the fire he saw a pot,
> Of sav'ry viands smoking hot,
> Said he, "They shan't enjoy that stew,"
> Then "Boots and Saddles" loudly blew.
>
> . . .
>
> But soldiers, you were made to fight,
> To starve all day and watch all night,
> And should you chance get bread and meat,
> That bugler will not let you eat.

And then, interestingly enough, the song ends on a wistful note of wishing for peace:

> Oh hasten, then, that glorious day,
> When buglers shall no longer play,
> When we through peace shall be set free,
> From "Tattoo," "Taps," and "Reveille."

"The Soldier's Fare" is another good-natured Confederate "gripe song," this one written by a soldier who thought enough of his verses to write a stanza containing his signature—in good folk song tradition:

> Not many you good people know
> What we poor soldiers undergo.
>
> . . .
>
> Sometimes we lie on the cold ground,
> Where there's no shelter to be found.
>
> . . .
>
> But as to grog we get enough,
> Although our beef is lean and tough;
> But as to that we'll not complain—
> We hope to get good beef again.
>
> Our doctor is a man of skill,
> And every day he gives a pill,
> And if that pill does not prove well,
> He gives a dose of calomel.

> You want to know who composed this song,
> I'll tell you now, it won't take long;
> It was composed by J. P. Hite,
> On his post on one rainy night.

The disdain of the professional soldier for the conscript is revealed in "The Soldier's Amen," a Civil War version of one of the most popular soldier songs in the English-speaking world, sometimes known as "The Soldier and the Sailor" or "The Soldier's Prayer":

> As a couple of good soldiers were walking one day,
> Said one to the other—"Let's kneel down and pray!
> I'll pray for the ear, and the good of all men—
> And whatever I pray for, do you say 'Amen.' . . ."
>
> "We'll pray for the privates, the noblest of all:
> They do all the work and get no glory at all.
> May good luck and good fortune them always attend!"
> "And return crowned with laurels!" said the Soldier's Amen.
>
> "We'll pray for the Conscript with frown on his brow,
> To fight for his country, he won't take the vow;
> May bad luck and bad fortune him always attend":
> "And die with dishonor"—said the Soldier's Amen.

Typical of Northern complaint songs was "Would You Be a Soldier, Laddy?" which seems to have been designed to work up enthusiasm for enlistment, though it is questionable how verses such as these could help rouse any young man to ardor for army life:

> Would you be a soldier, laddy?
> Come and serve old Uncle Sam!
> Come and serve old Uncle Sam!
> He henceforth must be your daddy,
> And Columbia your dam.
>
> Do you like salt-horse and beans?
> Do you know what hardtack means?
> Jolly hard-tack, tack, tack, tack,
> That's the stuff you have to crack,
> Do you like salt-horse and beans?

Of course, almost all soldier "griping" songs have that constant strain of irony and grim humor which help to make the burden of army discipline easier to bear. Far too many wars have proven beyond doubt that the soldier who gets his gripes off his chest in song or story or by swearing at his officers will be a better fighting man for it.

CONFEDERATE YANKEE DOODLE. With a stubborn streak of political and poetic perversity,

Confederate song writers adopted the melody and symbol of "Yankee Doodle" in their musical war with the Yankees. Pro-Southern "Yankee Doodle" parodies were written and sung throughout the South, striking a responsive note of defiance in Secession hearts.

The "Confederate Yankee Doodle," which seems to have been the best known of the parodies, lambasts the Unionists for every evil conceivable, from Puritan dining ("codfish and potatoes") and drunkenness to cowardice and thievery. Similarly, "A Farewell to Yankee Doodle" found fault with Puritanism and Yankee "do-gooders," with a few harsh words thrown in for John Brown in addition to a backhanded defense of slavery:

> Doodle's morbid conscience strains
> With Puritanic vigor,
> To loose the only friendly chains
> That ever bound a nigger.
>
> . . .
>
> Yankee Doodle sent us down
> A gallant missionary,
> His name was Captain Johnny Brown,
> The "Priest of Harpers Ferry."
>
> With pikes he tried to magnify
> The Gospel creed of Beecher,
> But old Virginia lifted high
> This military preacher.
>
> Yet glory to his name is sung,
> As if with sin untainted,
> The bloody wretch by justice hung,
> By bigotry is sainted.
>
> Yankee Doodle, now goodbye,
> We spurn a thing so rotten,
> Proud Independence is the cry
> Of Sugar, Rice, and Cotton.

The identification of the cause of the South with its most important products—sugar, rice, and, particularly, cotton—occurs in a number of songs. "Cotton Doodle," another "Yankee Doodle" parody, likewise carries out this theme:

> Hurrah for brave King Cotton!
> The Southerners are singing;
> From Carolina to the Gulf,
> The echo's loudly ringing;
> In every heart a feeling stirs
> 'Gainst Northern abolition!
> Something is heard of compromise,
> But nothing of submission.

> Cotton-doodle, boys, hurrah!
> We've sent old Yankee hissing;
> And when we get our Southern rights,
> I guess he'll turn up missing.
>
> Thank God his day is passing!
> He can no longer vex us;
> For, State by State, we'll firmly stand,
> From Maryland to Texas.
> King Cotton is a monarch
> Who'll conquer Abolition,
> And set his foot upon the neck
> Of treason and sedition.

I'LL BE A SERGEANT. This Civil War ancestor of the Second World War British marching song, "I've Got Six-Pence," must have a history that goes back to the earliest "common soldier" armies of England. "I'll Be a Sergeant" is credited to an unknown H. A. W. in this Civil War version, but it is quite apparently a reworking of an older song.

Even closer to the modern-day version is this Civil War variant:

> I love a six-pence,
> Jolly, jolly six-pence,
> I love a six-pence as I do my life;
> I'll save a penny of it,
> I'll spend a penny of it,
> I'll take four-pence of it home to my wife.
>
> For the pipe and the bowl shall greet us,
> Kind friends will ne'er deceive us,
> And happy is the man that shall meet us,
> As we go rolling home.

THERE WAS AN OLD SOLDIER. This folk song of Civil War days was, apparently, quite popular around both Confederate and Union campfires. At the end of the war, it passed into oral tradition via the returning soldiers and has, since, been collected in many parts of the country. An Indiana version seems to indicate some flickering connection with "Soldier's Amen" (see note above to "The Valiant Conscript").

A pair of contemporary folk-singers, Hermes Nye and Paul Clayton, connect the song directly with the Civil War through their informants, as does Carl Sandburg. The tune, of course, is a slight variant on the traditional square dance air, "Turkey in the Straw," a melody known to every country fiddler from Oregon to Georgia.

No one seems to know where the last verse

comes from or what its connection with the old soldier can possibly be, but Sam Hinton, a California folk singer, dubs it "a fine exercise in logic," which should be reason enough to sing it in this all too irrational world of ours.

JOHNNY IS MY DARLING. This simple Union song is a direct parody on one of the most popular Scottish Jacobite songs known, "Charlie Is My Darling," or "The Bold Chevalier." Folk singer Richard Dyer-Bennet sings a version of "Charlie" which seems as though it might have been the direct inspiration for the otherwise unidentified Father Reed to compose the Civil War parody:

> Charlie is my darling, my darling, my darling,
> Charlie is my darling, the young chevalier.
>
> 'Twas on a Monday morning,
> Right early in the year,
> When Charlie came to our town,
> The young chevalier.
>
> As he came marching up the street,
> The pipes played loud and clear,
> And all the folk came running out,
> To greet the chevalier.
>
> With Hieland bonnets on their heads
> And claymores bright and clear,
> They came to fight for Scotland's right
> And the young chevalier.

Some poorly conceived literary aspiration seems to have inspired Father Reed's final romantic verse which has no parallel in the original.

WHEN JOHNNY COMES MARCHING HOME. No matter how many patriotic, flag-waving, soul-inspiring martial songs may be written and sung in wartime, the most popular song of any war is bound to be, sooner or later, the one which has Johnny marching home rather than away.

Written in an age of lachrymose sentimentality, "When Johnny Comes Marching Home" is unique in being a musical hope for peace which rises above morbidity and heart-rending, tearful imagery. Perhaps this is why the song has grown in popularity with the passing of the years, and why many who know and sing it do not associate it with the Civil War. As a matter of fact, even though it was extremely popular during the war, the height of its popularity was achieved thirty-five years later during the Spanish-American War.

The most distinguishing characteristic of the song is, of course, its memorable melody—and therein lies a vexing problem of musical history. The first printed sheet music for the song bears the following legend:

Music introduced in the Soldier's Return March
By Gilmore's Band
Words & Music by Louis Lambert

Louis Lambert, however, was a pseudonym for Patrick S. Gilmore, bandmaster of the Union Army attached to General Butler's command in New Orleans. In later years, Gilmore confirmed his use of a pen name. But whether or not he actually composed the infectious tune became a subject for controversy which still rages. Gilmore himself had, on occasion, stated that he had learned the tune from an unidentified Negro singer and that it was really a traditional Negro air. The most casual listening, however, would contradict this highly astonishing statement. As one critic put it, "the Negro's name may have been Pat Reilly."

A New Hampshire Civil War musician states with absolute certainty that Gilmore "adapted the words to a rollicking old Irish air," and it is hard to find any person of Irish background who does not emphatically declare that the melody belongs to the Irish.

Unfortunately, none of those who claim the tune for the Irish can back up their assertion with demonstrable facts. I am willing to concede that the melody *sounds* like an Irish folk song, but subjective instinct is a poor substitute for evidence. The most frequently advanced argument is that the tune comes from the traditional Irish anti-war ballad, "Johnny I Hardly Knew Ye." Unfortunately for the proponents of this assertion, however, none can prove that the song was known and sung before the American Civil War. Some attribute "Johnny I Hardly Knew Ye" to the Crimean War, but we have already had some experience with this war, having been informed by various historians and singers that "Just Before the Battle, Mother" and "Battle Hymn of the Republic" were also products of the conflict which seems to have been best known heretofore for the typically senseless "Charge of the Light Brigade." With the experience of such unreliable musicology fresh in our minds, we will require more tangible proof than assertion before we consign "Johnny's" melody to the Crimean War.

Now what about Gilmore? Born in Ireland in the village of Ballygar (Galway County) on Christmas Day, 1829, Patrick S. Gilmore displayed a rare musical gift while still a youngster. He came to America in the 1840's, along with so many others who were fleeing the "famine" of those years ("Oh the praties they grow small, over here. . . ."), and embarked upon a musical career. Wartime found him Bandmaster for the United States Army, and in the post-war years Gilmore organized Monster Peace Jubilees which featured orchestras of a thousand musicians and choruses of 10,000 voices.

Despite this musical activity, which included a life of composing as well, Gilmore never again displayed the creative genius which may have produced "Johnny." Perhaps the real answer to the problem lies somewhere between the two obvious possibilities. Perhaps Gilmore, fresh from the Emerald Isle, reached back into his own portion of Irish folk memory to recall—and reconstruct—a tune. Who is to say that such a melody is not folk? And who is to say that Gilmore did not bring a creative effort to the air which justifies his individual stamp on it?

Certainly, we must say that the burden of proof falls on Gilmore's detractors, and that in the absence of such tangible evidence, Gilmore's claim should be acknowledged.

While the authorship of the song may be slightly clouded, there can be no doubt of the song's popularity and lasting appeal. Soldiers in both armies sang and identified with "Johnny," while singers, bands, and professional song writers added verses to and also parodied the original. Typical of the verses added to the song after its introduction were these stanzas of the California minstrel, Ben Cotton:

> We've got most glorious news today,
> Hurrah! hurrah!
> For Johnny's coming home, they say,
> Hurrah! hurrah!
> A soldier of the "loyal band,"
> Returning to his "native land,"
> And we'll all feel gay
> When Johnny comes marching home.

> When Johnny comes home, the girls will say,
> Hurrah! hurrah!
> We'll have sweethearts now to cheer our way,
> Hurrah! hurrah!
> And if they lost a leg, the girls won't run,
> For a half a man is better than none,
> And we'll all feel gay
> When Johnny comes marching home.

FOR BALES. Wartime parodies to "When Johnny Comes Marching Home" were popular throughout the North. Typical of these parodies was the chorus line:

> And we'll all drink stone blind,
> Johnny fill up the bowl.

The "Hurrah" refrain was also changed in most cases, with some variant of the word "bowl" substituted—"for bales," "for bowls," "foot balls," etc. Ellen Stekert, a young folklorist who has collected many Civil War songs in New York State, tells me that the song, as actually sung, has a decidedly less delicate and rather obvious earthy expression in the refrain.

One of the earliest parodies was titled "Johnny Fill Up the Bowl" and was published within a few months of the original:

> A soldier I'm just from the war,
> Footballs, footballs,
> A soldier I'm just from the war,
> Footballs, says I.
> A soldier I'm just from the war,
> Where thundering guns and cannons roar,
> And we'll all drink stone blind,
> Johnny fill up the bowl.

The song runs on for seventeen verses, containing a mixture of topical references and characteristic soldier irreverences. Here are a few:

> At first they led us to Bull Run,
> But "changed our base" for Washington.

> The Merrimac was all the talk,
> But the little Monitor made her walk.

> There was a man went to the war,
> The greatest fool you ever saw.

> He had a hat but ne'er a coat,
> So he buttoned his pantaloons up to his throat.

> The ladies fell in love with him,
> His maiden name, I think, was Jim.

A "Copperhead" parody also used the title "Johnny Fill Up the Bowl":

> Abram Lincoln, what yer 'bout?
> Hurrah! hurrah!
> Stop this war: for it's played out—
> Hurrah! hurrah!
> Abram Lincoln what yer 'bout?
> Stop this war for it's all played out!
> We'll all drink stone blind—
> Johnny, fill up the bowl!

The irrepressible Tony Pastor, staunch Democrat, critic of Lincoln, ardent Unionist, added a note of jingoism:

> The Union cause is going ahead,
> Ahead! Ahead!
> The Rebel cause will soon be dead,
> Be dead! Be dead!
> Their game is up and their hope is fled,
> And we'll make them pay for the blood they shed,
> We'll all drink to Uncle Sam,
> Johnny fill up the bowl!
>
> When we strike Rebellion a final blow,
> Ho, ho! You know—
> Unto the world our power we'll show,
> Oh, ho! That's so.
> We'll send some troops to Mexico,
> And a few more into Canada'll go!
> And we'll all drink to Uncle Sam—
> Johnny fill up the bowl!

Another parody, "We Are the Boys of Potomac's Ranks," was sung in the Third Corps in the fall of 1863. Its eight verses constitute a parade of Union generals—not in praise but in exasperation!

> We are the boys of Potomac's ranks, etc.
> We ran with McDowell, retreated with Banks,
> And we'll all drink stone blind,
> Johnny fill up the bowl. . . .

McClellan, Burnside, Hooker, and Meade ("a slow old plug") all came in for their share of abuse, with poor John Pope delivered a particularly stinging stanza:

> He said his headquarters were in the saddle,
> But Stonewall Jackson made him skedaddle.

This interesting Confederate parody, "For Bales," was written by the New Orleans song publisher, A. E. Blackmar. The original song was extremely popular in New Orleans in 1863 and 1864 since Gilmore had written it while stationed in that Union-occupied city.

"For Bales" is apparently based on an unsuccessful Union attempt to seize some bales of cotton stored up Red River. Blackmar, using the broadest kind of double meaning, sang sarcastically for the benefit of the Union government in New Orleans:

> Now let us all give praise and thanks,
> For the victory (?) gained by General Banks.

The sheet music is "Dedicated to those Pure Patriots who were afflicted with Cotton on the Brain and who saw the Elephant."

THE REBEL SOLDIER. This folk song of Civil War times was collected in the Southern Appalachian Mountains by the noted British folklorist, Cecil Sharp, in 1918. Sharp actually came across seven different versions in various parts of Virginia and Kentucky. This version was sung for him by Mrs. Lawson Gray of Montvale, Virginia.

An interesting topical reference is made in a West Virginia version. The state of West Virginia was formed during the war when mountaineers in the western part of Virginia rebelled against the Act of Secession declared in Richmond. Pro-Confederate mountaineers in the area were in the minority, as this variant reveals:

> The Union men and Yankees
> Have forced me to roam;
> I am a Rebel soldier
> And far from my home.
>
> .   .   .
>
> Miss Marley, Miss Marley,
> You've caused me to roam,
> To follow John H. Morgin [sic]
> And in his arms I'll roam.

An Arkansas version lets us in on a slice of domestic unrest. The Price referred to is General Sterling Price, former Governor of Missouri, who became an officer in the Confederate Army:

> I'll go to Price's army,
> At home I can't stay,
> For the home quarrels and Federals
> Have driven me away.

A Texas variant has the singer a "Rebel Prisoner," which gives the song an added note of poignancy. General Price gets into this one also:

> Go build me a cottage
> On yonder mountain high,

176

Where old General Price
Will help me to cry.
Where Southern boys will greet me
And help me to mourn—
I am a Rebel prisoner
And Dixie is my home!

"Farewell to old Texas!"
I could no longer stay,
For hard times and the Federals
Drove me away;
Hard times and Abe Lincoln
Have caused me to roam,
I am a Rebel prisoner
And Dixie is my home.

A Missouri version, under the title "A Roving Soldier," has the singer a Union man:

I eat when I get hungry,
I drink when I get dry,
And if the Rebels don't kill me,
I'll live until I die.

In the post-war years, Civil War veterans heading west would take the song with them and fashion it into a rip-snorter of a cowboy ballad with wild verses and a roaring tune best known under the title "Rye Whiskey."

THE SOUTHERN SOLDIER. This pro-Southern folk song would seem to have a literary forebear somewhere in the past, but so far none has been found. John A. Lomax collected this song for the Library of Congress from Mrs. Minta Morgan of Bells, Texas, in 1937.

PAT MURPHY OF THE IRISH BRIGADE. The favorite butt for mid-nineteenth-century American comics and singers was the Negro, in "black-face" minstrel form. But following close behind were Paddy O'Reilly and Mick McGuire —the "stage Irishmen." Typical of "comic Irish" songs with a Civil War motif was "Who Will Care for Mickey Now?" in another section of this collection.

The Irish, naturally, responded to the derogatory stereotypes with indignation and, in New York City and Boston, the Democratic Party. With their wonderful national tradition of song and dance behind them, Irish singers and comics began to take the stage in their own behalf. Irish song writers and parodists met each musical indignity with a score of replies. Some even employed the character of the "stage Irish" to make their point. A pre-Civil War song, "No Irish Need Apply," is typical:

I'm a decent boy just landed from the town of Ballyfad,
I want a situation and I want it very bad.
I have seen employment advertised, " 'Tis just the thing," says I,
But the dirty spalpeen ended with "NO IRISH NEED APPLY."

The song goes on to relate how the prospective employer was convinced that he had erred:

I couldn't stand it longer, so a-hold of him I took,
And gave him such a welting as he'd get at Donnybrook.
He hollered "Millia Murther" and to get away did try,
And swore he'd never write again, "NO IRISH NEED APPLY."

With the outbreak of hostilities, the Irish responded with enthusiasm, which turned into heroism in the stress of battle. Songs of the period identified the Union struggle against slavery with Ireland's centuries-old battle for freedom and national independence:

The war trump has sounded, our rights are in danger,
Shall the brave sons of Erin be deaf to the call,
When Freedom demands of both native and stranger
Their aid, lest the greatest of nations shall fall?

... Oh long may our flags wave in Union together,
And the harp of green Erin still kiss the same breeze,
And brave every storm that beclouds the fair weather,
Till our Harp, like the Stars, floats o'er rivers and seas.

Songs of Pat's courage under fire and of the martyrdom of the Irish, as "Pat Murphy of the Irish Brigade," were widely sung and remembered. The New York "69th" and other Irish regiments were celebrated in song, along with leaders like Corcoran, Ellsworth, and Meagher:

On the twenty-first of July,
Beneath a burning sun,
McDowell met the Southern troops
In battle at Bull Run;
Above the Union vanguard
Was proudly dancing seen,
Beside the starry banner,
Old Erin's flag of green.

Colonel Corcoran led the Sixty-Ninth
On that eventful day,
I wish the Prince of Wales were there
To see him in the fray.

Folk singer Frank Warner sings what may be the distant folk descendant of the above broadside sheet. Warner collected this in upper New York State:

This day will be remembered by America's noble sons,
If it hadn't a-been for Irishmen, what would our Union done?
'Twas hand to hand we fought 'em all in the broiling sun,
Stripped to the pants we did advance at the Battle of Bull Run!

There were songs celebrating Irish bravery, Irish loyalty, and the special regiments of Irishmen who marched off to war together. In 1861 they sang of Colonel Meagher and his newly-organized Brigade:

You gallant sons of Erin's isle, attend to what I say,
A brother, driven to exile, is up alive today;
He is of the good Hiberian blood that never frets nor fears,
He has arranged a new brigade of Irish volunteers.

But three years later, in 1864, the song of the Irish Brigade was somewhat different:

... They went forth to die in the swamps of the South,
And in the sunny green glade,
Lie the soldiers who fought in the Irish Brigade.

The pride of the Irish as a people, as a nation, as a group subjected to indignity and discrimination, and as loyal patriots faithful to their newly adopted land was expressed in scores of songs. Many were sung in the music halls of New York where Irish performers played such an important role. One of the best-known of such singers was Joe English, whose nightly turns covered a wide range of topical fare. In "Paddy and the Know-Nothings," Joe English ridicules anti-Irish prejudice, has warm words for Irish heroism, and winds up, naturally, singing the praises of "Little Mac":

A few years ago I came out to this country,
Being forced by misfortune abroad for to roam;
But the blaggards, they laughed, and called me a Micky,
And asked me, "Arrah, Pat, will ye ever go home?"
I felt mighty bad then—I got mighty mad then,
I pulled off my coat for to raise a big row;
When a friend, Barney Casey, says, "Larry, be aisy,
It's but the Know-Nothings that's after you now."
"Know-Nothings?" says I, "Faith, the name is a good one;
Sure, the devil a hap'orth these fellows can know!"

. . .

The President called on the land for an army,
And straightway to arms each patriot flew!

And they found that the men that they had scorned and slighted—
The Irish Brigade—to the Union was true.

. . .

And when the war's over and peace is restored,
And our brothers down South to the Union come back,
We'll join hands together and vote Democratic,
And for our next President elect the brave Little Mac.

With the Confederacy taking an Irish song, "The Irish Jaunting Car," and changing it into a Southern anthem, "Bonnie Blue Flag," it was natural for Irish Unionists to attempt to reclaim the melody. Another Joe English song, "The Irish Volunteer," uses the old tune and includes a typically Irish anti-British, anti-royalist verse:

When the Prince of Wales came over here and made a hubbaboo,
Oh everybody turned out, you know, in gold and tinsel too;
But then the good old Sixty-Ninth didn't like these Lords or peers—
They wouldn't give a d—n for kings, the Irish volunteers!
We love the land of Liberty, its laws we will revere,
"But the divil take nobility!" says the Irish volunteer.

"The Bonnie Green Flag" was an obvious answer to the Confederate song, and also made some comments about Northern discrimination against the Irish at the same time:

There are many around don't know what they're at,
When they laugh and they jeer and make game of poor Pat;
With his sprig of shillaleh and shamrock so green;
There are others you know oft tell a big lie,
When they say that the Irish need not apply;
But when soldiers they want, in the front there is seen,
The sprig of shillaleh and shamrock so green.

. . .

Here's to the Bonny Green Flag! and long may it wave,
With the Stars and the Stripes in the land of the brave,
With the sprig of shillaleh and shamrock so green;
And at no distant day it will once more float free,
On that dear little island over the sea.

The Confederacy could not allow Union song writers a monopoly on the musical and popular Irish, but it is doubtful whether any substantial number of newly arrived Irishmen served in Southern ranks. The Southern "Private Ma-Guire" is a typical "stage-Irish" piece which has the ring of non-Irish composition. ("I'm spilin' to meet ye, Abe Lincoln, Esquire"), while "Kelley's Irish Brigade" seems to be a reworking of a Northern broadside with Confederate symbols substituted where necessary.

SONGS THE SOLDIERS SANG

Only a few of these songs of the Irish and their fighting brigades have survived the passage of years, but history tells us that the songs of Irish bravery and devotion in the Civil War do not overstate the case. "Pat Murphy" is one of the few which an occasional singer will recall from a distant and hazy folk memory—and with it the "Irish Brigade" still marches into battle, its bright flag of green waving high alongside the Stars and Stripes.

HERE'S YOUR MULE. The title of this Confederate camp song is one of those soldier expressions which crop up in every war in the manner of "Kilroy Was Here" of the Second World War. Harwell believes that the phrase originally had some connection with the disappearance of livestock and goods whenever Morgan's famous raiders pitched camp in any area. Since the song appears to have been particularly popular in Tennessee and Kentucky, and since the tune was further identified with Morgan in a subsequent parody, this theory seems eminently plausible. In any event, it's a good singing song—its blunt soldier humor, supposedly based on an actual incident of camp life, supported by a rollicking tune.

HOW ARE YOU, JOHN MORGAN? The military career of John Hunt Morgan, "Morgan the Raider," was as meteoric as it was colorful. He enlisted as a scout in the Confederate Army in 1861, and became, successively, a captain, a colonel, and finally a brigadier general as his daring guerrilla raids struck terror in the hearts of pro-Union border state citizens. In time, many brigands and cutthroats joined his forces and these did not limit their activities to Union sympathizers, but considered any farmer or merchant or man of property fair game for their raids, no matter what his politics.

In 1863, Morgan was captured in Ohio after a series of dramatic forays into Southern Indiana and Ohio. A few months later, the energetic raider managed to escape from the Federal Penitentiary at Columbus, inspiring this song (originally published as "A Sequel to Here's Your Mule"), and at least one other, "Three Cheers for Our Jack Morgan":

> The dungeon dark and cold
> Could not his body prison,

> Nor tame a spirit bold
> That o'er reverse had risen;
> Then sing the song of joy,
> Our toast be lovely woman,
> And Morgan he's the gallant boy
> To plague the hated foeman!

A little less than a year later, Morgan, then aged thirty-nine, was killed by Union soldiers at Greenville, Tennessee.

I CAN WHIP THE SCOUNDREL. A Civil War story, possibly more colorful than accurate, tells of the Southern girl who wrote a letter to her cousin, a prisoner of war at Camp Morton, Indianapolis:

I will be for Jeffdavise till the tenisee river freezes over, and then be for him and scratch on the ice—
> Jeffdavise rides a white horse,
> Lincoln rides a mule,
> Jeffdavise is a gentleman,
> And Lincoln is a fule.

True or not, there is no doubt of the widespread usage of the four-line verse. It turns up in dozens of Southern folk songs, sometimes as an added stanza to some other ballad, as if a distant folk memory cannot erase the image and must constantly bring it out and fit it to a melody.

The persistent little quatrain appears as one of two stanzas found in Florida from which I have borrowed the title for this song. Folk singer Hermes Nye, in a ballad about General Patterson, sings about the white horse and the mule, and Mrs. Emma Dusenberry of Arkansas found it a favorite stanza to fit with other songs.

"I Can Whip the Scoundrel" is obviously a close first cousin (if not a more familiar relative) to a North Carolina prisoner of war song, "As I Went Down to Newbern":

> As I went down to Newbern,
> I went down there on the tide;
> I just got there in time
> To be taken by old Burnside.

> Old Burnside tuck me prisoner;
> He used me rough, 'tis true;
> He stole the knapsack off my back,
> And he did my blanket, too.

> And we'll lay five dollars down,
> Count them one by one,
> And every time we fight them
> The Yankees they will run.

179

The first verse is a reference to the Union's ill-fated Florida campaign of February, 1864. Baldwin represented the peak of the Yankee advance in the unsuccessful attempt to sever Florida from the Confederacy. Interestingly enough, the Fifty-fourth Massachusetts Regiment (Colored), whose song "Give Us a Flag," appears in another section, below, was also involved in this engagement.

CUMBERLAND GAP. This wild mountain banjo tune undoubtedly was a staple part of Appa-lachian musical fare before the Civil War. With its simple little two-line stanzas, it became an ideal vehicle for writing topical verses, as some of the most important fighting of the Civil War took place at this meeting point for the three states of Virginia, Kentucky, and Tennessee. This "Rebel" version stops with Confederate General Bragg's victory over George Morgan, but Union troops under the command of General Ambrose E. Burnside captured Cumberland Gap for the North in September of 1863 and it remained under Union control for the rest of the war.

Tenting on the Old Camp Ground

Words and music by Walter Kittredge

SONGS THE SOLDIERS SANG

2. We've been tenting tonight on the old camp
   ground,
   Thinking of days gone by,
   Of the loved ones at home that gave us the hand,
   And the tear that said, "Goodbye!"   (Chorus)

3. We are tired of war on the old camp ground,
   Many are dead and gone,
   Of the brave and true who've left their homes,
   Others been wounded long.   (Chorus)

4. We've been fighting today on the old camp ground,
   Many are lying near;
   Some are dead and some are dying,
   Many are in tears.

Final Chorus:
   Many are the hearts that are weary tonight,
   Wishing for the war to cease;
   Many are the hearts that are looking for the right
   To see the dawn of peace.
     Dying tonight, dying tonight,
     Dying on the old camp ground.

Tenting on the Old Camp Ground, II

Words: anonymous
Music by Walter Kittredge

1. We are tenting tonight on the old camp ground,
   The fires are flickering low,
   Still are the sleepers that lie around,
   And the sentinels come and go.

Chorus:
   Many are the hearts that are weary tonight,
   Waiting for the war to cease;
   Many are the eyes watching for the light
   To see the dawn of peace.
     Tenting tonight, tenting tonight;
     Tenting on the old camp ground.

2. Alas for the comrades of days gone by,
   Whose forms we miss tonight.
   Alas for the young and true who lie
   Where the battleflag braved the fight.
     (Chorus)

3. No more on march or field of strife
   Shall they lie down tired and worn;
   Nor rouse again to hope and life
   When the kettledrums beat at morn.   (Chorus)

4. The lone wife kneels and prays with a sigh,
   That God his watch will keep,
   O'er the dear one away and the little ones nigh,
   In the trundlebed fast asleep.   (Chorus)

5. She prays for him who with soldierly tread
   No more into ranks shall fall,
   Till the angel rallies the quick and the dead
   And the trumpet tone wakens all.   (Chorus)

6. Nearer and nearer the darkness draws,
   The hopes of the past lie low.
   The embers die with the dying cause;
   And the sentinels come and go.

Final Chorus:
   Many are the hearts that are weary tonight,
   Waiting for the war to cease,
   Many are the hopes, the hopes once high and
     bright,
   That sleep with those at peace.
     Dying tonight, dying tonight;
     Dying on the old camp ground.

Goober Peas

Anonymous

SONGS THE SOLDIERS SANG

185

SONGS THE SOLDIERS SANG

2. When a horseman passes, the soldiers have a rule,
   To cry out at their loudest, "Mister, here's your mule!"
   But another pleasure enchantinger than these,
   Is wearing out your grinders, eating goober peas!   (Chorus)

3. Just before the battle the Gen'ral hears a row,
   He says, "The Yanks are coming, I hear their rifles now."
   He turns around in wonder, and what do you think he sees?
   The Georgia Militia—eating goober peas!   (Chorus)

4. I think my song has lasted almost long enough,
   The subject's interesting, but rhymes are mighty rough,
   I wish this war was over, when free from rags and fleas,
   We'd kiss our wives and sweethearts and gobble goober peas!   (Chorus)

The New York Volunteer

Words: anonymous
Music: "Lincolnshire Poacher"

'Twas in the days — of sev-en-ty-six, When Free-men young and old, — All fought for In-de-pen-dence then, Each he-ro brave and bold! — 'Twas then the no-ble Stars and Stripes In tri-umph did — ap-

SONGS THE SOLDIERS SANG

pear, And de - fend - ed by — brave pa - tri - ots, The

Yan - kee Vol - un - teers. 'Tis ___ my de - light ___ to

Chorus

march and fight Like a New York Vol - un - teer. ___

2. Now, there's our City Regiments,
   Just see what they have done:
   The first to offer to the State
   To go to Washington,
   To protect the Federal Capital
   And the flag they love so dear!
   And they've done their duty nobly,
   Like New York Volunteers. (Chorus)

3. The Rebels out in Maryland,
   They madly raved and swore,
   They'd let none of our Union troops
   Pass through Baltimore;
   But the Massachusetts Regiment,
   No traitors did they fear;
   But fought their way to Washington,
   Like Yankee Volunteers. (Chorus)

188

Drink It Down

Anonymous

SONGS THE SOLDIERS SANG

down, drink it down, — drink it down.

2. Here's success to Sherry,
   Drink it down, drink it down,
   Here's success to Sherry,
   Drink it down, drink it down.
   Here's success to Sherry,
   For it makes the heart beat merry,
   Drink it down, drink it down, drink it down.

3. Here's success to Whiskey,
   For it makes the spirits frisky.

4. Here's success to Cider,
   For it makes the frame grow wider.

5. Here's success to Brandy,
   Just enough to make us handy.

6. Here's success to Ale,
   When it's made us strong and hale.

7. Here's success to Punch,
   With a little social lunch.

8. Here's success to Porter,
   While we use it as we oughter.

9. Here's success to Water,
   Heaven's draught that does no slaughter.

190

Farewell to Grog

Words by Caspar Schenk, U.S.N.
Music: "Landlord Fill the Flowing Bowl"

Come, mess-mates, pass the bot-tle 'round, Our time is short, re-mem-ber, For our grog must stop, our spir-its drop, On the first day of Sep-tem-ber.

SONGS THE SOLDIERS SANG

2. Farewell old rye, 'tis a sad, sad word,
   But alas! It must be spoken,
   The ruby cup must be given up,
   And the demijohn be broken.   (Chorus)

3. Jack's happy days will soon be gone,
   To return again, oh never!
   For they've raised his pay five cents a day,
   But stopped his grog forever.   (Chorus)

4. Yet memory oft' will backward turn,
   And dwell with fondness partial,
   On the days when gin was not a sin,
   Nor cocktails brought court martial.   (Chorus)

5. All hands to split the main brace, call,
   But split it now in sorrow,
   For the spirit-room key will be laid away
   Forever, on tomorrow.   (Chorus)

Wait for the Wagon

Words and music attributed to R. Bishop Buckley

SONGS THE SOLDIERS SANG

2. Where the river runs like silver
   And the birds they sing so sweet,
   I have a cabin, Phillis,
   And something good to eat;
   Come listen to my story,
   It will relieve my heart;
   So jump into the wagon,
   And off we will start.   (Chorus)

3. Do you believe, my Phillis, dear,
   Old Mike, with all his wealth,
   Can make you half so happy
   As I, with youth and health?
   We'll have a little farm,
   A horse, a pig and cow;
   And you will mind the dairy,
   While I do guide the plough.   (Chorus)

4. Your lips are red as poppies,
   Your hair so slick and neat,
   All braided up with dahlias,
   And hollyhocks so sweet.
   It's ev'ry Sunday morning,
   When I am by your side,
   We'll jump into the wagon,
   And all take a ride.   (Chorus)

5. Together, on life's journey,
   We'll travel till we stop,
   And if we have no trouble,
   We'll reach the happy top;
   Then come with me, sweet Phillis,
   My dear, my lovely bride,
   We'll jump into the wagon,
   And all take a ride.   (Chorus)

The Old Union Wagon

Words by John Hogarth Lozier
Music: "Wait for the Wagon"

1. In Uncle Sam's Dominion in Eighteen Sixty-One,
   The fight between Secession and Union was begun;
   The South declared they'd have the "rights" which Uncle Sam denied,
   Or in their Secesh Wagon they'd all take a ride!

   Chorus: Hurrah for the wagon,
   The old Union wagon,
   We'll stick to our wagon
   And all take a ride.

2. The makers of our wagon were men of solid wit,
   They made it out of "Charter Oak" which would not rot or split.
   Its wheels are of material, the strongest and the best,
   And two are named the North and South, and two the East and West.   (Chorus)

3. Our wagon bed is strong enough for any "revolution,"
   In fact it is the "hull" of the old "Constitution";
   Her coupling's strong, her axle's long, and anywhere you get her,
   No Monarch's frown can "back her down"—no Traitor can upset her.   (Chorus)

4. This good old Union Wagon, the nation all admired,
   Her wheels had run for four score years and never once been "tired,"
   Her passengers were happy as along her way she whirled,
   For the good old Union Wagon was the glory of the world.   (Chorus)

5. But when old Abraham took command, the South wheel got displeased,
   Because the *public fat* was gone that kept her axle greased;
   And when he gathered up the reins and started on his route,
   She plunged into Secession and knocked some "fellers" out.   (Chorus)

6. Now while in this Secession mire the wheel was sticking tightly,
   Some Tory passengers got mad and cursed the driver slightly;
   But Abraham "couldn't see it"—so he didn't heed their clatter,
   There's too much black mud on the wheel, says he—"That's what's the matter."   (Chorus)

7. So Abra'm gave them notice that in Eighteen Sixty-Three,
   Unless the Rebels "dried it up" he'd set their niggers free;
   And then the man that led the van to fight against his nation
   Would drop his gun and home he'd run, to fight against starvation.   (Chorus)

8. When Abra'm said he'd free the slaves that furnished their supplies,
   It opened Northern traitors' mouths and Southern traitors' eyes.
   "The slaves," said they, "will run away if you thus rashly free them!"
   But Abra'm guessed, perhaps they'd best go home and oversee them.   (Chorus)

9. Around our Union Wagon, with shoulders to the wheel,
   A million soldiers rally, with hearts as true as steel;
   And of all the Generals, high or low, that help to save the nation,
   There's none that strikes a harder blow than General Emancipation!   (Chorus)

The Southern Wagon

Words: anonymous
Music: "Wait for the Wagon"

1. Come all ye sons of freedom,
   And join our Southern band,
   We are going to fight the Yankees
   And drive them from our land.
   Justice is our motto,
   And Providence our guide,
   So jump into the wagon
   And we'll all take a ride.

Chorus:
   So wait for the wagon!
   The dissolution wagon!
   The South is the wagon,
   And we'll all take a ride.

2. Secession is our watchword,
   Our rights we all demand;
   To defend our homes and firesides
   We pledge our hearts and hands;
   Jeff Davis is our President,
   With Stephens by his side;
   Brave Beauregard, our General,
   Will join us in the ride.   (Chorus)

3. Our wagon is the very best,
   The running gear is good;
   Stuffed 'round the sides with cotton,
   And made of Southern wood.
   Carolina is the driver,
   With Georgia by her side,
   Virginia holds the flag up,
   And we'll all take a ride.   (Chorus)

4. There are Tennessee and Texas
 Also in the ring;
 They wouldn't have a government
 Where cotton wasn't king.
 Alabama and Florida
 Have long ago replied;
 Mississippi and Louisiana
 Are anxious for the ride.   (Chorus)

5. Old Lincoln and his Congressmen
 With Seward by his side,
 Put old Scott in the wagon
 Just for to take a ride;
 McDowell was the driver,
 To cross Bull Run he tried,
 But there he left the wagon
 For Beauregard to ride.   (Chorus)

6. Manassas was the battleground;
 The field was fair and wide;
 The Yankees thought they'd whip us out,
 And on to Richmond ride;
 But when they met our "Dixie" boys,
 Their danger they espied;
 They wheeled about for Washington,
 And didn't wait to ride.   (Chorus)

7. The Tennessee boys are in the field,
 Eager for the fray;
 They can whip the Yankee boys
 Three to one, they say;
 And when they get in conflict
 With Davis by their side,
 They'll pitch into the Yankee boys,
 And then you'll see them slide.   (Chorus)

8. Our cause is just and holy,
 Our men are brave and true;
 We'll whip the Lincoln cutthroats,
 Is all we have to do.
 God bless our noble army;
 In Him we all confide;
 So jump into the wagon,
 And we'll all take a ride.   (Chorus)

The Brass-Mounted Army

Words: an anonymous soldier of Col. A. Buchel's Regiment
Music: adapted from "Wait for the Wagon"

Oh, sol - diers I've con - clud - ed to
an - y be of - fend - ed at

make a lit - tle song, And if I tell no
what I have to sing, Then sure - ly his own

false - hood there can be noth - ing wrong; If
con - science ap - plies the bit - ter sting. Oh,
(to chorus)

198

SONGS THE SOLDIERS SANG

Chorus

how do you like the ar-my The brass-mount-ed ar-my, The
high-fa-lu-tin' ar-my, Where ea-gle but-tons rule?

2. Whisky is a monster, and ruins great and small,
   But in our noble army, Headquarters gets it all;
   They drink it when there's danger, although it seems too hard,
   But if a private touches it they put him "under guard."   (Chorus)

3. And when we meet the ladies we're bound to go it sly,
   Headquarters are the pudding, and the privates are the pie!
   They issue Standing Orders to keep us all in line,
   For if *we* had a showing, the *brass* would fail to shine.   (Chorus)

4. At every big plantation or Negro-holder's yard,
   Just to save the property, the general puts a guard;
   The sentry's then instructed to let no private pass—
   The rich man's house and table are fixed to suit the "brass."   (Chorus)

5. I have to change this story, so beautiful and true,
   But the poor man and widow must have a line or two;
   For them no guard is stationed, their fences oft are burned,
   And property molested, as long ago you've learned.   (Chorus)

6. The army's now much richer than when the war begun,
   It furnishes three tables where once it had but one;
   The first is richly loaded with chickens, goose, and duck,
   The rest with pork and mutton, the third with good old buck.   (Chorus)

SONGS THE SOLDIERS SANG

7. Our generals eat the poultry, and buy it very cheap,
   Our colonels and our majors devour the hog and sheep;
   The privates are contented (except when they can steal),
   With beef and corn bread plenty to make a hearty meal.   (Chorus)

8. Sometimes we get so hungry that we're bound to press a pig,
   Then the largest stump in Dixie we're sure to have to dig;
   And when we fret, an officer who wears long-legged boots,
   With neither judge nor jury, puts us on "double roots."   (Chorus)

9. These things, and many others, are truly hard to me,
   But still I'll be contented, and fight for Liberty!
   And when the war is over, oh what a jolly time!
   We'll be our own commanders and sing much sweeter rhymes.   (Chorus)

10. We'll see our loving sweethearts, and sometimes kiss them too,
    We'll eat the finest rations, and bid old buck adieu;
    There'll be no generals with orders to compel,
    Long boots and eagle buttons, forever fare ye well!

Final Chorus:

   And thus we'll leave the army, the brass-mounted army,
   The high-faluting army, where eagle buttons rule.

The Valiant Conscript

Words: anonymous
Music: "Yankee Doodle"

SONGS THE SOLDIERS SANG

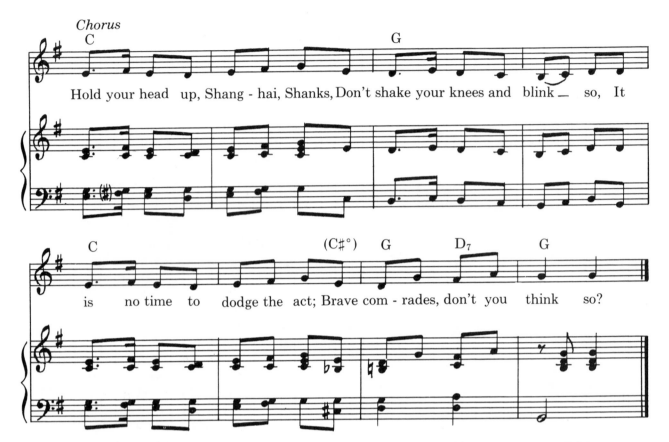

Chorus

Hold your head up, Shang - hai, Shanks, Don't shake your knees and blink _ so, It

is no time to dodge the act; Brave com - rades, don't you think so?

2. I was a ploughboy in the field,
   A gawky, lazy dodger,
   When came the conscript officer
   And took me for a sodger.
   He put a musket in my hand,
   And showed me how to fire it;
   I marched and counter-marched all day;
   Lord, how I did admire it!   (Chorus)

3. With corn and hog fat for my food,
   And digging, guarding, drilling,
   I got as thin as twice-skimmed milk,
   And was scarcely worth the killing.
   And now I'm used to homely fare,
   My skin as tough as leather,
   I do guard duty cheerfully
   In every kind of weather.   (Chorus)

4. I'm brimful of fight, my boys,
   I would not give a "thank ye"
   For all the smiles the girls can give
   Until I've killed a Yankee.
   High private is a glorious rank,
   There's wide room for promotion;
   I'll get a corporal's stripes some day,
   When fortune's in the notion.   (Chorus)

5. 'Tis true I have not seen a fight,
   Nor have I smelt gunpowder,
   But then the way I'll pepper them
   Will be a sin to chowder.
   A sergeant's stripes I now will sport,
   Perhaps be color-bearer,
   And then a captain—good for me—
   I'll be a regular tearer.   (Chorus)

6. I'll then begin to wear the stars,
   And then the wreaths of glory,
   Until the army I command,
   And poets sing my story.
   Our Congress will pass votes of thanks
   To him who rose from zero,
   The people in a mass will shout,
   Hurrah, behold the hero!   (Chorus)

He fires his gun by accident

7. What's that? oh dear! A boiler's burst,
   A gaspipe has exploded,
   Maybe the Yankees are hard by
   With muskets ready loaded.
   Oh, gallant soldiers, beat 'em back,
   I'll join you in the frolic,
   But I've a chill from head to foot,
   And symptoms of the colic.   (Chorus)

Confederate Yankee Doodle

Words: anonymous
Music: "Yankee Doodle"

1. Yankee Doodle had a mind
   To whip the Southern "traitors,"
   Because they didn't choose to live
   On codfish and potatoes.
   > Yankee Doodle, doodle-doo,
   > Yankee Doodle dandy,
   > And so to keep his courage up
   > He took a drink of brandy.

2. Yankee Doodle said he found
   By all the census figures,
   That he could starve the Rebels out
   If he could steal their niggers.
   > Yankee Doodle, doodle-doo,
   > Yankee Doodle dandy,
   > And then he took another drink
   > Of gunpowder and brandy.

3. Yankee Doodle made a speech;
   'Twas very full of feeling:
   I fear, says he, I cannot fight,
   But I am good at stealing.
   > Yankee Doodle, doodle-doo,
   > Yankee Doodle dandy,
   > Hurrah for Lincoln, he's the boy
   > To take a drop of brandy.

4. Yankee Doodle drew his sword,
   And practiced all the passes;
   Come, boys, we'll take another drink
   When we get to Manassas.
   > Yankee Doodle, doodle-doo,
   > Yankee Doodle dandy,
   > They never reached Manassas plain,
   > And never got the brandy.

5. Yankee Doodle soon found out
   That Bull Run was no trifle;
   For if the North knew how to steal,
   The South knew how to rifle.
   > Yankee Doodle, doodle-doo,
   > Yankee Doodle dandy,
   > 'Tis very clear I took too much
   > Of that infernal brandy.

6. Yankee Doodle wheeled about,
   And scampered off at full run,
   And such a race was never seen
   As that he made at Bull Run.
   > Yankee Doodle, doodle-doo,
   > Yankee Doodle dandy,
   > I haven't time to stop just now
   > To take a drop of brandy.

7. Yankee Doodle, oh! For shame,
   You're always intermeddling;
   Let guns alone, they're dangerous things;
   You'd better stick to peddling.
   > Yankee Doodle, doodle-doo,
   > Yankee Doodle dandy,
   > When next I go to Bully Run
   > I'll throw away the brandy.

8. Yankee Doodle, you had ought
   To be a little smarter;
   Instead of catching woolly heads,
   I vow you've caught a tartar.
   > Yankee Doodle, doodle-doo,
   > Yankee Doodle dandy,
   > Go to hum, you've had enough,
   > Of Rebels and of brandy.

I'll Be a Sergeant

Anonymous (soldier's song)

Rolling along ♩ = 132

I'll be a Ser-geant, an or-der-ly Ser-geant, I'll be a Ser-geant, on that just bet your life; I'll make the boys so sick of drill-ing on the dou-ble quick, They'll be glad to turn in, to dream of a wife.

SONGS THE SOLDIERS SANG

For the girls, they must love and a - dore us, Who __ fight for the coun - try that bore us, And __ hap-py shall we be, If they kiss __ you and me, When we come march - ing home. March - ing home, march-ing home, march-ing home, __ March-ing home to the roll of the

SONGS THE SOLDIERS SANG

drum, _____ When ___ peace shall call us back from the camp and biv-ou-ac, And the drum taps, "March - ing home."

2. She sha'nt be Cap'n, that must not happen,
   She sha'nt be Cap'n, but play the second fife;
   We can bear the colors best,
   She shall wear them on her breast,
   Salute us, and "dress," and in short be our wife.
   (Chorus)

3. Should I be Col'nel, gazetted in the Journal,
   Oh, should I be Colonel, to lead in the strife,
   For her sake, so proud I'd be,
   And let every Rebel see,
   How a man can fight for a flag and a wife!

Final Chorus:
   For, dear girls, we soldiers adore you;
   Make us brave through your love, we implore
        you!
   Then happy shall we be
   To bend the suppliant knee,
   When we come marching home.
   Marching home, marching home, marching home,
   Marching home to the roll of the drum.
   Then, freed from war's alarms,
   To you we'll yield our arms,
   When the drum taps, "Marching home!"

There Was an Old Soldier

Traditional American folk song

Oh, there was an old sol-dier and he had a wood-en leg. He had no to-bac-co, no to-bac-co could he beg. An-oth-er old sol-dier, as sly as a fox, He al-ways kept to-bac-co in his

old to-bac-co box. He al-ways kept to-bac-co in his old to-bac-co box.

2. Said the one old soldier, "Won't you give me a chew?"
   Said the other old soldier, "I'll be hanged if I do,
   Just save up your money and put away your rocks,
   And you'll always have tobacco in your old tobacco box,
   And you'll always have tobacco in your old tobacco box."

3. Well, the one old soldier, he was feeling mighty bad,
   He said, "I'll get even, I will begad!"
   He goes to a corner, takes a rifle from the peg,
   And stabs the other soldier with a splinter from his leg,
   And stabs the other soldier with a splinter from his leg.

4. Now there was an old hen and she had a wooden foot,
   And she made her nest by the mulberry root,
   She laid more eggs than any hen on the farm,
   And another wooden leg wouldn't do her any harm.
   And another wooden leg wouldn't do her any harm.

Johnny Is My Darling

Words by Father Reed
Music: "Charlie Is My Darling"

SONGS THE SOLDIERS SANG

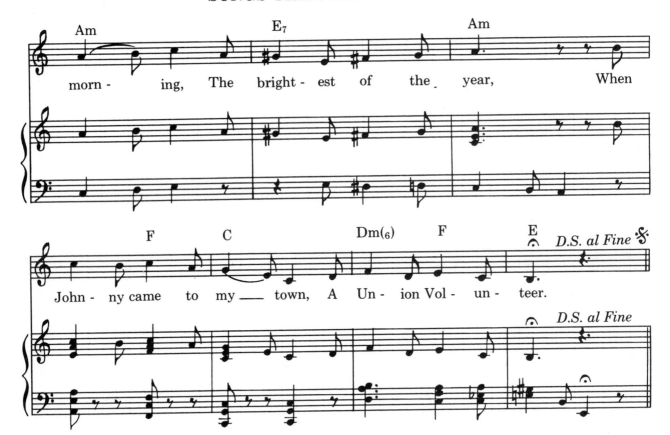

morn - ing, The bright - est of the year, When

John - ny came to my ___ town, A Un - ion Vol - un - teer.

2. As he came marching up the street,
   The bands played loud and clear;
   And everyone came out to greet
   The Union Volunteer.   (Chorus)

3. With proudly waving starry flags
   And hearts that knew no fear;
   He came to fight for Freedom's rights,
   A Union Volunteer.   (Chorus)

4. But though he's gone to glory win,
   And I left lonely here,
   He'll soon return to me again
   As *Cupid's Volunteer.*   (Chorus)

When Johnny Comes Marching Home

Words and music by Patrick S. Gilmore

SONGS THE SOLDIERS SANG

rah! _____ The _ men will cheer, — the boys will shout, The

la - dies, they _ will all turn out, And we'll all feel

gay when John - ny comes march - ing home. _____

SONGS THE SOLDIERS SANG

2. The old church bell will peal with joy,
   Hurrah, hurrah!
   To welcome home our darling boy,
   Hurrah, hurrah!
   The village lads and lassies say,
   With roses they will strew the way,
   And we'll all feel gay when Johnny comes
   marching home.

3. Get ready for the Jubilee,
   Hurrah, hurrah!
   We'll give the hero three times three,
   Hurrah, hurrah!
   The laurel wreath is ready now
   To place upon his loyal brow,
   And we'll all feel gay when Johnny comes
   marching home.

4. Let love and friendship on that day,
   Hurrah, hurrah!
   Their choicest treasures then display,
   Hurrah, hurrah!
   And let each one perform some part,
   To fill with joy the warrior's heart,
   And we'll all feel gay when Johnny comes
   marching home.

Abe Lincoln Went to Washington

Words: anonymous
Music: "When Johnny Comes Marching Home"

1. In eighteen hundred and sixty one,
   For bowls, for bowls,
   In eighteen hundred and sixty one,
   For bowls, says I.
   In eighteen hundred and sixty one,
   Abe Lincoln went to Washington,
   And we'll all drink stone blind,
   Johnny fill up the bowl!

2. In eighteen hundred and sixty two
   Old Abe he put the rebellion through.

3. In eighteen hundred and sixty three
   Old Abe he set the darkies free.

4. In eighteen hundred and sixty four
   Old Abe he called for a million more.

5. In eighteen hundred and sixty five
   John Wilkes Booth took Lincoln's life.

For Bales

Words and music by A. E. Blackmar

1. We all went down to New Orleans,
   For Bales, for Bales;
   We all went down to New Orleans,
   For Bales, says I;
   We all went down to New Orleans
   To get a peep behind the scenes,
   "And we'll all drink stone blind,
   Johnny fill up the bowl."

2. We thought when we got in the "Ring,"
   For Bales, for Bales;
   We thought when we got in the "Ring,"
   For Bales, says I;
   We thought when we got in the "Ring,"
   Greenbacks would be a dead sure thing,
   "And we'll all drink stone blind,
   Johnny fill up the bowl."

3. The "Ring" went up, with bagging and rope,
   For Bales, for Bales;
   Upon the "Black Hawk" with bagging and rope,
   For Bales, says I;
   Went up "Red River" with bagging and rope,
   Expecting to make a pile of "soap,"
   "And we'll all drink stone blind,
   Johnny fill up the bowl."

4. But Taylor and Smith, with ragged ranks,
   For Bales, for Bales;
   But Taylor and Smith, with ragged ranks,
   For Bales, says I;
   But Taylor and Smith, with ragged ranks,
   Burned up the cotton and whipped old Banks,
   "And we'll all drink stone blind,
   Johnny fill up the bowl."

5. Our "Ring" came back and cursed and swore,
   For Bales, for Bales;
   Our "Ring" came back and cursed and swore,
   For Bales, says I;
   Our "Ring" came back and cursed and swore,
   For we got no cotton at Grand Ecore,
   "And we'll all drink stone blind,
   Johnny fill up the bowl."

6. Now let us all give praise and thanks,
   For Bales, for Bales;
   Now let us all give praise and thanks,
   For Bales, says I;
   Now let us all give praise and thanks,
   For the victory (?) gained by General Banks,
   "And we'll all drink stone blind,
   Johnny fill up the bowl."

The Rebel Soldier

Southern Appalachian folk song
From the singing of Mrs. Lawson Grey

SONGS THE SOLDIERS SANG

2. It's grape shot and musket,
   And the cannons lumber loud,
   There's many a mangled body,
   The blanket for their shroud;
   There's many a mangled body
   Left on the fields alone,
   I am a Rebel soldier
   And far from my home.

3. I'll eat when I'm hungry,
   I'll drink when I am dry,
   If the Yankees don't kill me,
   I'll live until I die;
   If the Yankees don't kill me
   And cause me to mourn,
   I am a Rebel soldier
   And far from my home.

4. Here's a good old cup of brandy
   And a glass of nice wine,
   You can drink to your true love,
   And I will drink to mine;
   And you can drink to your true love,
   And I'll lament and mourn,
   I am a Rebel soldier
   And far from my home.

5. I'll build me a castle on the mountain,
   On some green mountain high,
   Where I can see Polly
   As she is passing by;
   Where I can see Polly
   And help her to mourn,
   I am a Rebel soldier
   And far from my home.

The Southern Soldier

Southern mountain folksong
From the singing of Mrs. Minta Morgan

SONGS THE SOLDIERS SANG

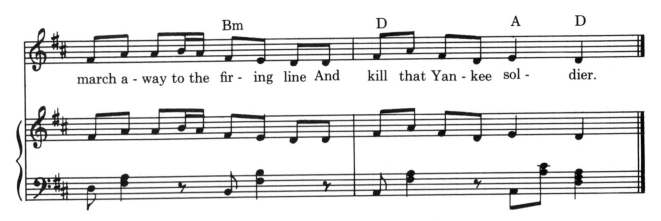

march a - way to the fir - ing line And kill that Yan - kee sol - dier.

2. I'll bid farewell to my wife and child,
   Farewell to my aged mother,
   And go and join in the bloody strife,
   Till this cruel war is over,
   Till this cruel war is over,
   I'll go and join in the bloody strife,
   Till this cruel war is over.

3. If I am shot on the battlefield,
   And I should not recover,
   Oh, who will protect my wife and child,
   And care for my aged mother?
   And care for my aged mother,
   Oh, who will protect my wife and child,
   And care for my aged mother?

4. And if our Southern cause is lost,
   And Southern rights denied us,
   We'll be ground beneath the tyrant's heel
   For our demands of justice,
   For our demands of justice,
   We'll be ground beneath the tyrant's heel
   For our demands of justice.

5. Before the South shall bow her head,
   Before the tyrants harm us,
   I'll give my all to the Southern cause,
   And die in the Southern army,
   And die in the Southern army,
   I'll give my all to the Southern cause,
   And die in the Southern army.

6. If I must die for my home and land,
   My spirit will not falter,
   Oh, here's my heart and here's my hand
   Upon my country's altar,
   Upon my country's altar,
   Oh, here's my heart and here's my hand
   Upon my country's altar.

7. Then Heaven be with us in the strife,
   Be with the Southern soldier,
   We'll drive the mercenary horde
   Beyond our Southern border,
   Beyond our Southern border,
   We'll drive the mercenary horde
   Beyond our Southern border.

Pat Murphy of the Irish Brigade

Anonymous

Says Pat to his moth-er, "It looks strange to see Broth-ers fight-ing in such a queer man-ner, ——— But I'll fight till I die if I nev-er get killed for A-mer-i-ca's bright star-ry

SONGS THE SOLDIERS SANG

Chorus

ban - ner." ____ Far a - way in the East was a dash - ing young blade, And the song he was sing - ing so gai - ly, ____ — 'Twas hon - est Pat Mur - phy of the I - rish Bri - gade, And the song of the splin - tered shil - le - lagh. ____

2. The morning soon broke and poor Paddy awoke,
He found Rebels to give satisfaction,
And the drummers were beating the Devil's sad
tune,
They were calling the boys into action. (Chorus)

3. Sure, the day after battle, the dead lay in heaps,
And Pat Murphy lay bleeding and gory,
With a hole through his head by some enemy's
ball
That ended his passion for glory.   (Chorus)

4. No more in the camp will his letters be read,
Or his song be heard singing so gaily,
But he died far away from the friends that he
loved,
And far from the land of shillelagh.   (Chorus)

Here's Your Mule

Words: anonymous
Music by C. D. Benson

With humor ♩. = 126

A farm - er came to camp one day, With milk and eggs to sell, Up - on a mule that oft would stray To where no one could tell. The farm - er tir - ed

SONGS THE SOLDIERS SANG

of his tramp, For hours was made a fool, By

ev - 'ry one he met in camp With, "Mis - ter, here's your mule."____

Chorus

Come on, ___ come on, come on, ___ old man, And don't ___ be made a fool, By

ev - 'ry - one you meet in camp With, "Mis - ter, here's your mule."____

2. His eggs and chickens all were gone,
   Before the break of day;
   The mule was heard of all along,
   That's what the soldiers say;
   And still he hunted all day long,
   Alas! a witless tool,
   Whilst every man would sing the song
   Of, "Mister, here's your mule."   (Chorus)

3. The soldiers run in laughing mood,
   On mischief were intent;
   They lifted muley on their back,
   Around from tent to tent;
   Through this hole and that, they pushed
   His head and made a rule,
   To shout with hum'rous voices all,
   "I say! Mister, here's your mule."   (Chorus)

4. Alas, one day the mule was missed!
   Ah, who could tell his fate?
   The farmer, like a man bereft,
   Searched early and searched late,
   And as he passed from camp to camp,
   With stricken face—the fool,
   Cried out to ev'ryone he met,
   "Oh, Mister, where's my mule?"   (Chorus)

How Are You, John Morgan?

Words: anonymous
Music: "Here's Your Mule"

1. A famous Rebel once was caught,
   With sabre bright in hand,
   Upon a mule he never bought,
   But pressed in Abra'm's land.
   The Yankees caught his whole command,
   In the great Ohio State;
   And kept the leader of the band,
   To change for Colonel Streight.

Chorus:
   Then raise the shout, the glorious shout,
   John Morgan's caught at last,
   Proclaim it loud, the land throughout,
   He's into prison cast.

2. A felon's cell was then prepared,
   At David Tod's request,
   And in Columbus prison shared
   The convict's *shaven crest.*
   And thus the Rebel chieftain's pride,
   They sought to humble low,
   But Southern valor don't subside
   Nor less in prisons grow.   (Chorus)

3. But prison fare he did not like,
   And sought a time to leave,
   And with greenbacks and pocket knife,
   The keepers did deceive.
   They say he dug a tunnel 'neath
   Its grated walls so grand,
   And from the North he took "French leave"
   Away for Dixie's land.   (Chorus)

4. John Morgan's gone like lightning flies,
   Through every State and town;
   Keep watch, and for the famous prize,
   Five thousand dollars down.
   But he is gone, too late, too late,
   His whereabouts to find,
   He's gone to call on Master Jeff,
   Way down in Richmond town.

Final Chorus:
   Upon his mule, he's gone, they say,
   To Dixie's promised land,
   And at no very distant day
   To lead a new command.

I Can Whip the Scoundrel

Adapted from the singing of Hermes Nye

SONGS THE SOLDIERS SANG

lay ten dol - lars down, Or twen - ty if you choose, For
I can whip the scoun- drel that stole old Ab - ner's shoes.

2. Jeff Davis was a gentleman,
   Abe Lincoln was a fool.
   Jeff Davis rode a dapple gray,
   Abe Lincoln rode a mule.   (Chorus)

3. The Yankees took me prisoner,
   They used me rough, it's true;
   They took from me my knapsack,
   And stole my blankets too.   (Chorus)

4. The Yankees took me prisoner,
   And if I can get parole,
   I'll go right back and fight them,
   I will, upon my soul.   (Chorus)

Cumberland Gap

Southern mountain folksong

Lay down, boys, and take a lit-tle nap,
(Like a 5-string banjo)
Lay down, boys, and take a lit-tle nap, Lay down, boys, and take a lit-tle nap,
Four-teen miles to the Cum-ber-land Gap.

SONGS THE SOLDIERS SANG

1. The first white man in Cumberland Gap,
   The first white man in Cumberland Gap,
   The first white man in Cumberland Gap,
   Was Doctor Walker, an English chap.

2. Daniel Boone on Pinnacle Rock,
   He killed Indians with an old flintlock.

3. Cumberland Gap is a noted place,
   Three kinds of water to wash your face.

4. Cumberland Gap with its cliff and rocks,
   Home of the panther, bear, and fox.

5. September mornin' in sixty-two,
   Morgan's Yankees all withdrew.

6. They spiked Long Tom on the mountain top,
   And over the cliffs they let him drop.

7. They burned the hay, the meal, and the meat,
   And left the Rebels nothing to eat.

8. Braxton Bragg with his Rebel band,
   He run George Morgan to the blue-grass land.

9. The Rebels now will give a little yell,
   They'll scare the niggers all to Hell.

10. Ol' Aunt Dinah, ef you don't keer,
    Leave my little jug settin' right here.

11. Ef it's not here when I come back,
    I'll raise Hell in Cumberland Gap.

12. Ol' Aunt Dinah took a little spell,
    Broke my little jug all to Hell.

13. I've got a woman in Cumberland Gap,
    She's got a boy that calls me "pap."

14. Me and my wife and my wife's grand'pap,
    All raise Hell in Cumberland Gap.

It's All About That Terrible Fight

SONGS OF BATTLES AND CAMPAIGNS

Oh, shipmates, come gather
And join in my ditty,
Of a terrible battle
That happened of late.

From Sumter to Appomattox, the battles of the Civil War have been commemorated in song. Folk singers North and South have relived and refought almost every important battle and scores of comparatively minor engagements to the accompaniment of banjo, guitar, or fiddle—or with no accompaniment at all.

The use of a ballad to tell the story of a particular event is as old as ballad-making. At the time of the Civil War, with modern journalism still in its infancy, the news-relating function of balladry was still very much alive. In rural areas, banjo-picking mountaineers and strong-voiced farmers still fashioned crude narrative songs out of the military events of the day. In the cities, the stall-ballad or broadside writers still plied their trades, frequently "scooping" the newspapers with the details of some important event—and in any case, taking poetic license to embellish natural and human tragedies such as floods, murders, and pitched battles with a high degree of personalized fiction.

The most popular battle as a song subject was Bull Run (Manassas), with scores of ballads written either celebrating the Confederate victory or bemoaning the Union defeat. (See introduction to "Flight of Doodles" later in this section for more material on Bull Run songs.)

Grant's successful six-week siege of Vicksburg also produced a host of songs, most of these, surprisingly enough, Confederate. Perhaps the hardship and drama of life under siege conditions are responsible for the number of lighthearted Southern efforts which attempt to minimize the effects of the encirclement and to lighten the burden of the city's defenders and population.

One such, to the tune of "A Life on the Ocean Wave," was not overly appreciative of the Confederate command under the leadership of Lieutenant General John Clifford Pemberton:

> Old Grant is starving us out,
> Our grub is fast wasting away,
> Pemb don't know what he's about,
> And he hasn't for many a day.
>
> . . .

A life on the Vicksburg bluff,
A home in the trenches deep,
Where we dodge Yank shells enough,
And our old "pea bread" won't keep.

Sep Winner's famous melody, "Listen to the Mocking Bird," provided the tune for another Southern Vicksburg song on the lighter side:

> 'Twas at the siege of Vicksburg,
> Of Vicksburg, of Vicksburg,
> 'Twas at the siege of Vicksburg,
> When the parrot shells were whistling through the air.
> Listen to the parrot shells,
> Listen to the parrot shells,
> The parrot shells are whistling through the air.

In a more serious vein were songs like "Bombardment of Vicksburg" and "The Battle of Vicksburg," the latter a reworking of the much-used and much-abused "Bingen on the Rhine," a classic of supine sentimentality.

While many battle songs began life as popular songs or topical broadsides, except for some occasional soldier parodies, only a few became a part of the stream of our folk music. And, despite the fact that most songs, naturally enough, dealt with victories from a partisan point of view, the folk survivals tend to be mostly accounts of bloody defeats, or, at best, extremely costly victories.

Two Shiloh songs are included in this section, and in addition I have come across songs concerning the following battles: Antietam Creek, Gettysburg, Mill Springs, Cedar Creek, Fisher's Hill, Elkhorn Tavern, Stone River, New Orleans ("New Ballad of Lord Lovel"—a satire on the Confederate defender of that city), Fort Donelson, Murfeesboro, Charleston, Sumter, Fredericksburg, Mission Ridge, Pea Ridge, Port Royal, and dozens of others. The majority of these, like most topical songs, are primarily of historical interest, although an absorbing, if not thoroughly accurate history of the Civil War could be written by arranging such ballads in proper chronological sequence.

One Southern soldier began such a musical chronology in a single song, but after covering

SONGS OF BATTLES AND CAMPAIGNS

Bull Run, Shiloh, and Gainesville, he got bogged down in McClellan's inactivity:

> Now the last I've heard of McClellan, the third,
> He was down on James River bogged up in the mud,
> In a bend of the river, near a big pond,
> The want of more news puts an end to my song.

If the Civil War on land produced a great quantity of ballads, the Civil War on the sea produced some of the finest songs to emerge from the conflict. Included here are two songs dealing with the historic battle between the U.S.S. *Cumberland* and the Confederate *Merrimac,* the first ironclad in modern naval history. While there are songs dealing with the *Monitor's* victory over the *Merrimac,* I have not been able to find any with enough musical and literary worth to be included in this collection. A typical song is "The Monitor and the Merrimac":

> Behold the smoke and flame,
> And hear the angry voice of War,
> Around the wrathful giant
> Moves the nimble *Monitor!*
> On every side he plants his blows—
> He has not wasted one:
> And now the monster moves,
> Too wise to stay, too proud to run.
>
> With a Whack Row de Dow,
> Three cheers for the *Monitor;*
> Whack Row de Dow,
> How are you *Merrimac?*

See "Roll, Alabama, Roll" and "Cairo" (included here because the city's strategic value was naval rather than military) for other examples of Civil War "sea-battle" songs. A typical folk "Come-all-ye" ballad tells the story of one Confederate victory at sea:

> Come all ye brave Texians, come join in my song,
> Let joy and Thanksgiving and praises abound;
> Come, give your attention, and hear what I say,
> While I tell of our victory on Galveston Bay.

Another Southern ballad relates the story of "The Florida's Cruise," a twenty-verse account of Confederate naval victories which seems to employ a degree of "poetic embellishment" on the historical facts. Among other Union ships either defeated, sunk, or outmaneuvered by *The Florida,* according to the song, were *The Cuyler, The Estelle, The Sonoma, The Bulldog, The Star, The Lapwing,* and *The Mary Jane Colcord,* plus a few unnamed merchant vessels. The words are credited to an anonymous "foretop-man of the C.S.S. *Florida."* Here is a sample:

> We next took a schooner well-laden with bread,
> What the devil got into Uncle Abe's head?
> To send us such biscuit is such a fine thing,
> It sets us all laughing as we sit and sing:
>
> Huzza! Huzza! for the Florida's crew!
> We'll range with bold Maffitt the world through and
>   through.

The next few pages contain a dozen or so Union and Confederate songs relating to specific battles. I have not included in this section such songs as "Drummer Boy of Shiloh," which, while relating to a specific battle, really has nothing to do with the events or personalities of the engagement.

By and large, the songs included here are of the "Come-all-ye" style of folk song, which tell a story simply and directly, either in the first person or with a strong sense of personal identification on the part of the narrator.

FLIGHT OF DOODLES. The Battle of Bull Run was the first major military encounter of the Civil War. The battle took place on July 21, 1861, and resulted in a complete rout of the Union forces under the command of General McDowell. (It was in this engagement, incidentally, that Thomas Jonathan Jackson won his name Stonewall.)

The South was jubilant. Under the leadership of General Beauregard, they had repulsed the first serious Union attack on the newly organized Confederacy. The green Northern troops had given a poor account of themselves in their baptism of fire.

The Southern victory produced scores of songs, one of the most widely sung of which was "Flight of Doodles," the title obviously referring to the headlong dash back to Washington by the "Yankee Doodles." Apparently the song started out as a narrative of the battle, sometimes known as Manassas after Manassas Junction, a key railroad link at the center of the fighting. But after four stanzas, the anonymous author ran out of verses about Bull Run and switched to that favorite theme of all Rebel songs, the parade of secession.

The tune of "Flight of Doodles" was one of the most popular minstrel melodies of the day, "Root Hog or Die." While the tune was widely known, serving as the basis for scores of parodies on a wide range of subjects, little is known about the authorship of the original. The first printed sheet music is dated 1856, with the New York edition containing the following inscription:

Sung by J. H. Budworth at George Christy and Wood's Minstrels, arranged for the piano by G. W. H. Griffin.

A Boston edition merely says "as sung by Ordway's Aeolians." However, the New York Public Library credits Griffin as the composer, and in the absence of a contrary claim, we can concede the likelihood, at least, of Griffin having written it. Griffin was one of the most prominent men of New York black-face minstrelsy in the period immediately preceding the Civil War. He was well known, particularly, as an "interlocutor," that sad-faced, dignified, burnt-cork master of ceremonies who always winds up the loser in every clash of wits with those two rascals, Tambo and Bones. Among Griffin's other compositions were "I Am Lonely Tonight" and "Pleasant Dreams of Long Ago."

The phrase "root, hog, or die" seems to have a wide range of meanings, depending mostly on the context in which it is sung. Basically, however, it would seem to mean that one must "work like the devil under terrible conditions" in order to survive, although, at times, it seems to stand for "eating crow," and, at other times it is used as a shout of defiance. Mrs. Emma Dusenberry, of Arkansas, who proved one of the richest sources of traditional song to collectors, sang a version of "Root, Hog, or Die" to Waldemar Hille and then went on to explain:

All of us have got to work to make our own living. Hogs has to root in the woods or starve, and you have to work or starve.

Here's a verse and chorus from the original song:

I'm right from old Virginny wid my pocket full ob news,
I'm worth twenty shillings right square in my shoes;
It doesn't make a dif of bitterence to neither you nor I,
Big pig or little pig, root hog or die.

I'm chief cook and bottle-washer, cap'n ob de waiters,
I stand upon my head when I peel de apple dumplin's.

Bull Run remained a favorite Southern song subject throughout the war and Confederate writers celebrated the great victory with a mas-sive literary output. A single verse seems to sum up the Southern victory best:

> King Abraham is very sick,
> Old Scott has got the measles,
> Manassas we have won at last,
> Pop goes the weasel!

ROOT HOG OR DIE (Southern Version). Almost as soon as it was introduced in 1856, "Root Hog or Die" was used as a vehicle for topical verses. The Boston edition of the sheet music, under the heading "Another version adapted to the same music" includes a seven-verse history of British-American relations:

I'll tell you of a story that happened long ago,
When the English came to America, I s'pose you all know,
They couldn't whip the Yankees, I'll tell you the reason why,
Uncle Sam made them sing, Root hog or die.

With the outbreak of the war, the well-known, lively little tune was put to work by both sides. The song printed here tells the story of the fall of Fort Sumter from the Southern point of view. The North replied in kind with a song called "The Union":

> Away down in South Carolina,
> They're kicking up a muss;
> By bombarding Fort Sumter
> They surely make it worse:
> They cannot split the Union,
> I'll tell you the reason why,
> The Newburg boys will make them sing:
> Root hog or die.
>
> • • •
>
> As for Jeff Davis,
> We will put him back apace,
> We will whip his Southern traitors
> With the very best of grace;
> They will not stand or make a show,
> I'll tell you the reason why—
> The Union boys will make them sing:
> Root hog or die.

A Texas parody, "Run Yanks, or Die," is interesting because it presents a rare example of the explicit defense of slavery in the refrain:

Now if you all will listen while I relate,
About the cause of freedom you're here to calculate;
Old Abe tried to enslave us, but soon it was the cry,
Oh Liberty for Southern boys! Run Yanks, or die!

Hurrah for slavery, for Southerners are the boys,
For singing and fighting and stopping Yankee noise!

The young Confederacy is getting on quite spry,
Ho! Big Yank! Little Yank! Run Yanks, or die.

. . .

We're going out to Richmond to get all the news,
We're coming back by Washington to get old Lincoln's
shoes;
And as we walk the streets, the Yankees they will fly,
They'll holler out, "It's Southern boys; Run Yank, or
die!"

The notorious "Trent Affair," in which a Union warship stopped a British mail packet on the high seas and forcibly removed the newly appointed Confederate Commissioners to Great Britain and France, James M. Mason and John Slidell, inspired another Southern "Root Hog or Die" parody, "Death of the Lincoln Despotism":

> 'Twas out upon 'mid-ocean,
> That the San Jacinto hailed
> An English neutral vessel,
> While on her course she sailed;
> Then sent her traitor Fairfax
> To board her with his crew,
> And beard the British Lion
> With his "Yankee-doodle-doo."

The anonymous Southern author believed, as did many in the North, that the incident would lead to British involvement in the war, a prospect which the South viewed with joy:

> Then while old England's cannon
> Are booming on the sea,
> Our Johnson, Smith, and Beauregard
> Dear Maryland will free,
> And Johnston in Kentucky
> Will whip the Yankees too,
> And start them to the lively tune
> Of "Yankee-doodle-doo."

"Root Hog or Die" was also a popular melody for topical rhymes by Northern broadsiders. H. De Marsan, a New York broadside publisher, lists at least five of a pro-Union character. Here is a sample of one of them:

> Come, listen to my story,
> And a good one I'll relate,
> 'Bout the Burnside Expedition
> In North Carolina State.
> We've whipped the Southern Chivalry,
> And blowed their forts sky-high;
> Colonel Hawkins and his red-caps
> Made 'em sing: "Root hog or die."

THE BATTLE OF SHILOH. One of the bloodiest, bitterest, and least decisive battles of the Civil War was fought for two days in April of 1862 at the tiny river port town of Pittsburg Landing in Western Tennessee. Starting on the morning of April 6 and lasting through April 7, a Confederate Army of some 40,000 men under the command of General Beauregard attacked a Union force of slightly larger size near the old Shiloh Meeting House on the Tennessee River. Both armies suffered casualties of approximately 25 percent in killed, wounded, and missing in a battle which ended in a stalemate.

Many Southerners chose to interpret it as a victory because of the initial rout of the Union forces. This folk song, sung by a Virginia woman in 1918 for the noted collector, Cecil Sharp, reflects an obviously partisan Southern folk memory:

> Each loyal Southerner's heart to cheer,
> With the victory gained at Shiloh.

Indeed, if the battle had ended at the close of the first day, the song might very well stand as an almost accurate historical memento. But on April 7, Grant's beleaguered army was reinforced and the Union troops managed to stem and eventually throw back the Rebel tide. And while the Union could not claim a victory, the fact that what appeared to be another Bull Run had been averted was an extremely important military and political event.

Somewhere over the years, the date of the battle has been moved up some ten days, but this was obviously of little importance to the people who preserved the song in the folk tradition.

THE BATTLE OF SHILOH HILL. Here is another Confederate point of view on the Battle of Shiloh, but this one seems somewhat more realistic, confining itself to a brutal description of the fighting and the bloodshed, and ignoring any claim to victory. The song apparently entered Southern mountain oral tradition after the war, with collectors in Missouri, North Carolina, and Mississippi coming across various abridged versions.

While the author of this song, supposedly a Texas soldier, M. B. Smith, Company C, Second Regiment, Texas Volunteers, was accurate enough in his dates, the folk process has embellished the casualty figures to make the narrative bloodier and more dramatic. The original version of the song says "thousands of brave soldiers had fell to rise no more," whereas a version collected in Missouri in 1928 reports that "ten thousand men was killed" in the second day's fighting alone. Bloody as Shiloh was, the official figure of men killed on both sides, together, was some 3,500, with another 2,500 listed as missing.

Shiloh, perhaps because it was so indecisive and yet so fierce a battle, helped develop a strange kinship between Rebel and Union soldiers—a sentiment reflected in the last stanza of this song in which the author asks God to "save the souls of *all* who fell" at Shiloh.

CAIRO. The Southern Illinois riverport town of Cairo was a key military objective in the battle of the Mississippi and the struggle for control of the West. Cairo stands astride the juncture of the Ohio and Mississippi Rivers, only a relatively few miles below the meeting of the Missouri with the Mississippi at St. Louis, so control of Cairo meant control of a substantial portion of America's mightiest waterway during the Civil War.

Before the outbreak of hostilities, Cairo and its environs were, if not pro-Southern in outlook, ardently anti-Abolitionist and anti-Republican in politics. Bordering on Southwestern Kentucky and only a few miles above Tennessee and Arkansas, Cairo was, geographically, further South than either Louisville or Richmond. It was in a similar section of Illinois that the fiery Abolitionist editor, Elijah Lovejoy, was lynched by a proslavery mob in the 1830's. In the days before the war, the Cairo *Times* wrote that there would "be no underground railroad from Cairo as the climate there does not agree with Abolitionists."

In the momentous election of 1860, Cairo best revealed its political views by casting 347 votes for Stephen Douglas and 76 votes for Abraham Lincoln. But when war broke out, Cairo followed the example of the "Little Giant," pledging its support to Lincoln and the Union in the hour of crisis. In response to Lincoln's first call for volunteers in 1861, Cairo sent more men than could be enrolled.

The strategic importance of Cairo was well understood by both the Confederate and Union commands. Major General John C. Fremont, then in command of the "Western Department," embracing Illinois and all states west of the Mississippi, wrote in a post-war analysis:

Among the various points threatened, Cairo was the key to the success of my operations. The waterways and the district around Cairo were of first importance. Upon the possession of this district depended the descent and control of the Mississippi Valley by the Union armies, or the inroad by the Confederate forces into the loyal states.

Learning of a Confederate plan to attack the city in the summer of 1861, Fremont reinforced the undermanned garrison, discouraging the Rebel venture and securing Cairo for the Union for the duration of the war.

This song, written during the first year of the war, must have been composed by a song-writing strategist who delighted in melodic military analyses. The reference to "Southern chivaligators" is typical of many Union topical songs which derided Rebel claims to the tradition of "Southern chivalry" and gentility.

"Bold Prentiss" in the last verse apparently refers to Major General Benjamin M. Prentiss, then in charge of the Cairo garrison, while "Jim Lane" is probably Brigadier-General James H. Lane, at the time commander of a Kansas Brigade in Fremont's Department.

BROTHER GREEN. This sad narrative ballad seems to be one of the most widely known, genuine folk songs of the Civil War. Unlike most other Civil War folk songs which had a printed origin and later entered the oral folk tradition, "Brother Green" appears to have originated among the folk in the manner of the traditional ballads, and its entire life has been spent in the folk memory— the song staying alive solely through the "word-of-mouth" process.

It has been found by folk-song collectors in North Carolina, West Virginia, Missouri, Illinois, Ohio, Arkansas, Kentucky, and Indiana. The version printed here was sung by Mrs. Emma Dusenberry of Arkansas for my good friend, Waldemar Hille, who collected more than 100 traditional songs from this grand old woman, who died in 1948. While she lived she was esteemed as "a repository of American folk song."

While there is no known author of the words to "Brother Green," folklorists have come across various claims to the song. An Illinois contributor asserted that the song had been "composed by Rev. L. J. Simpson, late chaplain in the army . . . on the death of a brother who was killed at Fort Donelson, February, 1862."

The North Carolina version learned from manuscript copies ends the song with the following notation: "Joseph Green, his song ballet, Sep. the 1 1877." Vance Randolph reports having heard one version in which the text had been changed to make the dying soldier a Confederate shot down by the "Northern foe." Randolph further reports that "several old-timers insist that the song was written by a Federal officer named Sutton, wounded at the battle of Wilson's Creek, near Springfield, Missouri." Mr. O. F. Kirk, of Oakland City, Indiana, 79 years old at the time, told a collector back in 1935 that "this song has been in our family ever since I can recollect. I don't know who we learned it from, or any more of its history."

Most versions are fairly close to each other in text, and most of the melodies used, as the one printed below, seem to be some variant on the great old English ballad tune, "Barbara Allen."

ROLL, ALABAMA, ROLL. When the Civil War broke out, almost all American merchant shipping was in the hands of the North. In a massive effort to counter the effective Union blockade and to impair Northern economy and trade, the Confederacy set out to destroy as much Northern shipping as possible.

Accordingly, the South dispatched a special agent, J. D. Bulloch, to arrange for the construction of a vessel which could strike terror into the hearts of Yankee sea captains. Bulloch ordered the vessel from Jonathan Laird & Sons, shipbuilders of Liverpool, England. The British Government was strongly pro-Southern during the war, but pressure from British workingmen who sympathized with the antislavery struggle of the North, as well as typical British caution, fearing an alignment with the losing side of the fight, forced the Crown to maintain a shaky pro-Confederate neutrality.

As a result, it was possible for the South to get a ship built in England, but it then had to go to the Azores to be outfitted and armed. It was through such fiction that the British claimed nonpartisanship in the conflict.

Jonathan Laird's ship for the South was built in Birkenhead, England, on the river Mersey in 1862. After taking on arms, supplies, and the balance of her crew at the Azores, the ship was officially named the *Alabama* and proceeded on a two-year career of naval warfare directed against Yankee merchantmen.

After preying on American shipping in Atlantic and Caribbean waters for many months, and reaping a toll of an estimated 56 merchant vessels captured and sunk, the *Alabama,* early in 1864, ventured into the China Seas, paralyzing American trade in that area.

The officers of the *Alabama,* in a wartime account of their exploits, reported the presence of music and ballad-making aboard the ship:

The Alabama had the usual quota of wits and fun-makers among her crew. An Irish fiddler on board is the life of the forecastle. When the men are off-duty he sets them dancing to his lighter strains, or, dividing them into Northerners and Southerners, like a true Irishman, he gets up a sham fight to the spirit-stirring strains of a march, in which the Northerners are, of course, invariably beaten. Another sailor, Frank Townshend, is no mean poet, as will be seen from the verses which here follow. He had sung the exploits of their beloved ship to his messmates in rude and vigorous fashion.

The verses referred to tell the story of the fight of the American gunboat *Hatteras* and the *Alabama* on January 11, 1863. Here are two of the stanzas:

Off Galveston, the Yankee fleet, secure at anchor lay,
Preparing for a heavy fight they were to have next day;
Down came the *Alabama,* like an eagle o'er the wave.
And soon their gunboat *Hatteras* had found a watery grave.

. . .

And now, to give our foes their due, they fought with all their might,
But yet they could not conquer us, for God defends the right;
One at a time the ships they have to fight us, they may come,
And rest assured that our good ship from them will never run.

But a year and a half later, in the summer of 1864, the *Alabama* herself went to a watery grave. The final battle took place on June 19, 1864, outside the French port of Cherbourg, where the man-of-war U.S.S. *Kearsarge* finally caught up with and sank the daring sea-raider. The fierce battle, witnessed by Parisians down to the coast for the event and British sportsmen out in their pleasure yachts for the occasion, was fought after a challenge from the *Kearsarge* had brought the *Alabama* out of Cherbourg harbor.

A Union song, "The Kearsarge and the Alabama," celebrated the sinking of the Confederate blockade-runner:

> The *Alabama* she is gone,
> She'll cruise the seas no more,
> She met the fate she well deserved
> Along the Frenchman's shore;
> Then here is luck to the *Kearsarge,*
> We know what she can do,
> Likewise to Captain Winslow
> And his brave and gallant crew.
>
> Hoist up the flag, and long may it wave,
> Over the Union, the home of the brave!
> Hoist up the flag, and long may it wave,
> God bless America, the home of the brave!

An earlier sea chanty, "Roll the Cotton Down," believed to have originated among Negro longshoremen in Southern ports, helped provide the melody for "Roll, Alabama, Roll." Perhaps the reference to Alabama in the longshoreman's song inspired some unknown singing sailor to borrow the tune:

> Down in Alabama I was born,
> Roll the cotton down;
> Way down in Alabama I was born,
> And I rolled the cotton down.

VIRGINIA'S BLOODY SOIL. A quiet, sweet-smelling wooded area in Northern Virginia, not too many miles below the Rapidan River on the road to Richmond from Washington, was the scene of one of the fiercest battles of the Civil War. Known as the Battle of the Wilderness, which took place early in May of 1864, the bloody carnage raged for three full days, from May 5 through May 7, with losses in killed, wounded, and missing estimated at some 17,000 for each side.

The net result was a Union victory of attrition, a few stubborn inches gained on Lee by Grant, and the Confederate Army of Northern Virginia seriously weakened by the substantial loss of rapidly dwindling personnel.

Folk singer and folk-song collector Frank Warner learned this song from the late "Yankee John" Galusha of Minerva, New York. Frank Warner's wife, Anne, reports that the song was written by an unknown ballad-maker of Minerva about a local hero who was killed in the Battle of the Wilderness.

THE CUMBERLAND AND THE MERRIMAC. The most important naval engagement of the Civil War took place on March 8, 1862, just off Newport News in Chesapeake Bay. Two wooden warships, the frigate *Congress* and the sailing-sloop *Cumberland,* impressive-looking men-of-war, lay at anchor in the bay that morning, when a strange-looking craft came steaming up the channel from Norfolk. This vessel, "something like a house-top," was the Confederate ironclad *Virginia,* now known to history as the *Merrimac,* after the sunken United States frigate of that name which the Confederates had raised and reconstructed.

As the *Merrimac* steamed up the channel, it is doubtful that the Union seamen aboard the ill-fated ships were aware that a momentous event of history was in the making. But by day's end, with the *Congress* run aground and set afire, and the *Cumberland* at rest on the floor of Chesapeake Bay, the age of wooden navies was at an end. Perhaps Civil War ballad-makers were aware that the sinking of the *Cumberland* was a dramatic and tragic symbol of progress in the art of naval warfare, for ballads of the famous battle and of the heroic crew of the *Cumberland* quickly appeared.

The military advantage to the Confederacy lasted but a day, or as long as it took the Union iron-clad, *Monitor* ("the cheese box on a raft"), to prove that the North could meet iron with iron; but the ballads stressed the *Merrimac's* victory over the wooden ships, sensing, perhaps, that theirs would be final musical tributes to a vanished era of the sea.

The version of "Cumberland and Merrimac" printed here comes from Ellen Stekert, who learned it from an old New York State lumberjack, Ezra "Fuzzy" Barhight. The original of this song, however, was a printed broadside published by Johnson of Philadelphia.

THE CUMBERLAND CREW. Of the *Cumberland's* 376-man crew, 117 men were lost when the *Merrimac* sent the Union vessel to the bottom of Chesapeake Bay on March 8, 1862. The drama of the engagement, the historical significance of the first ironclad attack on traditional warships, and the terrible losses suffered by the Union crews, focused national attention on the men of the *Cumberland*.

In New York City, a citizen's committee tendered a giant reception at the Academy of Music on April 10, 1862, for "the survivors of the Officers and Crews of the U.S.S. Frigates *Cumberland* and *Congress*."

Of the many songs written about the mighty naval battle (and the events of the following day in which the Union *Monitor* evened the odds once again), "The Cumberland Crew" seems to have taken the fastest hold on the folk memory. Perhaps because a large number of crewmen were New Yorkers, the song has survived in many areas of New York State, with variants collected from seamen in New York City and various others upstate. Apparently, the original song was somewhat on the pretentious side, containing such a glorious summation as:

In Columbia's sweet birthright of Freedom's communion,
Our flag never floated so proudly before.
May the spirits of those that died for the Union,
Beneath its proud folds exultingly soar.

But the folk process has weaned out the literary pretensions of the original and fashioned a ballad which is a genuine expression of sorrow and tribute to the men of the *Cumberland's* crew.

WHEN SHERMAN MARCHED DOWN TO THE SEA. General William T. Sherman's "March to the Sea" in late 1864 was a military venture of daring and high strategy, whose success, capped by the fall of Savannah shortly before Christmas, insured Union victory in the bloody fratricidal war. (For further details on this campaign, see introductory notes to "Marching Through Georgia.")

The songs inspired by this dramatic feat reflected Union exultation at the sight of victory not far in the future. The most famous of these songs, of course, was Henry C. Work's "Marching Through Georgia," which has lasted until today as a popular patriotic marching song. Other efforts made up in military knowledgeableness what they lacked in literary and musical achievement:

Atlanta next was Sherman's aim,
Though Dalton blocked the way;
But flanking was the kind of game
That Sherman knew would pay.

Joe Johnston found that to retreat
Was all the way to do;
For it was dangerous to meet
The Bonny Boys in Blue.

The words to "When Sherman Marched Down to the Sea" were written by a Union Lieutenant from Iowa, S. H. M. Byers, at the time a prisoner of war in Charleston, South Carolina. The 800 Federal prisoners heard only the vaguest of rumors about Sherman's historic march; then, according to one story, a Charleston Negro smuggled a newspaper into the prison by hiding it in a loaf of bread. It was, supposedly, from this newspaper account, that Byers wrote the lyrics for this song. Another Union prisoner, a Lieutenant Rockwell of a New York regiment, set Byer's ballad to music and, so the story goes, the song was eventually smuggled *out* of the prison and passed on to Sherman's army.

Subsequently, after the fall of Columbia and the evacuation of Charleston, Byers was found by Sherman's army where he heard the troops singing his song. The song became immensely popular, but it was an age of musical piracy, and scores of publishers brought out their own versions of the song, frequently with different melodies, and Byers never realized very much money for his effort.

The version printed here is in a musical setting by E. Mack of Philadelphia; it is a more professional tune than Rockwell's and not so readily available in print. Mack, incidentally, specialized in marches, producing such items as the "Monitor Grand March," "Major General Sheridan's Grand Victory March," "General Grant's Grand March," and many others.

THE FALL OF CHARLESTON. At the conclusion of the successful "March to the Sea," Sherman swung his army northward, aiming at an eventual giant nutcracker in which Grant from the North and Sherman from the South would crush the remnants of Lee's fast-crumbling army.

On February 17, 1865, Sherman's northward march overran Columbia, South Carolina, making the maintenance of a Confederate hold over Charleston completely untenable. On the following day, February 18, Charleston was evacuated by Southern troops. This event, of only minor military significance at the time, had great symbolic meaning for the North, for it was in Charleston harbor that the first shots of the terrible conflict had been fired almost four years earlier.

This song, the creation of a minstrel-stage writer, Eugene T. Johnston (nicknamed "The Professor") employed a standard burnt-cork tune, "Whack Row De-Dow," which had already seen service in the war both as a minstrel number and as a naval ballad. The minstrel song, written in 1861, by Miss Fanny Herring, had the usual McClellan verse:

> Down South there's General Beauregard,
> With his bully little crew,
> Who says he'll make us Northern folks
> Nip up de doo den doo;
> But we guess as how the Rebel rout
> Had better mind what they're about,
> For they'll find that Gen'ral McClellan
> Will be ready for a fight to give 'em
> Whack! row de dow!

The naval ballad, written by a seaman aboard the U.S.S. *Vandalia* during the successful attack on Port Royal in November, 1861, used the same melody to describe the engagement:

> When we were seen advancing,
> They laughed with foolish pride,
> And said that soon our Northern fleet
> They'd sink beneath the tide;
> And with their guns trained carefully,
> They waited our advance,
> And the gallant Wabash soon struck up
> The music of the dance.

> Whack row de dow,
> How are you, old Port Royal?
> Whack row de dow,
> How are you, Secesh?

> Each ship advanced in order,
> Each captain wore a smile,
> Until the famed *Vandalia*
> Brought up the rear in style,
> And as our guns were shortest
> We balanced to the right,
> And brought us to the enemy,
> The closest in the fight.

Another parody of Johnston's, which appears elsewhere in this collection, is "Who Will Care for Micky Now?"

Flight of Doodles

Words: anonymous
Music: "Root Hog or Die"

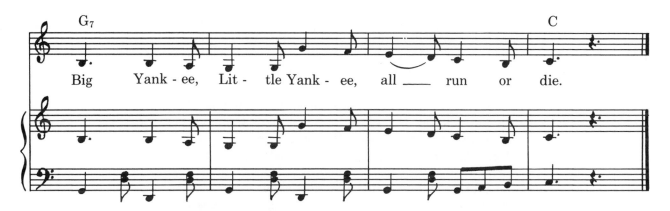

Big Yank - ee, Lit - tle Yank - ee, all ___ run or die.

2. I saw all the Yankees at Bull Run,
   They fought like the devil when the battle first begun.
   But it don't make a niff-a-stiff'rence to neither you nor I,
   They took to their heels, boys, and you ought to see 'em fly.

3. I saw old Fuss-and-Feathers Scott, twenty miles away,
   His horses stuck up their ears, and you ought to hear 'em neigh;
   But it don't make a niff-a-stiff'rence to neither you nor I,
   Old Scott fled like the devil, boys, root, hog, or die.

4. I then saw a "Tiger," from the old Crescent City,
   He cut down the Yankees without any pity;
   Oh! It don't make a diff-a-bitt'rence to neither you nor I,
   We whipped the Yankee boys and made the boobies cry.

5. I saw South Carolina, the first in the cause,
   Shake the dirty Yankees till she broke all their jaws;
   Oh! It don't make a niff-a-stiff'rence to neither you nor I,
   South Carolina give 'em Hell, boys, root, hog, or die.

6. I saw old Virginia, standing firm and true,
   She fought mighty hard to whip the dirty crew;
   Oh! It don't make a niff-a-stiff'rence to neither you nor I,
   Old Virginia's blood and thunder, boys, root, hog, or die.

7. I saw old Georgia, the next in the van,
   She cut down the Yankees almost to a man;
   Oh! It don't make a niff-a-stiff'rence to neither you nor I,
   Georgia's some in a fight, boys, root, hog, or die.

8. I saw Alabama in the midst of the storm,
   She stood like a giant in the contest so warm;
   Oh! It don't make a niff-a-stiff'rence to neither you nor I,
   Alabama fought the Yankees, boys, till the last one did fly.

9. I saw Texas go in with a smile,
  But I tell you what it is, she made the Yankees bile,
  Oh! It don't make a niff-a-stiff 'rence to neither you nor I,
  Texas is the devil, boys, root, hog, or die.

10. I saw North Carolina in the deepest of the battle,
  She knocked down the Yankees and made their bones rattle;
  Oh! It don't make a niff-a-stiff 'rence to neither you nor I,
  North Carolina's got the grit, boys, root, hog, or die.

11. Old Florida came in with a terrible shout,
  She frightened all the Yankees till their eyes stuck out;
  Oh! It don't make a niff-a-stiff 'rence to neither you nor I,
  Florida's death on Yankees, boys, root, hog, or die.

Root Hog or Die (Southern Version)

Words: anonymous
Music: "Root Hog or Die"

1. Old Abe Lincoln keeps kicking up a fuss,
   I think he'd better stop it, he'll only make it worse,
   We'll have our Independence—I'll tell you the reason why,
   Jeff Davis he will make them sing "Root Hog or Die!"

2. When Lincoln went to reinforce Sumter for the fight,
   He told his men to pass through the harbor in the night.
   He said to them, be careful, I'll tell you the reason why,
   The Southern boys are mighty bad on "Root Hog or Die!"

3. Then Beauregard he called a halt according to the style,
   The Lincolnites they faced about and looked mighty wild;
   They couldn't give the password, I'll tell you the reason why,
   Beauregard's countersign was "Root Hog or Die!"

4. They anchored out a battery upon the waters free,
   It was the queerest looking thing that ever you did see—
   It was the fall of Sumter, I'll tell you the reason why,
   It was the Southern alphabet of "Root Hog or Die!"

5. They telegraphed to Abraham they took her like a flirt;
   They underscored another line—"There was nobody hurt."
   We are bound to have the Capitol, I'll tell you the reason why,
   We want to teach Old Abe to sing "Root Hog or Die!"

6. When Abra'm read the dispatch, the tear came in his eye,
   He walled his eyes to Bobby, and Bob began to cry.
   They prayed for Jeff to spare them, I'll tell you the reason why,
   They didn't want to *mark time* to "Root Hog or Die!"

7. The "Kentucky Braves" at Trenton are eager for the fight—
   They want to help the Southern boys to set old Abra'm right;
   They had to leave their native State, I'll tell you the reason why,
   Old Kentucky wouldn't sing, "Root Hog or Die!"

The Battle of Shiloh

Southern Appalachian folk song
From the singing of Philander Fitzgerald

All you South-ern-ers now draw near, Un-to my sto-ry ap-proach you here, Each loy-al South-ern-er's heart to cheer, With the vic-t'ry gained at Shi-loh.

2. Oh it was on April, the sixteenth day,
   In spite of a long and muddy way,
   We landed safe at Corinth Bay,
   All on our route to Shiloh.

3. That night we lay on the cold ground,
   No tents nor shelters could we find;
   And in the rain we almost drowned,
   All on our way to Shiloh.

4. Next morning a burning sun did rise,
   Beneath the eastern cloudless sky,
   And General Beauregard replied:
   Prepare to march to Shiloh.

5. And when our Shiloh hove in view,
   It would the bravest hearts subdue
   To see the Yankee melody* crew
   That held the works at Shiloh.

6. For they were strongly fortified,
   With batteries on the riverside.
   Our generals viewed the plains and cried:
   "We'll get hot work at Shiloh."

7. And when those batteries strove to gain,
   The balls fell around us thick as rain,
   And many a hero there was slain,
   Upon the plains of Shiloh.

8. The thirty-third and the Zouaves,
   They charged the batteries and gave three cheers,
   And General Beauregard rang the airs
   With Southern steel at Shiloh.

9. Their guns and knapsacks they threw down,
   They ran like hares before the hounds.
   The Yankee Dutch could not withstand
   The Southern charge at Shiloh.

10. Now many a pretty maid did mourn
    A lover who'll no more return;
    The cruel war has from her torn—
    His body lies at Shiloh.

* Presumably "motley"

The Battle of Shiloh Hill

Words by M. B. Smith (Company C, 2d Regiment, Texas Volunteers)
Music: "Wandering Sailor"

Come all you val-iant sol-diers, A sto-ry I will tell, A-bout the blood-y bat-tle That was fought on Shi-loh hill; It was an aw-ful strug-gle And will cause your blood to chill, It

SONGS OF BATTLES AND CAMPAIGNS

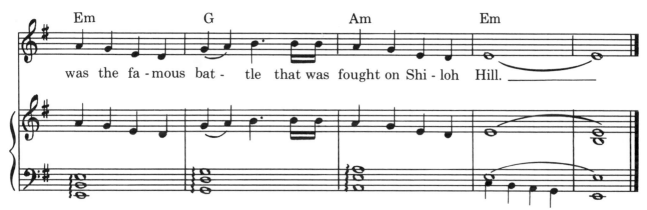

was the fa-mous bat - tle that was fought on Shi - loh Hill. _____

2. It was the Sixth of April,
   Just at the break of day,
   The drums and fifes were playing
   For us to march away;
   The feeling of that hour
   I do remember still,
   For the wounded and the dying
   That lay on Shiloh Hill.

3. About the hour of sunrise
   The battle it began,
   And before the day had vanished
   We fought them hand to hand;
   The horrors of the field
   Did my heart with anguish fill,
   For the wounded and the dying
   That lay on Shiloh Hill.

4. There were men from every nation
   Laid on those bloody plains,
   Fathers, sons, and brothers
   Were numbered with the slain,
   That has caused so many homes
   With deep mourning to be filled,
   All from the bloody battle
   That was fought on Shiloh Hill.

5. The wounded men were crying
   For help from everywhere,
   While others, who were dying,
   Were offering God their prayer,
   "Protect my wife and children
   If it is Thy holy will!"
   Such were the prayers I heard
   That night on Shiloh Hill.

6. And early the next morning
   We were called to arms again,
   Unmindful of the wounded
   And unmindful* of the slain,
   The struggle was renewed
   And ten thousand men were killed;
   This was the second conflict
   Of the famous Shiloh Hill.

7. The battle it raged on,
   Though dead and dying men
   Lay thick all o'er the ground,
   On the hill and on the glen;
   And from their deadly wounds
   The blood ran like a rill;
   Such were the mournful sights
   That I saw on Shiloh Hill.

8. Before the day was ended
   The battle ceased to roar,
   And thousands of brave soldiers
   Had fell to rise no more;
   They left their vacant ranks
   For some other ones to fill,
   And now their mouldering bodies
   All lie on Shiloh Hill.

9. And now my song is ended
   About those bloody plains,
   I hope the sight by mortal man
   May ne'er be seen again;
   But I pray to God, the Saviour,
   "If consistent with Thy will,
   To save the souls of all who fell
   On bloody Shiloh Hill."

* In the Randolph text, the words *unuseful to* have been substituted here—a distinct improvement which deepens the imagery and speaks volumes for the sublety of the folk process.

Cairo

Words: anonymous
Music: "White Cockade"

There's a place out West where the Un - ion troops Take toll from the Reb - el — ships and sloops; And if down the riv - er a craft would go, She must rec - og - nize a cus-tom house at Ca - i - ro.

SONGS OF BATTLES AND CAMPAIGNS

2. The rolling Mississippi was a highway free,
   When the people down in Dixie acted honestly;
   But since like plunderers they've cut up so,
   They'll have to pay a floating tax to Ca-i-ro!
   Ca-i-ro, Oh, Ca-i-ro!
   The Southrons say it's a precious go,
   That they can't send a boat for a bit of tow,
   But it has to take an overhaul at Ca - i - ro.

3. The Southern chivaligators now, they say,
   To capture the place are on their way;
   But if they'd take *my* advice they'd never try to go
   Within telescopic range of Ca-i-ro!

Ca-i-ro, Oh, Ca-i-ro!
The Union guns are mounted so,
That if once sighted at a nearby foe,
They'd make a perfect graveyard of Ca-i-ro.

4. Bold Prentiss holds the chief command,
   And prime Jim Lane is close at hand;
   They are bound by their honors to do nothing
       slow,
   But to take a river revenue at Ca-i-ro!
   Ca-i-ro, Oh, Ca-i-ro!
   There's no giving that the slip, you know;
   And if down the river the traitors want to go,
   They'll have to get their baggage *checked* at
       Ca-i-ro!

Brother Green

Words: anonymous
Music: "Barbara Allen"   From the singing of Mrs. Emma Dusenberry

2. The Southern foe has laid me low,
   On this cold ground to suffer,
   Dear brother stay, and put me away,
   And write my wife a letter.

3. Tell her I know she's prayed for me,
   And now her prayers are answered,
   That I might be prepared to die
   If I should fall in battle.

4. Go tell my wife she must not grieve,
   Go kiss my little children,
   For I am going to Heaven to live
   To see my dear old mother.

5. Dear sister may have gone there, too,
   She lives and reigns with angels,
   And Jeffer's son who died when young,
   I know I'll see their faces.

6. I have one brother in this wide world,
   He's fighting for the Union,
   But oh, dear wife, I've lost my life,
   To put down this Rebellion.

7. Tell my wife she must not grieve,
   And kiss the little children,
   For they will call their pa in vain,
   When he is up in Heaven.

8. My little babes, I love them well,
   Oh could I once more see them,
   That I might give a long farewell
   And meet them all in Heaven.

Roll, Alabama, Roll

Traditional (adapted by Hermes Nye)

When the Al - a - bam - a's keel was laid, ___

Roll, Al - a-bam - a, roll, 'Twas — laid in the yard of

Jon - a-than Laird, Oh, roll, Al - a-bam - a, roll.

2. 'Twas laid in the yard of Jonathan Laird,
   Roll, Alabama, roll.
   'Twas laid in the town of Birkenhead,
   Roll, Alabama, roll.

3. Down the Mersey ways she rolled then,
   Roll, Alabama, roll.
   Liverpool fitted her with guns and men,
   Roll, Alabama, roll.

4. From the Western Isles she sailed forth,
   Roll, Alabama, roll,
   To destroy the commerce of the North,
   Roll, Alabama, roll.

5. To Cherbourg port she sailed one day,
   Roll, Alabama, roll,
   To take her count of prize money,
   Roll, Alabama, roll.

6. Many a sailor lad he saw his doom,
   Roll, Alabama, roll,
   When the Ke-arsarge it hove in view,
   Roll, Alabama, roll.

7. Till a ball from the forward pivot that day,
   Roll, Alabama, roll,
   Shot the Alabama's stern away,
   Roll, Alabama, roll.

8. Off the three-mile limit in sixty-five,
   Roll, Alabama, roll,
   The Alabama went to her grave,
   Roll, Alabama, roll.

Virginia's Bloody Soil

Traditional
As sung by Frank Warner and
   learned from "Yankee" John Galusha

Slow ad lib.

Em

Come all you loy - al Un - ion - ists, wher - ev - er you may be, ___ I

G   B₇

hope you'll pay at - ten - tion and lis - ten un - to me; ___ For

Em   G

well you know the blood and woe, the mis - e - ry and toil, ___ It

SONGS OF BATTLES AND CAMPAIGNS

took to down Se - ces - sion on Vir - gin - ia's blood- y soil.

2. When our good old flag, the Stars and Stripes, from Sumter's walls was hurled,
   And high o'erhead on the forwardest walls the Rebels their flag unfurled,
   It aroused each loyal Northern man and caused his blood to boil
   For to see that flag—Secession's rag—float o'er Virginia's soil.

3. Then from o'er the hills and mountain tops there came that wild alarm:
   Rise up! ye gallant sons of North, our country calls to arms!
   Come from the plains, o'er hill and dale, ye hardy sons of toil,
   For our flag is trampled in the dust on Virginia's bloody soil!

4. And thousands left their native homes, some never to return,
   And many's the wife and family dear were left behind to mourn.
   There was one who went among them who from danger would ne'er recoil;
   Now his bones lie bleaching on the fields of Virginia's bloody soil.

5. In the great fight of the Wilderness, where's many the brave men fell,
   Our captain led his comrades on through Rebel shot and shell;
   The wounded 'round they strewed the ground, the dead lay heaped in piles,
   The comrades weltered in their blood on Virginia's bloody soil.

6. The Rebels fought like fury, or tigers drove to bay;
   They knew full well if the truth they'd tell they could not win the day.
   It was hand to hand they fought 'em, the struggle was fierce and wild,
   Till a bullet pierced our captain's brain on Virginia's bloody soil.

7. And now our hero's sleeping with thousands of the brave;
   No marble slab does mark the place that shows where he was laid.
   He died to save our Union, he's free from care and toil—
   Thank God! the Stars and Stripes still wave above Virginia's soil!

The Cumberland and the Merrimac

Anonymous

It was on last Mon-day morn-ing, __ just at the break of day, __ When the good ship called *The Cum - ber - land* lay an - chored in her way, __ And the man up on our look-out __ to those be - low did say, __ "I see

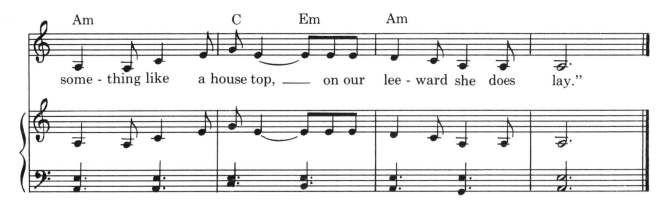

some - thing like a house top, —— on our lee - ward she does lay."

2. Our captain seized his telescope and he gazed far o'er the blue,
   And then he turned and spoke to his brave and loyal crew,
   "That thing which yonder lies floating, that looks like some turtle's back,
   It's that infernal Rebel steamer, and they call her *Merrimac*."

3. Our decks were cleared for action and our guns were pointed through,
   But still she kept a-coming up across the water blue,
   And on, still on, she kept coming, till no distance stood apart;
   When she sent a ball a-humming, stilled the beat of many a heart.

4. It was then we fired our broadside into her ribs of steel,
   And yet no break in her iron made, no damage did she feel,
   Till at length that Rebel pirate unto our captain spoke,
   Saying, "Haul down your flying colors now, or I'll sink your Yankee boat."

5. Our captain's eyes did glisten and his cheeks turned pale with rage,
   And then in tones of thunder, to that Rebel pirate said:
   "My men are brave and loyal, too, they're true to every man,
   And before I'll strike my colors down, you may sink me in the sand."

6. Well, *The Merrimac* she left us then for a hundred yards or more,
   Then with her whistles screaming out, on our wooden side she bore;
   She struck us at our midship, and her ram went crashing through,
   And the water came a-pouring in on our brave and loyal crew.

7. Well, our captain turned unto his men and unto them he did say,
   "I never will strike my colors down while *The Cumberland* rides the wave,
   But I'll go down with my gallant ship for to meet a watery grave,
   And you, my loyal comrades, you may seek your lives to save."

8. They swore they never would leave him, but would man their guns afresh,
   Poured broadside after broadside, till the water reached their breasts;
   And then they sank far down, far down into the watery deep,
   The Stars and Stripes still flying from her mainmast's highest peak.

The Cumberland Crew

Anonymous

tear of sad pit - y When he thinks of the once gal - lant Cum - ber - land's fate. The

eighth day of March that told a ter - ri - ble sto - ry, When

man - y a brave tar to this world bid "a - dieu," Our flag __ was wrapped in a

man - tle of glo - ry by the he - ro - ic deeds of the Cum - ber - land's Crew.

2. That ill-fated day, about ten in the morning,
   The sky it was cloudless and bright shone the sun;
   The drums of the Cumberland sounded a warning
   That told every man to stand by his gun.
   When an iron-clad frigate down on us came bearing,
   High up in the air her base Rebel flag flew;
   An emblem of treason she proudly was wearing,
   Determined to conquer the Cumberland Crew.

3. They fought us three hours with stern resolution,
   Till those Rebels found cannon could never decide;
   For the flag of Secession had no power to quell them,
   Though the blood from our scuppers did crimson the tide.
   She struck us amidships, our planks she did sever,
   Her sharp iron prow pierced our noble ship through;
   And slowly we sank in Virginia's dark waters,
   "We'll die by our guns," cried the Cumberland Crew.

4. Oh, slowly she sank in the dark rolling waters,
   Their voices on earth will be heard never more.
   They'll be wept by Columbia's brave sons and fair daughters,
   May their blood be avenged on Virginia's old shore.
   And if ever sailors in battle assemble,
   God bless our dear banner—the red, white, and blue;
   Beneath its proud folds we'll cause tyrants to tremble,
   Or sink at our guns like the Cumberland Crew.

When Sherman Marched Down to the Sea

Words by S. B. M. Meyers
Music by E. Mack

Our camp-fires shone bright on the moun - tains, That

frowned on the riv - er be - low; While we stood by our guns in the

morn - ing, And ea - ger - ly watched for the foe; When a

261

SONGS OF BATTLES AND CAMPAIGNS

2. Then shout upon shout for bold Sherman
Went up from each valley and glen;
And the bugles re-echoed the music
That rose from the lips of the men;
For we know that the stars in our banners
More bright in their splendor would be,
And that blessings from North land would
greet us,
When Sherman marched down to the sea;
And that blessings from North land would
greet us,
When Sherman marched down to the sea.

3. Then forward, boys, forward to battle,
We marched on our wearisome way;
And we stormed the wild hills of Resacca,
God bless those who fell on that day!
Then Kenesaw, dark in its glory,
Frowned down on the flag of the free,
But the East and the West bore our standards,
When Sherman marched down to the sea;
But the East and the West bore our standards,
When Sherman marched down to the sea.

4. Still onward we pressed till our banners
Swept out from Atlanta's grim walls,
And the blood of the patriot dampened
The soil where the Traitor flag falls.
We paused not to weep for the fallen,
That slept by each river and tree,
But we twined them a wreath of the laurel,
When Sherman marched down to the sea;
But we twined them a wreath of the laurel,
When Sherman marched down to the sea.

5. Proud, proud was our army that morning,
That stood where the pine darkly towers,
When Sherman said, "Boys, you are weary,
But today, fair Savannah is ours."
Then we all sang a song for our Chieftain,
That echoed o'er river and lea,
And the stars on our banners shone brighter,
When Sherman marched down to sea;
And the stars on our banners shone brighter,
When Sherman marched down to the sea.

The Fall of Charleston

Words by Eugene T. Johnson
Music: "Whack Row de Dow"

2. The South Carolina chivalry,
   They once did loudly boast;
   That the footsteps of a Union man
   Should ne'er pollute their coast.
   They'd fight the Yankees two to one,
   Who only fought for booty;
   But when the "mudsills" came along,
   It was "Legs do your duty!"
      With a whack row de dow!
      Babylon is fallen;
      Whack row de dow,
      The end is drawing near.

3. And from the "Sacred City,"
   This valiant warlike throng
   Skedaddled in confusion,
   Although thirty thousand strong—
   Without a shot, without a blow,
   Or least sign of resistance,
   And leaving their poor friends behind,
   With the "Yankees" for assistance.
      With a whack row de dow!
      How are you Southern chivalry?
      Whack row de dow!
      Your race is nearly run.

4. And again o'er Sumter's battered walls,
   The Stars and Stripes do fly,
   While the Chivalry of Sixty-One
   In the "last ditch" lie;
   With Sherman, Grant, and Porter, too,
   To lead our men to glory;
   We'll squash poor Jeff's Confederacy,
   And then get "Hunkydory."
      With a whack row de dow!
      How are you neutral Johnny Bull?
      Whack row de dow!
      We'll settle next with you.

Let My People Go!

NEGRO SPIRITUALS, ABOLITIONIST SONGS,

SONGS OF THE NEGRO SOLDIER

Go down, Moses,
Way down in Egypt's land,
Tell old Pharoah,
To let my people go.

The seeds of the Civil War were planted when the first slaves from Africa were imported to these shores early in the seventeenth century. Likewise, the songs of the Civil War date back to the first mournful cry of protest uttered by an African in chains in the hold of a slave ship sailing across the Atlantic.

The history of the Civil War is the history of slavery; and the history of slavery in America becomes, more and more, the history of the United States as the fateful days of 1860 approach. Every important political event immediately prior to, during, and in the wake of the Civil War revolved around the issue of slavery—from the Missouri Compromise to the Fugitive Slave Law, from the Dred Scott decision to the Emancipation Proclamation, from the execution of John Brown to the enactment of the Thirteenth, Fourteenth, and Fifteenth Amendments to the Constitution.

No collection of songs of the Civil War can be complete or truly representative unless it includes the music of the men and women whose lives and physical persons were at the heart of the conflict. For the war against slavery is as old as slavery itself, and the music created by the Negro in America is a part of that struggle.

Today we have no way of knowing the variety and extent of pre-Civil War Negro music in America. We know that the Negro brought from Africa a plethora of musical cultures, some raw and primitive, some highly developed and sophisticated. When the various African cultures came into contact with the Anglo-Saxon and Scotch-Irish musical traditions of the white South in the circumstances of slavery, a powerful musical explosion occurred—a musical fission which has been responsible for every subsequent significant American musical style.

One of the first results of this gigantic eruption was the Negro spiritual—a body of song with a multiplicity of variegated roots in both the African and Anglo-Saxon cultures, but with a life and art and soul-deep expression which could only have been produced by the Negro in America under the conditions of slavery.

For a variety of reasons, mostly sociological, the main musical expression of the Negro before the Civil War seems to have taken the form of the spiritual. (At least, it is this body of music from that era which has been best preserved.) And running through this great body of music like a many-colored thread, sometimes a bright and flaming scarlet, sometimes an elusive will-o'-the-wisp sky blue, is the theme of deliverance and freedom.

In most cases, of course, the yearning for deliverance was embodied in a longing for Heaven and the salvation of the soul. This was only natural, however, for these songs were sung on plantations within the hearing of overseer and master. Not that the longing for Heaven was a mere subterfuge, for the life after death in which "All God's children have shoes" and "Me and my God gwine to do as we please" also represented deliverance from a life of slavery and oppression on earth. But a people who could withstand the lashings, the privations, the physical and emotional tortures of slavery, did not restrict its vision of deliverance to the next world. Many of the songs, some subtly, some in remarkably explicit terms, proclaimed the yearning for freedom. Some of the songs, in fact, were used as actual vehicles in the antislavery struggle, the words and music sometimes carrying secret signals and hidden, double meanings.

Not all of the spirituals, of course, fall into the above categorizations. Many are straight and simple beautiful expressions of devotion. Some are undoubtedly keyed to another world, forsaking the wickedness and sinfulness of this one. But for the purposes of this collection, I have selected those Negro spirituals which, in varying degree, express the protest against servitude and the hope (and sometimes the call) for freedom.

In addition to these pre-Civil War songs of the Negro, this section includes songs of the Negro

269

soldier in the Civil War and post-Emancipation Proclamation songs, all of which bear a marvelous similarity to the earlier spirituals in construction and melody, but which tend to a more secular imagery.

Despite the emotional and political intensity of the Abolitionist movement, relatively few songs of lasting merit were produced by the great crusade against slavery in the North. Two such are included here as representative of a movement whose evangelical spirit and moral fervor helped to arouse and inflame an entire nation.

But with the coming of the war, musical expressions against slavery began to pour forth. It is no accident, in my opinion, that the most successful inspirational songs of the war were written by composers who, from the beginning, were zealous antislavery advocates—Henry C. Work and George F. Root.

Work came from a family famous in Abolitionist annals—his father was tried and convicted in Quincy, Illinois, for helping slaves to escape via the Underground Railroad. Root's anti-slavery sentiments were expressed in the summer of 1862 when the composer of "Battle Cry of Freedom" and "Just Before the Battle, Mother" signed a petition—an appeal to the President calling for a decree of Emancipation, as "a sign of national repentance as well as a military necessity."

Not included in this section are spurious Negro dialect songs, many of which were extremely sympathetic to the Negro. These, I believe, more appropriately belong in another section of this book, as expressions of the white popular and theatrical tradition in the form of minstrel stage songs.

In presenting these traditional Negro songs, I have avoided the use of dialect (except for the occasional dropping of a final "g" or similar stylistic expressions), believing that there is no single Negro dialect and that these songs were sung in a variety of accents and inflections. I have therefore edited these songs using generally accepted spelling, just as I have endeavored to reproduce some of the mountain folk songs in this collection without trying to simulate local Appalachian accents.

GO DOWN, MOSES. The slaveowners believed that religion had a placating and salutary effect on the Negro slave, teaching him humility, patience, and that the rewards of Heaven were for the meek. But the Bible may be all things to all men, and the Negro preacher searching for his Sunday text was sooner or later bound to stumble across the fiery prophets of the Old Testament whose God was a God of war and whose faith was a faith in freedom.

And soon the giants of Israel were living once again in the Negro spirituals, whose plaintive melodies and sadly beautiful refrains belied the turbulence of their expression. Songs of Joshua, David, Daniel, and Ezekiel were sung on plantations throughout the South, the Negroes finding personal identification with these Biblical figures. But of all the mighty leaders of the Old Testament, none held greater attraction or appeal than Moses who went "way down in Egypt land" to "tell old Pharoah, Let my people go."

According to legend, partially confirmed by the reminiscences of former slaves, the great Negro woman Abolitionist leader and ex-slave, Harriet Tubman, was the Moses of the song. As a tireless Underground Railroad conductor, Harriet Tubman made scores of journeys into "Egypt's land," returning to the North after each trip with a band of runaway slaves, and amassing a record of never having lost a soul.

The song was a favorite among Negro troops during the Civil War, from whom it was learned and notated by the Reverend L. C. Lockwood, chaplain of the "contrabands" (refugee slaves) at Fort Monroe, Virginia. Lockwood notes that "this song has been sung for about nine years by the slaves of Virginia."

FOLLOW THE DRINKING GOURD. The most effective weapon employed by the Negro slaves in the war of attrition against their white masters was escape. Each year, hundreds of thousands of dollars in valuable slave property vanished from the South—borne mysteriously on the midnight trains of the Underground Railroad. This highly secret Abolitionist organization earned its name through the extra-legal activities of thousands of Negro and white Americans who maintained a continuous line of way-stations and hiding places for fleeing Negroes. The Fugitive Slave Law came into existence in a vain effort to stem this annual floodtide of escape.

NEGRO AND ABOLITIONIST SONGS

This song is based on the activities of an Underground Railroad "conductor" by the name of "Peg Leg Joe." Joe was a white sailor who wore a wooden peg in place of his right foot which had been lost in some seafaring mishap.

Peg Leg Joe would travel from plantation to plantation in the South, offering to hire out as a painter or carpenter or handyman. Once hired, Joe would quickly strike up an acquaintance with many of the young Negro men on the plantation and, in a relatively short period of time, the sailor and the slaves would be singing this strange, seemingly meaningless song. After a few weeks, Joe would hobble on and the same scene would be enacted at another plantation. Once the sailor had departed, he was never heard of again.

But the following spring, when "the sun come back and the first quail calls," scores of young Negro men from every plantation where Peg Leg Joe had stopped would disappear into the woods. Once away from the hounds and the posses, the escaping slaves would follow a carefully blazed trail—a trail marked by the symbol of a human left foot and a round spot in place of the right foot.

Traveling only at night, the fleeing man would "follow the drinking gourd," the long handle of the Big Dipper in the sky pointing steadfastly to the North Star—and freedom. Following the river bank, which "makes a mighty good road," the slave would eventually come to the place "where the great big river meets the little river"—the Ohio River. There, "the old man was a-waiting"—and Peg Leg Joe or some other agent of the Underground Railroad was ready to speed the escapee on his way to Canada.

A good story, perhaps, or is it just an old folk legend? H. B. Parks of San Antonio, Texas, one-time chief of the Division of Apiculture in the State Research Laboratory, writes:

One of my great-uncles, who was connected with the (underground) railroad movement, remembered that in the records of the Anti-Slavery Society there was a story of a peg-legged sailor, known as Peg Leg Joe, who made a number of trips through the South and induced young Negroes to run away and escape.... The main scene of his activities was in the country immediately north of Mobile, and the trail described in the song followed northward to the head waters of the Tombigee River, thence over the divide and down the Tennessee River to the Ohio.

Parks's uncle went on to confirm the story of the sailor's use of the song as a guide to the escaping slaves.

STEAL AWAY. It is hard to think of a melody in any music more plaintive, more fragile, less militant in spirit and tempo than this, one of the most beautiful of the old spirituals. And yet, history shows that "Steal Away" was one of the most widely used "signal" songs employed by the slaves when they wanted to hold a secret conclave somewhere off in the woods.

And on closer examination, the song is seen to abound with the subterfuge and double-meaning imagery which a secret message would require. The "green trees bending" and the "tombstones bursting" certainly might refer to specific meeting places, and it takes little imagination to visualize the lightning-struck hollow tree or abandoned barn meant by the singer as he sang out, "He calls me by the lightning."

One researcher believes that the song was written by Nat Turner, leader and organizer of one of the most famous of the early nineteenth-century slave revolts. In any event, the song has lasted as a memory of secret, clandestine revolt, and as a musical testament to the creative capacity of the people whose heritage it is.

CLEAR THE TRACK. A special niche in the history of American music and in the study of the songs of the Civil War belongs to the group of singers known as The Hutchinson Family. Since the Hutchinsons sang in the age before the phonograph record, we must rely on contemporary accounts for our judgment of them, but it is safe to say that no musical group in American history has stirred up such unmitigated enthusiasm and, at the same time, such adverse criticism, as the singing Hutchinsons.

Few critics attacked the Hutchinsons on musical grounds, however. In this area, it was generally acknowledged, they had no peers. But the Hutchinsons were singers with a mission. Children of an upright New Hampshire family, every Hutchinson went through life with a strong and active Puritan conscience. From the very beginning of their professional lives in 1841 (when Abby, Judson, John, and Asa Hutchinson organized the first quartet), the Hutchinsons were militant Abolitionists combining their music with their politics as a matter of principle.

In the very first year of their existence, the Hutchinsons attended and sang at the opening and closing of every session of the Boston Anti-Slavery Society. Within a few years, the Hutchinsons added frank antislavery appeals to their concert programs, and, when sufficient material of this nature could not be found, they proceeded to write their own. Such songs as "The Bereaved Slave Mother," "The Fugitive Slave to the Christian" ("The hounds are baying on my track, / Oh Christian! Will you send me back?"), and "The Slave's Appeal" were designed to play on the sympathies of their audiences in exposing the inhumanity of slavery. Songs containing outspoken pleas for abolition were also a part of their repertoire; the most successful of these was this one, "Clear the Track." In introducing it, the Hutchinsons wrote:

Words composed and adapted to a slave melody, advocating the emancipation of the slave, and illustrating the onward progress of the anti-slavery cause in the United States.

Written in 1844 by Jesse Hutchinson to the tune of Dan Emmett's highly popular "Old Dan Tucker" (which the Hutchinsons mistakenly believed to be a slave melody), the song was greeted enthusiastically at Abolitionist meetings throughout the country. The steam engine had just become a reality and the imagery of the railroad created tremendous excitement among the listeners. Nathaniel P. Rogers, editor of a leading Abolitionist newspaper, *Herald of Freedom,* wrote:

It represented the railroad in characters of living light and song, with all its terrible enginery and speed and danger. And when they came to the chorus cry that gives name to the song—when they cried to the heedless pro-slavery multitude that were stupidly lingering on the track, and the engine "Liberator" coming hard upon them, under full steam and all speed, the Liberty Bell loud ringing and they standing like deaf men right in its whirlwind path, the way they cried "Get off the track!" in defiance of all time and rule was magnificent and sublime.

While the Abolitionist and Free Soil press were among the most enthusiastic of the Hutchinson admirers, the more conservative newspapers viewed their singing with alarm. After one concert

in 1846, the Philadelphia *Courier* offered the Hutchinsons some unsolicited advice:

It is really time that someone should tell these people, in a spirit of friendly candor, that they are not apostles and martyrs, entrusted with a "mission" to reform the world, but only a company of common song-singers, whose performances sound very pleasant to the great mass of the people ignorant of real music, and finding an innocent gratification in listening to melodious sounds which they are capable of understanding.

But if the Hutchinsons' singing left Philadelphia in an uproar, that was exactly what the singing Abolitionists intended. In fact, their advance posters capitalized on the controversial nature of their performances and the Hutchinsons made sure that prospective customers knew exactly what they were in for when they bought a concert ticket. Here is the content of a typical Hutchinson Family advance poster:

LOWELL IN AN UPROAR. What is the cause? THE HUTCHINSON FAMILY, (half a dozen or more) are to sing in the CITY HALL on Thursday evening, Feb. 6, '51 . . . many new songs, trios and quartettes &c., such as awaken the deepest emotions of the heart, OPPOSITION to SLAVERY and OPPRESSION, and a desire to elevate WOMAN TO HER EQUAL RIGHTS. . . . Women half-price, because her wages are but half the price paid men. . . . It is understood that the performers have a right to talk, and the people the same right to believe or disbelieve what is said. . . . Old bachelors, accompanied with a sympathizing associate of the gentle sex, free gratis for nothing; and Fugitive Slaves not only free, but every one who will prove himself such, shall be presented with a *dollar and a quarter.*

WE WAIT BENEATH THE FURNACE BLAST. With the coming of the Civil War, the Hutchinson Singers (considerably reorganized and now including the children of some of the original quartet) raised their voices in the Union cause, singing throughout the North to inspire recruiting and to raise morale. They were among the first to sing such songs as "Battle Cry of Freedom" and "We Are Coming Father Abraham," and they were primarily responsible for the success of "Tenting Tonight."

Along with many other ardent Abolitionists, such as General Fremont and the fiery Pennsylvania Congressman, Thaddeus Stevens, the Hutchinsons were impatient with the Lincoln Government for its hesitancy in making the war an all-out crusade against slavery. Fremont, in fact, had been removed from his command for issuing a "premature" Emancipation Proclamation in the West. Many of the top Union generals, including McClellan, were firmly opposed to Abolition and deplored every step in the direction of Emancipation. (Does this help explain McClellan's caution in pursuit of the war?)

In 1862, while the great debate continued on all levels of government, the Hutchinsons embarked on a singing trip to entertain troops in the Army of the Potomac. True to the tradition of the famous singing family, the Hutchinsons managed to include some incendiary material on their program, singing for a New Jersey regiment, along with many nonpolitical songs, this John Greenleaf Whittier poem, set to the melody of Martin Luther's famous chorale, "Ein Feste Burg."

A near riot was narrowly averted at the concert itself upon the conclusion of the song, and the singers were haled before General Kearny, who forbade the group to perform in the army again, saying: "You are Abolitionists. I think as much of a Rebel as I do of an Abolitionist." The matter went further, however, and Brigadier General Franklin finally asked to see copies of all the Hutchinson songs. After reading Whittier's hymn, the general was supposed to have declared, "I pronounce that incendiary; if these people are allowed to go on, they will demoralize the army." The incident finally went to McClellan, and "Little Mac" sustained his generals and revoked the Hutchinsons' pass.

The offending song was finally brought to the attention of Lincoln and his Cabinet, and, according to the Hutchinsons, Lincoln said, "It is just the character of song that I desire the soldiers to hear." A compromise was finally worked out whereby the group could sing for troops in the army upon the invitation of the specific commander.

But Whittier was not alone in putting the plea for vigorous antislavery into song. Charles Carroll Sawyer, who would later write such songs as "Weeping Sad and Lonely" and "Who Will Care for Mother Now?" penned the following, under the title, "Uncle Sam What Ails You?"

> Confiscate their stocks and farms,
> Do it with a vigor,
> If it will our Union save,
> Confiscate the nigger.

Meanwhile, another of the literary "greats" of the era, James Russell Lowell, wrote of "The Present Crisis":

> Once, to every man and nation,
> Comes the moment to decide,
> In the strife of truth with falsehood,
> For the good or evil side;
> Some great cause, God's *new* Messiah,
> Offering each the bloom or blight,
> Parts the goats upon the left hand,
> And the sheep upon the right,
> And the choice goes by forever
> 'Twixt that darkness and that light.

MY FATHER, HOW LONG? While the Negro spirituals made effective use of hidden and double meanings to express the yearning for freedom without raising the wrath of the slaveowners, some of the songs were more directly outspoken than others. One of the early slave-song collectors, Colonel T. W. Higginson, who led a regiment of Negro troops during the Civil War, reports that for singing this song,

negroes (sic) had been put in jail at Georgetown, S. C., at the outbreak of the Rebellion. "We'll soon be free" was too dangerous an assertion, and though the chant was an old one, it was no doubt sung with redoubled emphasis during the new events. "De Lord will call us home" was evidently thought to be a symbolical verse; for, as a little drummer boy explained it to me, ... "Dey tink *de Lord* mean for say *de Yankees.*"

THE GOLD BAND. Pre-war spirituals employed the symbols of travel as part of the two-way meaning of their imagery. Thus, such songs as "Walk in Jerusalem," "Swing Low, Sweet Chariot," "Get on Board, Little Children," etc., meant, on the surface, travel to Heaven; but they also meant travel the dark ways of the Underground Railroad to freedom or, in the most general sense, get away from slavery.

But with the outbreak of hostilities and the recognition that slavery would fall or flourish by the outcome of the conflict, the imagery of war and fighting came into the spirituals. In this one, the Negro who could "march away in de gold band" would be fighting for his own and his people's liberty. A Negro gospel hymn, collected many years later, may have developed from this song or, as seems more likely, may have a common root with "The Gold Band."

> Oh sinner man, where you going to run to?
> Oh sinner man, where you going to run to?

Oh sinner man, where you going to run to?
All on that day.

Most unusual, from a musical point of view, is the rendition of the verse and final six bars of music in three-quarter time; in fact, it is hard to call to mind another Negro spiritual sung in that meter, which leads one to suspect that this may very well be a slight adaptation of a "white" song with the more typical Negro refrain added.

OH FREEDOM. There is no precise way to date the creation of most Negro spirituals, since their imagery and mood are so general and all encompassing. The spirituals, by the very circumstances of their creation, could not be topical, although plantation incidents were undoubtedly worked into many verses in ante-bellum days.

Despite the problem of dating, it is doubtful that this song, called by Alan Lomax "the greatest of all the spirituals," could possibly have come into being prior to January 1, 1863, when the Emancipation Proclamation was issued. In fact, it is more than likely that "Oh Freedom" grew out of the Proclamation and developed and was sung as a communal reaction to the news of freedom.

For many years after the war it was one of the best-known and most frequently sung spirituals of the Negroes in the South. Thirty years after the war, it was found as a "cradle song" among North Carolina Negroes, the lines including:

No more sighing, etc.
No more crying, etc.
No more weeping, etc.
No more slavery, etc.

Half a century after the war was over, Negroes in the tens of thousands marched down the streets of Atlanta, Georgia, singing the old spiritual as a protest against anti-Negro riots and as an affirmation of racial solidarity.

GIVE US A FLAG. The Massachusetts Fifty-fourth Regiment (Colored) was the first all-Negro regiment organized outside the South, and on its bright silk regimental flags and the cocked bayonets of its thousand fighting men rested the hopes of tens of thousands of Northern Negroes and white Abolitionists. The Fifty-fourth was a "test" regiment, a military band designed to prove that the Negro could fight and that the tales of racial

inferiority were myths which could only aid the Rebel cause.

One of the leading spirits in organizing the regiment was Massachusetts Governor John A. Andrew, who realized the tremendous significance of the undertaking when he obtained permission from Secretary of War Stanton to organize the Fifty-fourth. But a comparative handful of Negroes lived in Massachusetts in the first days of 1863, and after six weeks of recruiting, a mere one hundred volunteers had responded to the call. Andrew then enlisted the aid of Negro leaders and undertook recruiting for the regiment throughout the North. In a short time the quota had been filled and one thousand Negroes, representing every state in the Union, including a corps from Canada as well, were in basic training. Among the recruits were Lewis and Charles Douglass, the two sons of the famous Negro Abolitionist, Frederick Douglass.

Chief complaint of the Northern Negroes was that the regimental officers were white, although Andrew's intention, far from reflecting prejudice, seems to have been to obtain the most experienced officers possible for this "showcase" regiment. Andrew described the qualities he wanted in his regimental officers:

Young men of military experience, of firm Anti-slavery principles, ambitious, superior to the vulgar contempt of color, and having faith in the capacity of colored men for military service.

The Fifty-fourth's "baptism of fire" took place on July 18, 1863, when the Negro regiment led a fierce and bloody charge against Confederate positions at Fort Wagner on Morris Island in South Carolina, a few miles from Charleston. The Union assault was repulsed by the Rebels and the attacking forces suffered huge losses, with the Fifty-fourth losing more men than any other regiment.

The engagement was a Union setback, but it proved to the entire country that Negro troops could stand up in battle and display courage and heroism with the best fighting men in America. Among the casualties at Fort Wagner was the regiment's commanding officer, Colonel Shaw. The Confederate Command at Wagner, as a gesture of disdain for the Negro troops, refused to give Shaw the military burial appropriate to his rank, but buried him in a common grave with his fallen Negro comrades.

Subsequently, the Fifty-fourth participated in the Florida campaign, and then was returned to the vicinity of Charleston for the balance of the war. When the South Carolina capital fell in the early days of 1865, two companies from the Fifty-fourth were among the first troops to enter the citadel of Rebellion.

The regimental song, "Give Us a Flag," was written by an anonymous member of Company A of the Fifty-fourth, shortly before the troops embarked for South Carolina. Many versions of the song appear without the last verse, which seems to have been added later, possibly after the engagement at Fort Wagner.

The tune, interestingly enough, was borrowed from Billy Holmes's "Hoist Up the Flag," published by Sep Winner; like other Winner songs, this one reflected the anti-Emancipation sentiments of many Northern Democrats:

> We'll fight for the Union, but just as it was,
> Nor care what Secesh or Abe-o-lition does,
> We'll stand by the flag, the sword, and the gun,
> To save from dishonor the land of Washington.

Was it accident or Abolitionist irony that seized upon this melody for the marching song of America's most famous Negro regiment?

MANY THOUSAND GONE. As the war went on and long-awaited milestones in the struggle against slavery were passed to the tempo of soldiers' marching feet, so the Negro spirituals became more and more secular in imagery and increasingly direct and outspoken in sentiment. Colonel Higginson said that this was a song "to which the Rebellion had actually given rise. . . . The peck of corn and pint of salt were slavery's rations."

FREE AT LAST. This spiritual of "deliverance" still employs religious imagery to convey its meaning and, as such, it undoubtedly reflects a transitional period in which the newly liberated slaves were bold enough to use the word "free," but still cautious enough to couch it in the symbolism of the Bible. In later years, of course, with the victory over slavery established, the religious meaning came to predominate, but there is still too much of the very real jubilation of freedom in this song to permit a purely spiritual interpretation.

SLAVERY CHAIN DONE BROKE AT LAST. In the days of slavery, the Negro could express the burning longing for freedom with oblique songs like "Joshua Fit the Battle of Jericho." The chattel slave could identify with the embattled Joshua and his people as they stormed the walls at Jericho in their struggle for liberation and their own home; and yet, his song was based directly on the Bible and somehow managed to pass the stern censorship of overseer and master.

But with emancipation, the Negro could take the stirring melody of "Joshua" and more directly express the joy of freedom. And that is what he has done in this jubilant hymn of deliverance.

Go Down, Moses

Traditional Negro spiritual

NEGRO AND ABOLITIONIST SONGS

Tell ol' Phar-aoh, To let my peo-ple go.

2. Thus saith the Lord, bold Moses said,
   Let my people go,
   If not, I'll smite your first-born dead,
   Let my people go.   (Chorus)

3. No more shall they in bondage toil,
   Let them come out with Egypt's spoil.
   (Chorus)

4. The Lord told Moses what to do,
   To lead the Hebrew children through.
   (Chorus)

5. O come along Moses, you'll not get lost,
   Stretch out your rod and come across.
   (Chorus)

6. As Israel stood by the waterside,
   At God's command it did divide.   (Chorus)

7. When they reached the other shore,
   They sang a song of triumph o'er.   (Chorus)

8. Pharaoh said he'd go across,
   But Pharaoh and his host were lost.   (Chorus)

9. Jordan shall stand up like a wall,
   And the walls of Jericho shall fall.   (Chorus)

10. Your foes shall not before you stand,
    And you'll possess fair Canaan's Land.
    (Chorus)

11. O let us all from bondage flee,
    And let us all in Christ be free.   (Chorus)

12. We need not always weep and mourn,
    And wear these slavery chains forlorn.
    (Chorus)

Follow the Drinking Gourd

Words and music adapted and arranged by Lee Hays
and The Weavers from a traditional song

car - ry you to free-dom, If you fol-low the drink - in' gourd.

2. The riverbank will make a very good road,
   The dead trees show you the way,
   Left foot, peg foot, traveling on—
   Follow the drinking gourd.   (Chorus)

3. The river ends between two hills,
   Follow the drinking gourd,
   There's another river on the other side,
   Follow the drinking gourd.   (Chorus)

4. Where the great big river meets the little river,
   Follow the drinking gourd,
   The old man is a-waitin' for to carry you to
           freedom,
   If you follow the drinking gourd.   (Chorus)

Steal Away to Jesus

Traditional Negro spiritual

NEGRO AND ABOLITIONIST SONGS

trum-pet sounds with - in - a my soul, I ain't got long to stay here.

2. Green trees are bending,
   Poor sinner stands a-trembling;
   The trumpet sounds within-a my soul,
   I ain't got long to stay here.   (Chorus)

3. Tombstones are bursting,
   Poor sinner stands a-trembling;
   The trumpet sounds within-a my soul,
   I ain't got long to stay here.   (Chorus)

4. My Lord calls me,
   He calls me by the lightning;
   The trumpet sounds within-a my soul,
   I ain't got long to stay here.   (Chorus)

Clear the Track

Words: Jesse Hutchinson
Music: "Old Dan Tucker," by Daniel D. Emmett

Roll it along ♩ = 138

Ho, the car E - man - ci - pa - tion Rides ma - jes - tic through the na - tion,

Bear - ing on its train the sto - ry, Li - ber - ty! a na - tion's glo - ry.

Chorus:

Roll it a- long,   Roll it a- long,   Roll it a- long

283

NEGRO AND ABOLITIONIST SONGS

through the na - tion, Free - dom's car, E - man - ci - pa - tion. man - ci - pa - tion.

2. Men of various predilections,
   Frightened, run in all directions;
   Merchants, Editors, Physicians,
   Lawyers, Priests and Politicians.
      Get out of the way! Every station,
      Clear the track for 'mancipation.

3. All true friends of Emancipation,
   Haste to Freedom's Railroad Station;
   Quick into the cars get seated,
   All is ready and completed.
      Put on the steam! All are crying,
      And the Liberty Flags are flying.

4. Now again the Bell is tolling,
   Soon you'll see the car wheels rolling;
   Hinder not their destination,
   Chartered for Emancipation.
      Wood up the fire! Keep it flashing,
      While the train goes onward dashing.

5. Hear the mighty car wheel's humming!
   Now look out! *The Engine's coming!*
   Church and Statesmen! Hear the thunder!
   Clear the track! Or you'll fall under.
      Get off the track! All are singing,
      While the Liberty Bell is ringing.

6. On triumphant, see them bearing,
   Through sectarian rubbish tearing;
   The Bell and Whistle and the Steaming
   Startles thousands from their dreaming.
      Look out for the cars! While the Bell rings,
      Ere the sound your funeral knell rings.

7. See the people run to meet us;
   At the depots thousands greet us;
   All take seats with exultation,
   In the car Emancipation.
      Huzza! Huzza! Emancipation
      Soon will bless our happy nation.

We Wait Beneath the Furnace Blast

Words by John Greenleaf Whittier
Music: "Ein Feste Burg" (Martin Luther)

2. The hand-breadth cloud the sages feared,
   Its bloody rain is dropping;
The poison plant the fathers spared,
   All else is overtopping.
     East, West, South, North,
     It curses the Earth;
     All justice dies,
     And fraud and lies
Live only in its shadow.

3. What gives the wheat fields blades of steel?
   What points the Rebel cannon?
What sets the roaring rabble's heel
   On the old star-spangled pennon?
     What breaks the oath
     Of the men of the South?
     What whets the knife
     For the Union's life?—
Hark to the answer: SLAVERY!

4. Then waste no blows on lesser foes,
   In strife unworthy freemen;
God lifts today the veil, and shows
   The features of the demon!
     O North and South,
     Its victims both,
     Can ye not cry,
     "Let Slavery die!"
And Union find in freedom?

5. What though the cast-out spirit tear
   The nation in his going?
We who have shared the guilt must share
   The pang of his o'erthrowing!
     Whate'er the loss,
     Whate'er the cross,
     Shall they complain
     Of present pain,
Who trust in God's hereafter?

6. For who that leans on His right arm
   Was ever yet forsaken?
What righteous cause can suffer harm
   If He its part has taken?
     Though wild and loud,
     And dark the cloud,
     Behind its folds
     His hand upholds
The calm sky of tomorrow.

7. Above the maddening cry for blood,
   Above the wild war-drumming,
Let Freedom's voice be heard, with good
   The evil overcoming.
     Give prayer and purse
     To stay The Curse,
     Whose wrong we share,
     Whose shame we bear,
Whose end shall gladden heaven!

8. In vain the bells of war shall ring
   Of triumphs and revenges,
While still is spared the evil thing
   That severs and estranges.
     But blest the ear
     That yet shall hear
     The jubilant bell
     That rings the knell
Of Slavery forever!

9. Then let the selfish lip be dumb,
   And hushed the breath of sighing;
Before the joy of peace must come
   The pains of purifying.
     God give us grace,
     Each in his place
     To bear his lot,
     And murmuring not,
Endure, and wait, and labor!

My Father, How Long?

Traditional Negro spiritual

NEGRO AND ABOLITIONIST SONGS

won't _ be long, Poor sin-ner suf - fer here.

2. We'll soon be free,
   We'll soon be free,
   We'll soon be free,
   The Lord will call us home.   (Chorus)

3. We'll walk the miry road,
   Where pleasure never dies.   (Chorus)

4. We'll walk the golden streets,
   Of the new Jerusalem.   (Chorus)

5. My brothers do sing,
   The praises of the Lord.   (Chorus)

6. We'll fight for liberty,
   When the Lord will call us home.   (Chorus)

The Gold Band

Traditional Negro spiritual

2. Sister Mary goin' to hand down the robe,
   In the army, bye and bye;
   Goin' to hand down the robe and the gold band,
   In the army, bye and bye.   (Chorus)

Oh Freedom

Traditional Negro spiritual

NEGRO AND ABOLITIONIST SONGS

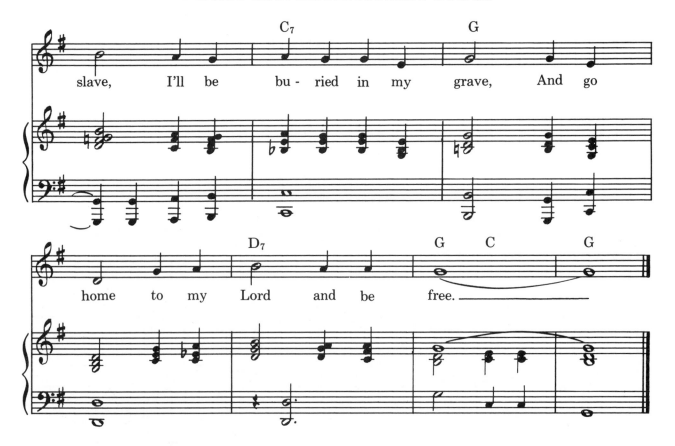

slave, I'll be bu - ried in my grave, And go home to my Lord and be free.

2. No more moaning, no more moaning,
   No more moaning over me.
   And before I'll be a slave,
   I'll be buried in my grave,
   And go home to my Lord and be free.

3. No more weeping, etc.

4. There'll be singing, etc.

Give Us a Flag

Words: anonymous
Music: "Hoist Up the Flag" (by Billy Holmes)

Oh, Fre - mont he told them when the war it first be - gun, How to save the — Un - ion and the way it should be done. But Ken - tuck - y swore so hard and Old Abe he had his fears, Till

293

NEGRO AND ABOLITIONIST SONGS

NEGRO AND ABOLITIONIST SONGS

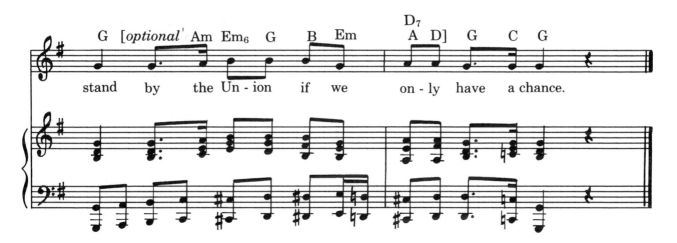

stand by the Un-ion if we on-ly have a chance.

2. McClellan went to Richmond with two hundred thousand brave;
   He said, "Keep back the niggers" and the Union he would save.
   Little Mac he had his way, still the Union is in tears,
   NOW they call for the help of the colored volunteers.   (Chorus)

3. Old Jeff says he'll hang us if we dare to meet him armed,
   A very big thing, but we are not at all alarmed;
   For he first has got to catch us before the way is clear,
   And that is "what's the matter" with the colored volunteer.   (Chorus)

4. So rally, boys, rally, let us never mind the past;
   We had a hard road to travel, but our day is coming fast;
   For God is for the right, and we have no need to fear,
   The Union must be saved by the colored volunteer.   (Chorus)

5. Then here is to the 54th, which has been nobly tried,
   They were willing, they were ready, with their bayonets by their side,
   Colonel Shaw led them on and he had no cause to fear,
   About the courage of the colored volunteer.   (Chorus)

Many Thousand Gone

Traditional Negro spiritual

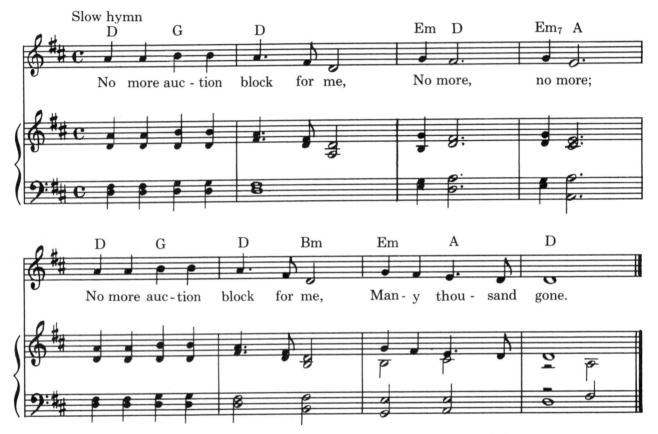

Slow hymn

No more auc - tion block for me, No more, no more;
No more auc - tion block for me, Man - y thou - sand gone.

2. No more peck of corn for me,
   No more, no more;
   No more peck of corn for me,
   Many thousand gone.

3. No more driver's lash for me.

4. No more pint o' salt for me.

5. No more hundred lash for me.

6. No more mistress' call for me.

Free at Last

Traditional Negro spiritual

NEGRO AND ABOLITIONIST SONGS

Way down   yon-der in the grave-yard walk,   I thank God I'm   free at   last,

Me and my   Je-sus gon-na   meet and talk, —   I thank God I'm   free at last. Oh

2. On my knees when the light passed by,
   I thank God I'm free at last,
   Thought my soul would rise and fly,
   I thank God I'm free at last.   (Chorus)

3. Some of these mornings, bright and fair,
   I thank God I'm free at last,
   Gonna meet my Jesus in the middle of the air,
   I thank God I'm free at last.   (Chorus)

Slavery Chain Done Broke at Last

Words: anonymous
Music: "Joshua Fit the Battle of Jericho"

NEGRO AND ABOLITIONIST SONGS

2. I did tell him how I suffer,
   In the dungeon and the chain;
   And the days I went with head bowed down,
   An' my broken flesh and pain.   (Chorus)

3. I did know my Jesus heard me,
   'Cause the spirit spoke to me,
   An' said, "Rise my chile, your children
   An' you too shall be free."   (Chorus)

4. I done p'int one mighty captain
   For to marshall all my hosts;
   An' to bring my bleeding ones to me,
   An' not one shall be lost.   (Chorus)

5. Now no more weary trav'lin',
   'Cause my Jesus set me free,
   An' there's no more auction block for me
   Since He give me liberty.   (Chorus)

Grafted into the Army

DIALECT, MINSTREL, AND COMIC SONGS

Our Jimmy has gone for to live in a tent,
They have grafted him into the army;
He finally puckered up courage and went,
When they grafted him into the army.

America of 1860–1865 was a land still in the process of fashioning a national idiom. Hesitant, self-conscious, still in awe of European tradition, literate America did not know what to make of the burgeoning native expression which came welling up out of the country west of the Atlantic seaboard. It was no accident that the two most gifted and prolific Civil War composers, George F. Root and Henry C. Work, did their finest work in Chicago, where geography kept them partially free of the European shadow.

Perhaps it took the fierce bloodletting of civil war together with a warmly human, compassionate, earthy man in the White House to help unleash the distinctively American imagery—broadly egalitarian, jingoistic, and proudly independent.

Included in this section are songs of personal and political satire from the days of the Civil War, songs reflecting a distinctive American humor, albeit a primitive humor. Much of it grew out of the literary shadow of England, even though the wording and the issues were American—songs like "Overtures from Richmond" and "High-Toned Southern Gentleman." But others, such as "Grafted into the Army" and "Billy Barlow" were assuming the new face and laughter of an emerging national image.

An important form of mid-nineteenth-century theatrical and musical expression was the dialect song, the ballad recitation delivered through faces smeared with burnt cork for its "Jim Crow" Negro or uttered in a brogue as broad as the Irish Channel for the representation of Paddy of Erin.

A number of songs representative of "dialect entertainment" appear in this section. (A few others are scattered throughout other portions of this volume.) I have not changed or modernized the lyrics to these songs since their creation in their original form is a matter of historical fact and significance. It is my view that scholarship and history must deal with authentic materials.

However, it is important to keep in mind that songs, unlike other subjects of study, have lives of their own independent of historical documentation. Undoubtedly many singers will be performing these songs in the next few years and, in the format of our entertainment media, it is extremely doubtful that it will be possible to place these dialect pieces in proper historical context.

For this reason, I offer the following bit of completely unsolicited advice to the would-be performer of these dialect songs. First, the so-called "dialect" employed in all these cases is nowhere near a truthful representation of the manner of speech of the Negroes, Irish, or Germans of the period. Rather, these are merely theatrical and musical conventions which developed out of ignorance, humor of the most primitive sort, and a certain feeling of racial superiority typical of the times. (And let it be said, here, that some of the most blatant examples of spurious Negro dialect occur in songs created out of the deepest sympathy for the Negro by men whose sentiments were staunchly Abolitionist.)

Accordingly, I would suggest that the artist who employs these materials should, where proper documentation is difficult, "translate" the dialect into a more reasonable form of English, which will serve the artistic purpose and will not offend the particular national group whose tongue is so impossibly reproduced.

Unlike the folk humor displayed in the songs in the section titled "Tenting on the Old Camp Ground," the songs here are all composed pieces of the period, most of them by established songsmiths and all with a more explicit literary tradition than the more common folk song. Even the "dialect" songs here fall more into the category of literary device than natural expressions of the Negro (or Irish or German).

Many of these songs were written for the stage—a theater dominated by the increasingly popular format of the black-face minstrel show. A number of the songs lend themselves readily to the addition of timely verses on the events of the day, and some such verses are included here.

Perhaps in microcosm, the songs in this section reflect all that was healthy and unhealthy about American popular music of the Civil War era. For along with the use of stereotyped dialect is the implicit recognition of a healthy musical force in American life flowing from the music of the Negro; and along with the primitive humor of the comic song is the beginning of an indigenous laughter, an American way of punning, cracking jokes, and puncturing the most inflated balloon on the political or artistic horizon.

GRAFTED INTO THE ARMY. After two years of bloody and costly war, the Union Government enacted the Conscription Act, which became law with Lincoln's signature on March 3, 1863. Born of the necessities of Civil War, the law made subject to the draft "all able-bodied males between 20 and 45." There was, however, one glaring exception to the act: A draftee could be excused from service upon the presentation of a substitute or upon payment to the government of $300. (The Confederacy enacted a draft law a year earlier which also contained provisions for substitution.)

The $300-exemption provision led to charges that this was "a rich man's war and a poor man's fight." These charges were buttressed by the exorbitant war profits of many Northern manufacturers together with the revelations of corruption, shoddy supplies, and similar scandals which plagued the Union leadership.

Henry C. Work's comic song, "Grafted into the Army," was a most inspired play on words—and while the malapropisms of the verses may strike us today as extremely primitive humor ("dressed up in his unicorn"), many a Union draftee, learning of rich men's sons' exemptions and the wartime profiteering of the wealthy must have ruefully acknowledged that he was, indeed, being "grafted into the army."

Many Civil War songs dealt with the vagaries of the "graft"; the famous minstrel, R. Bishop Buckley, sang:

Oh the dollars I have wasted on all sorts of things,
If I had them now, I reckon, grief would soon take wings.
Where are you $300? Where are you, I say?
They will sadly muss my collar if I do not pay.

The irrepressible Tony Pastor added his musical comment to the inflammable $300 controversy:

We are coming, Father Abraham,
Three hundred dollars more,
We're rich enough to stay at home,
Let them go out that's poor.
But Uncle Abe, we're not afraid,
To stay behind in clover,
We'll nobly fight, defend the right,
When this cruel war is over.

The "substitute" loophole inspired such songs as "Wanted—A Substitute" and "The Substitute Broker," the latter a description of a system similar to the one used to "Shanghai" sailors. "Come in Out of the Draft" told the sad story of a draftee who tried to marry his way out of conscription but could not enlist the aid of any obliging female, while Tony Pastor reflected on at least one positive accomplishment of the draft:

A dandy beau among the girls
Has passed for eight and twenty,
With whiskers black and jetty curls
From hair-dye used in plenty.
But suddenly, white locks appear,
Black hairs away are wafting;
He owns at last he's fifty near,
For to avoid the drafting.

Sep Winner also commented on draft-dodging techniques with a biting comment on the corruption of the time in "He's Gone to the Arms of Abraham":

He tried to be exempted,
A red head was his plea,
It was the same as being lame,
In hollow tones said he;
The surgeon "couldn't see it"—
He said it was "no go,"
But many say he might have passed,
A *greenback* did he show.

Some answered the call of the draft by "skedaddling," running off to Canada, Mexico, and South America. These draft dodgers came to be known as the "Skedaddle Rangers":

Oh never mind stopping this side of the sea,
Get anywhere out of the land of the free,
We want not the men that are weak in the knees,
So send for the North, or the South, if you please.
Skedaddle, skedaddle, go hither and thither,
Oh no matter whither, skedaddle, skedaddle-i-o.

Many a skedaddler went to Canada and, with the end of the war, songs greeted him upon his return; among these were "My Beau That Went to Canada" and "Can I Come Home from Canada?" subtitled, appropriately enough, "Mother, Is the Battle Over?"

But of all the draft songs written, none achieved the popularity of Work's oddly seriocomic piece. Perhaps its mixture of willingness to accept the duty of the draft, together with the implied knowledgeableness of the corruption, was the most accurate reflection of the temper of the people of the North; in addition, its raw humor and imaginative malapropisms undoubtedly appealed to popular taste in an age which gloried in bluntness of serious and comic emotion.

With the end of the war, a song writer tagged a happy ending to Jimmy's story. Subtitled "A Companion to 'Grafted into the Army'," the song was called, "He's Got His Discharge from the Army" and was written by William A. Field:

> My Jimmy's got home, I am ever so glad,
> He's got his discharge from the army,
> He behaved himself well and was a brave lad,
> So he got his discharge from the army.

BILLY BARLOW. One of the great stock characters of the nineteenth-century stage was the roguish, loud-mouthed braggart whose self-confidence was matched only by his disreputable appearance and outrageous lies. The personification of this character took many names, but one of the most popular was "Billy Barlow." One of the earliest references to "Billy Barlow" in our popular music is 1836, with a version sung by Jack Reeve including such verses as:

> As I went down the street the other fine day,
> I met two fair ladies just coming this way;
> Says one, "Now that chap, he isn't so slow,"
> "I guess not," says the other, "that's Mr. Barlow."

> I'm told there's a show coming into the town,
> Red lions and monkeys and porcupines brown;
> But if they should show, I'll beat them I know,
> For they've never a varmint like Billy Barlow.

> I went to the races on Long Island so gay,
> The man at the gate, he asked [me] to pay;
> "What pay!" says I, and I looked at him so—
> "Pass on, sir, I know you; you're Mr. Barlow!"

For the next quarter of a century ragged Billy kept bobbing up on the stage in New York, Philadelphia, Boston, and New Orleans, commenting on the times and blowing his horn. Early in 1861, shortly before the war broke out, Billy Barlow was singing in New York:

> Our country's excited 'bout this thing and that,
> Both North and the South hardly know what they're at.
> They secession, coercion and compromise blow,
> But it's talk and no cider—thinks Billy Barlow.

For once, Billy proved himself a poor political prophet. His prediction was belied by the attack on Fort Sumter, but he still managed to produce a couplet which deserves enshrinement along with the best of Mr. Dooley and Will Rogers:

> Our members of Congress have plenty to do,
> But it's seldom, if ever, they do it, 'tis true.

The version printed in this collection is a wartime set of lyrics. While the subject matter is military, Billy Barlow is still the same, modestly pointing out in a verse concerning the Union defeat at Bull Run:

> It's true they got routed, but then you all know,
> It was on account of the absence of Billy Barlow.

But all of the above is only half of the fascinating history of Mr. William Barlow. For Billy turns up in folk song, too, still an unreconstructed, obstreperous fellow in a traditional children's song. And this Billy Barlow traces his lineage back to fourteenth-century England through a score of characters such as John the Red-Nose and Robin the Bobbin.

The melody of the stage song is different, and so is the story, the trace of traditional folk song remaining only in the title and the character of the hero. But there is no doubt that it is, if not the same Billy Barlow, a reasonable and remarkable facsimile thereof—in tune with the times.

KINGDOM COMING (Year of Jubilo). To a German immigrant named Gottlieb Graupner goes the dubious credit of being the first authentic "blackface" performer on the American musical stage. Graupner's burnt-cork bow took place in Boston in 1799 with the performance of a song called "The Negro Boy" at the second act curtain of a play called "Oroonoko, or the Royal Slave." But it wasn't until some thirty years later that Negro minstrelsy became an established, accepted theatrical style when the famous Thomas Dartmouth "Daddy" Rice introduced the song which gave America one of its most pungent phrases:

Weel about and turn about
And do jis' so,
Eb'ry time I weel about,
I jump Jim Crow.

In 1843, the minstrel *show* was born, when a quartet of entertainers, including, appropriately enough, the composer of "Dixie," Dan Emmett, organized the first minstrel company. In a few short years, the black-face minstrel show, with its lively, zestful tunes and topical lyrics, its racist stereotypes, and vaudeville-show continuity became the single most important form of American stage entertainment. In time, the coal-black face, the thick lips and oversized mouth, the gaudy costumes, and white gloves became such a theatrical convention that performers did not limit themselves to so-called "darky" numbers in their pseudo-Negro make-up.

Despite the creation of many ingenious melodies and songs of lasting worth, the minstrel stage was, of course, demeaning of the Negro. At its best, it was merely patronizing of dark-skinned Americans; at its worst, it helped to create and perpetuate many of the vicious stereotypes which continue to plague so many white Americans in their view of the Negro. At the same time, the minstrel stage was the breeding ground for an American music which was beginning to make the real break with European culture and traditions.

Few white Americans, if any, were repelled or even annoyed by the black-face minstrel shows. Some of the most ardent antislavery crusaders of mid-century America employed the conventions and techniques of burnt-cork minstrelsy in the cause of abolition. During the Civil War, Henry Clay Work, from a staunch Abolitionist family, wrote one of the most popular antislavery songs of the day in this spurious Negro dialect, "Kingdom Coming." The song became extremely popular throughout the North among both Negroes and whites, and reportedly was sung by Negro troops as they marched into Richmond in the closing days of the war.

Written early in 1862, "Kingdom Coming" was promoted by its publishers, Root & Cady, with a week-long advertising campaign heralding the "coming" of the song. With audience interest built up through newspaper teaser ads and various "stunt" ads around Chicago, the song was finally introduced on April 23, 1862, by the famous Christy's Minstrels. The song's success was immediate and overwhelming.

In a short period of time, parodies, sequels, and answers were being created by the score. Among the parodies was an antidraft broadside which seems to have been inspired by the New York City riots of 1863:

Say, gents, hab you seen de enrolling officer,
Wid de muffstash on his face,
Go 'long dis block some time dis morning,
Like he gwine to leab de place?
He seen de smoke way up in Harlem,
Where de anti-draft men lay;
An' he took his books an' lef' berry sudden,
So I spec' he's run away.

De rich man run, ha, ha!
De poor man stay, ho, ho!
It mus' be now de Kingdom is comin'
In de year ob Jubilo.

(Harlem, at this time, was not yet the famous Negro "ghetto" of New York City; it was, in fact, more properly the outskirts of the city and a logical spot for anti-draft men to hide.)

In the later years of the war, and after the war was over, the song, for some reason, became extremely popular in the white South, entering the folk tradition in many areas and surviving, almost intact, for more than half a century. In recent years, versions fairly close to the original have been found in Missouri, Alabama, and North Carolina.

BABYLON IS FALLEN. Ever since some unknown genius back in days of darkest antiquity discovered a way to make a penny by supplying people with songs, music purveyors have operated on the principle that imitation is the sincerest form of profit. This concept has lasted until our own day, but in no period did it flourish more than the Civil War era. No successful song in that age failed to have a reply, a sequel, or a parody. (In addition, pirated editions of published originals were commonplace.)

After the success of Henry C. Work's "Kingdom Coming," the composer was prevailed upon (by his publisher, his pocketbook, or both) to try his hand at a sequel. "Babylon Is Fallen" was the result, and while the song never achieved the popularity of its predecessor, it was, nevertheless, widely sung.

Written in 1863, "Babylon Is Fallen" is as "advanced" a song, politically, as the most ardent Abolitionist could wish for (this, despite the anomaly of employing stereotyped Negro dialect, more accurately reflecting the fictional "stage" Negroes of the time than any real-life person). The song was obviously inspired by the recent decision to promote the recruitment of Negro troops in the Union army. It is doubtful that any sizeable number of Abolitionists could have been found who would subscribe to Work's statement:

> We will be de Massa,
> He will be de servant.

Despite its "radical" ideas, the song was in keeping with the emancipation spirit of the times. If songs are any reflection of a people's mood, the common people of the North undoubtedly supported Lincoln's Proclamation and welcomed the antislavery emphasis of the war. No song opposing the antislavery struggle (and there were many such) received any like support in the North.

DE DAY OB LIBERTY'S COMIN'. Another song inspired by the success of "Kingdom Coming" and written in frank imitation was George F. Root's "De Day ob Liberty's Comin'." The sheet music credits the song to "Wurzel," a pseudonym used by Root for his comic and dialect songs. "Wurzel" is the German equivalent of "root."

In addition to imitating Work's song, Root freely borrowed musical and text ideas from other songs, and we find remnants of Dan Emmett's "Dance, Boatmen, Dance" and the Negro spiritual, "Go Down Moses," in both the text and tune.

I GOES TO FIGHT MIT SIGEL. Another unwitting victim of mid-century musical stereotypes was the newly arrived German. During the nineteenth century, German immigrants came to America in greater numbers than those of any other nationality, with the Irish running a close second. One of the first effects of this wave of immigration was the stage "Dutchman," a thickly accented, beer-drinking, sauerkraut-slurping nincompoop, as lovable as he was dumb.

Typical of such songs in the era immediately preceding the Civil War was Sep Winner's "Der Deitcher's Dog," better known to us today as "Where Oh Where Has My Little Dog Gone?" Another popular German dialect piece was Henry C. Work's "Corporal Schnapps," more distinguished for its atrocious use of language than anything else:

> Mine heart ish proken into little pits,
> I tells you, friend, what for;
> Mine schweetheart, von coot patriotic kirl,
> She trives me off mit der war.
> I fights for her der pattles of de flag,
> I schtrikes so prave I can;
> Put now long times she nix remembers me,
> And coes mit another man.
>
> Ah! mine fraulein!
> You ish so ferry unkind!
> You coes mit Hans to Zhermany to live,
> And leaves poor Schnapps pehind.

Harry Macarthy, author of the Confederacy's "Bonnie Blue Flag," popularized a German dialect piece, "The Dutch Volunteer." This one, naturally, had a Southern bent, but it is doubtful that this reflected any sizeable number of Germans fighting under the Rebel flag. Macarthy, a consummate vaudevillian, was obviously employing a standard stage convention, his German volunteer characterized by a dialect rivaled only by Schnapps's and an intellect not distinguished by its alertness.

> My name is Yacob Schneider,
> Und I yust come here tonight,
> From Hood's Army up in Georgia,
> Ver all de times dey fight.
>
> Now, all young folks vot goes out dere,
> To fight your country's foes,
> Take my adfice, brepare yourself,
> Pefore out dere you goes.
>
> Take a couble parrels of sauerkraut,
> Und lots of schweitzer kase,
> Also, some perloona sausage,
> Und everything else you please.

Many German immigrants settled in the midwest, and with the outbreak of the war, enlisted under Union commanders in that area. The best known of these was Major General Franz Sigel, a German refugee from the ill-fated Revolution of 1848. Settling in St. Louis, Sigel became director of schools in that city and one of the most important figures in the German community. His immediate support of the Union cause after the outbreak of hostilities helped rally the Germans to the North. This song of a volunteer in Sigel's Army, while still employing the typical clichés of sauerkraut and lager beer, strikes a note of sympathetic camaraderie with the desire of a new American to fight for his adopted nation's liberty. The "Fighting Joe" of the last stanza refers to General Joseph Hooker, commander of the Union Army for a short period in 1863. Other printings of the song have "Little Mac" inserted here.

THE GIRL I LEFT BEHIND ME.

This traditional leavetaking song of the British army employs a delightful Irish melody which dates back at least 300 years. The version popular with the English was probably written by an unknown bard of an Irish regiment sometime around 1758:

> The dames of France are fond and free,
> And Flemish lips are willing,
> And soft the maids of Italy,
> And Spanish eyes are thrilling;
> Still though I bask beneath their smile,
> Their charms fail to bind me,
> And my heart falls back to Erin's isle,
> To the girl I left behind me.

As with so many other Irish songs, this one made the long journey to America, where it became popular as a stage song, a square dance tune and a pioneer song of leavetaking:

> If ever I travel this road again,
> And tears don't fall and blind me,
> I'm going back to Tennessee,
> To the gal I left behind me.

The lilting melody was enlisted by both troops and minstrels to fight the war, supplying the tune for "I Goes to Fight mit Sigel," and on its own as a song of heroism in the version printed here. Another broadside version, "The American Volunteer," less on the literary side, was also sung:

> I'm going to leave my native hills,
> And cross the mountains craggy,
> To fight the foe and traitor band,
> And part from my dear Maggie.
>
> . . .
>
> And when the war is at an end,
> We'll cross the mountains gaily,
> And kiss the girls we left behind,
> And pray for blessings daily.

SAMBO'S RIGHT TO BE KILT.

Should the Negro be permitted to fight for his own emancipation? The issue almost wrecked the North as the debate raged throughout the war over the advisability of recruiting Negroes into the armed forces. When, in 1863, following the Emancipation Proclamation, the Union embarked on a wholesale program of Negro recruitment, the decision was greeted with loud approbation in Abolitionist ranks and either violent objection or bitter resignation by opponents of the antislavery objectives of the war.

The majority of Northerners, however, undoubtedly felt that the biting irony of "Private" Miles O'Reilly was the voice of common sense.

> The right to be kilt I'll divide wid him,
> And devil a word I'll say.

A pair of Abolitionist ladies, Mrs. Kidder and Mrs. Parkhurst, tried to whip up enthusiasm for Negro troops with a song; but their dialect strained the limits of reason and O'Reilly undoubtedly won more adherents with his unpolitical song of self-interest than the ladies could possibly have won with verses such as:

> Dey said we wouldn't fight,
> Kase we's born so awful black,
> Kase we's lazy from de cranium to de toes;
> But dey'll find dese darkies some
> When de Rebel sojers come,
> If dey keep us well in powder for de foes.

"Private Miles O'Reilly" was actually Charles Graham Halpine, an Irish-born Union officer and journalist. He served as a private in the famous New York "Sixty-ninth" for a few months in 1861, before being mustered out. He subsequently volunteered again and served as an able staff officer for General David Hunter in South Carolina. It was in this latter capacity that Halpine prepared the order mustering into Federal Service one of the first troops of Negro soldiers. With the controversy stirred up by this move, Halpine defended his superior's action with "Sambo's Right to Be Kilt," which appeared in the New York *Herald* in 1862.

Halpine's versifying was not an accident, since his previous career had included, among other things, a position as private secretary to P. T. Barnum and a job writing advertising copy in verse. He was also Washington correspondent for the New York *Times* and private secretary to Stephen A. Douglas.

RICHMOND IS A HARD ROAD TO TRAVEL.

The road to the Confederacy's capital was paved with the good intentions and poor military strategy of the Union high command, and Southern rhymesters did not miss any opportunity to celebrate this fact in song. Written in 1863, this lengthy satiric tome was ironically dedicated to Union general Ambrose E. Burnside, and gleefully recounted the travails of his all-too-numerous predecessors.

The melody was from a minstrel song composed a decade earlier, most likely by Dan Emmett. Its original words, probably written by E. P. Christy of the famous minstrel company, were an invitation to future parodies:

> Of all the banjo songs that have been sung of late,
> There is none that is so often called on,
> As the one I sing myself and apply it to the times,
> It's called: On the Other Side of Jordan.

The Hutchinson Family Singers, always quick to recognize a catchy melody, used the tune for one of their most effective antislavery songs:

Slavery and Freedom, they both had a fight,
And the whole North came up behind 'em,
Hit Slavery a few knocks, with a free ballot box,
Sent it staggering to the other side of Jordan.
Then take off your coats, boys, roll up sleeves,
Slavery is a hard foe to battle, I believe.

. . . The day is drawing nigh that Slavery must die,
And every one must do his part accordin';
Then let us all unite to give every man his right, (and
    every woman, too),
And we'll get our pay the other side of Jordan.
Then rouse up, ye freemen, the sword unsheathe,
Freedom is the best road to travel, I believe.

In the election campaign of 1860, Lincoln supporters trotted out new lyrics in behalf of "Honest Abe":

> I hearkened in the East and I hearkened in the West,
> And I heard a fifing and a drumming,
> And my heart bobbed up in the middle of my breast,
> For I knew that the people were a-coming.
> Then pull off your coat and roll up your sleeve,
> Abe and the people are a-coming!
> Oh, pull off your coat and roll up your sleeve,
> Lincoln and the people are a-coming I believe.

John R. Thompson, who wrote the Confederate parody printed here, was well known as editor of *The Southern Literary Messenger* and *The Southern Field and Fireside*.

OVERTURES FROM RICHMOND.

Throughout the war, rumors of "peace overtures" emanating from Richmond swept the North. Dedicated antislavery men were constantly fearful of these "overtures," concerned lest some compromise be reached between North and South which would continue slavery and permit the Southern States to resume their dominant role in the government. This song is the reaction of a Northern Abolitionist to such rumors.

Professor Francis James Child, author of the lyrics, is best known as one of the great figures in the study of Anglo-American folk music, his five-volume work, *The English and Scottish Popular Ballads,* long recognized as the classic study in its field. But during the Civil War, Child devoted his energies and talents to the pursuit of the conflict. His *War Songs for Freemen* was a collection of propaganda songs, antislavery in outlook, designed to inspire Union troops. To this collection, Child himself contributed "Overtures from Richmond."

For his melody, Child borrowed the old English political tune, "Lilliburlero," a song credited with helping to defeat James II in 1688. The air was supposedly composed by Henry Purcell, appearing in print as early as 1686.

HIGH-TONED SOUTHERN GENTLEMAN.

A favorite claim of Southern poets and orators was the "genteel" tradition of the Confederacy, the courtliness, bravery, and chivalric heritage of the Southern aristocracy. It is no accident that a popular Confederate song saluted "The Cavaliers of Dixie," while another chanted the praises of "Chivalrous C.S.A." (Confederate States of America) to the tune of "Vive la Compagnie":

> Chivalrous, chivalrous people are they!
> Chivalrous, chivalrous people are they!
> In C. S. A.! In C. S. A.!
> Aye, in chivalrous C. S. A.!

In reply, Northern rhymesters delighted in poking fun at the Southern "chivaligators," belittling Rebel claims to the tradition of virtue and gentility with a fierce arsenal of satiric verse. "The

High-Toned Southern Gentleman" was one of the most pungent of such musical sallies.

Popular for many years as a minstrel song with the title "Fine Old Colored Gentleman," words generally credited to Dan Emmett, the song actually dates back to seventeenth-century England. Pepys notes in his Diary for June 16, 1668, a "song of the 'Old Courtier of Queen Elizabeth' and how he was changed." Pepys notes the song's opening lines as:

An old song made by an aged old pate,
Of an old worshipful gentleman, who had a great estate.

Almost a century and a half later, the song turned up again in London as "The Fine Old English Gentleman," the opening lines of which went:

I'll sing you an old ballad that was made by an old pate,
Of a poor old English gentleman who had an old estate.

The song eventually became the subject of a heated and hilarious copyright suit involving leading musicians and publishers in London. In 1843, Dan Emmett adapted the old song to the blossoming minstrel stage:

In Tennessee, as I've heard say, dare once did use to dwell,
A fine old Colored Gemman, and dis nigger knows him well,
Dey used to call him Sambo or somethin' near the same,
De reason why dey call him dat was because it was his name;
For Sambo was a Gemman, one of de oldest kind.

A few years later, the song turns up again as a tribute to "Old Rough and Ready" Zachary Taylor, the hero of the Mexican War, under the title, "The Fine Old Southern Gentleman." With the outbreak of the war, the version presented here became immensely popular throughout the North.

The North was not alone, however, in adapting the old song to the partisanship of Civil War. A Confederate parody, "The Yankee President," derided Lincoln and the Union cause:

I'll sing you a new-made song, made by a modern pate,
Of a real Yankee President, who took the helm of State,
In 1861, as history does relate,
And then began his mad career, with Seward as his mate.
   (*Previous to this he had let his whiskers grow.*)
Like a vain old vandal as he was, one of our modern beau.

The vandal left off splitting rails, and bade his friends goodbye,

And went straightway to Washington, to "conquer or to die!"
But ere he reached that model place he feared some danger nigh,
And clad himself in cloak and cap, and sneaked in like a spy,
   (*For fear somebody might lose a valuable President.*)
Like a brave old vandal as he was, one of these modern times.

HARD TIMES IN DIXIE. As the war progressed, it became increasingly apparent that time was on the side of the Union. With the Northern blockade effectively keeping Southern cotton from foreign shores, and the demands of the Rebel Army taxing Southern productive capacity to its meager limit, both Rebel soldier and Confederate civilian knew the hardships created by wartime exigencies. Such Southern songs as "Goober Peas" and "Short Rations" reflected the Rebel reaction to the hard times. But if the misfortunes of Dixie were bemoaned or laughed off in the South, they were greeted gleefully in the North. This comic lament was "respectfully" dedicated to Jeff Davis by its composer, who chose the name Eugarps for his credit, although the pseudonym is quite apparently the reversed spelling for Sprague.

JEFF IN PETTICOATS. On May 10, 1865, Jefferson Davis was taken prisoner by a detachment of Federal Cavalry near Irwinsville, Georgia. Newspaper reports of the capture of the Rebel leader claimed that Davis was attempting to escape disguised in woman's clothing and that, in fact, he was clad in his wife's dress and shawl at the moment of his apprehension. Naturally, such an ignominious end for the Confederate chieftain tickled the fancy of the North, and, despite the fact that subsequent research has cast grave doubt on the original story, the report inspired a good number of songs throughout the Union, of which this is a fine example.

Henry Tucker is represented elsewhere in this volume by the lyrics to "Weeping Sad and Lonely," and George Cooper's lyric to Stephen Foster's "For the Dear Old Flag I Die" is also in the present collection. Tucker and Cooper's most famous collaboration was on "Sweet Genevieve," written in 1869.

Grafted into the Army

Words and music by Henry C. Work

MINSTREL AND COMIC SONGS

ar - my. I told them the child was too young, a - las! At the cap-tain's fore-quar - ters, they said he would pass, They'd train him up well in the in - fan - try class, So they graft - ed him in - to the ar - my. Oh, Jim - my, fare - well! Your broth - ers fell Way down in A - la-

MINSTREL AND COMIC SONGS

bar - my; I thought they would spare — a lone wid - der's heir, But they graft - ed him in - to the ar - my.

2. Dressed up in his unicorn, dear little chap,
   They have grafted him into the army;
   It seems but a day since he sot in my lap,
   But they grafted him into the army.
   And these are the trousies he used to wear,
   Them very same buttons, the patch and the tear;
   But Uncle Sam gave him a bran' new pair
   When they grafted him into the army.
   (Chorus)

3. Now in my provisions I see him revealed,
   They have grafted him into the army;
   A picket beside the contented field,
   They have grafted him into the army.
   He looks kinder sickish—begins to cry,
   A big volunteer standing right in his eye!
   Oh, what if the ducky should up and die,
   Now they've grafted him into the army.
   (Chorus)

Billy Barlow

Words by Ed Clifford
Music: anonymous

MINSTREL AND COMIC SONGS

down on Se - ces - sion, is Bil - ly Bar - low.

Chorus

Oh! yes, I'm rough, I well know, But a

bul - ly old sol - dier is Bil - ly Bar - low.

2. Since last I saw you, to Richmond I've been;
   And during my stay, Mrs. Davis I've seen.
   She treated me kindly and smiled on me so. . .
   Old Jeff he got jealous of Billy Barlow.
       Oh! yes, I'm rough, I well know,
       But the ladies all like Mr. William Barlow.

3. Now the other night while out for a lark,
   I lost my way, it being quite dark;
   A sentinel grabbed me, to the guardhouse I did go.
   Oh! That was too rough on old Billy Barlow.
       Oh! yes, I'm rough, I well know,
       But they should not abuse old Billy Barlow.

4. Now I see on picket every time I go out,
   A nice little gal, her name is Lize Stout;
   They say she's Secesh, but I know that's not so;
   For she'll stand by the Union with Billy Barlow.
       Oh! yes, I'm rough, I well know,
       But a very good fellow is Billy Barlow.

5. Now, there's one thing I can't help but to look
       at—
   That is what keeps our Quartermaster so sleek
       and so fat;
   It may not be good living, but there's one thing
       I know:
   He'd get thin on the grub he gives Billy Barlow.
       Oh! yes, I'm rough, I well know,
       But I'm used to good living, is Billy Barlow.

6. It's down in Virginia, at a place called Bull Run,
   Where first our brave soldiers their fighting
       begun;
   It's true they got routed, but then you all know,
   It was on account of the absence of Billy Barlow.
       Oh! yes, I'm rough, I well know,
       But a bully old soldier is Billy Barlow.

7. Just a few words more, then I shall have done,
   And I hope what I've said, you'll take all in fun;
   If I have not done right, why, please tell me so,
   And I'll bid you good-night, will Billy Barlow.
       Oh! yes, I'm rough, I well know,
       But I hope you'll excuse poor old Billy Barlow.

Billy Barlow—On the Times

Words by H. Angelo
Music: "Billy Barlow"

1. I beg your attention, kind gentlefolks all,
   I hope no intrusion in making this call;
   It's been a long time since you've seen me, I
       know,
   But I'm the identical Billy Barlow.
       Oh! dear, I'm ragged, I know,
       But the times have affected poor Billy Barlow.

2. Our country's excited 'bout this thing and that,
   Both North and the South hardly know what
       they're at.
   They secession, coercion, and compromise blow,
   But it's talk and no cider, thinks Billy Barlow.
       Oh! dear, I'm ragged I know,
       But "Stand by the Union" will Billy Barlow.

3. If I had but the power I'd soon bring 'em to,
   Though this may be nonsense I'm singing to you.
   I'd hang of ringleaders a hundred or so,
   And choke off secession, would Billy Barlow.
       Oh! dear, I'm ragged, I know,
       Then times would be better, thinks Billy
       Barlow.

4. Our cities are flooded with traitors and spies,
   And our papers are filled with a strange pack of
       lies;
   They'll agitate questions for friend or a foe,
   Whilst they pocket the *rhino,* says Billy Barlow.
       Oh! dear, I'm ragged, I know,
       Self-interest they go for, thinks Billy Barlow.

5. Our members of Congress have plenty to do,
   But it's seldom, if ever, they do it, 'tis true;
   Political speeches for hours they'll blow,
   But it all 'mounts to nothing, says Billy Barlow.
       Oh! dear, I'm ragged, I know,
       Why don't they do something? says Billy
       Barlow.

6. Believe me, my friend, in my song I don't err,
   But the poor have to suffer when such things
       occur;
   And as I belong to that class, you must know,
   I'd fight for the Union, would Billy Barlow.
       Oh! dear, I'm ragged, I know,
       Hurrah for the Union! says Billy Barlow.

Kingdom Coming (Year of Jubilo)

Words and music by Henry C. Work

Say,— dar-kies, hab you seen de mas-sa, Wid de muff-stash on his face, Go long de road some time dis morn-in', Like he gwine to leab de place? He seen a smoke way

2. He six foot one way, two foot tudder,
   An' he weigh tree hundred pound,
   His coat so big, he couldn't pay de tailor,
   An' it won't go half way 'round.
   He drill so much dey call him Cap'n,
   An' he got so drefful tanned,
   I spec' he try an' fool dem Yankees
   For to tink he's contraband.   (Chorus)

3. De darkeys feel so lonesome libbing
   In de loghouse on de lawn,
   Dey move dar tings to massa's parlor
   For to keep it while he's gone.
   Dar's wine an' cider in de kitchen,
   An' de darkeys dey'll hab some;
   I spose dey'll all be cornfiscated
   When de Linkum sojers come.   (Chorus)

4. De oberseer he make us trouble,
   An' he dribe us 'round a spell;
   We lock him up in de smokehouse cellar,
   Wid de key trown in de well.
   De whip is lost, de han'cuff broken,
   But de massa'll hab his pay;
   He's ole enough, big enough, ought to known
      better
   Dan to went an' run away.   (Chorus)

Babylon Is Fallen

Words and music by Henry C. Work

Jubilantly ♩ = 120

Don't you see de black clouds Ris-in''ob-er yon - der,

Whar de Mas-sa's old plan-ta - tion am? Neb - er you be fright - ened,

Dem is on - ly dark - ies, Come to jine an' fight for Un-cle Sam. Look

MINSTREL AND COMIC SONGS

out dar, now! We's a-gwine to shoot! Look out dar, don't you un-der-stand? Ba-by-lon is fall-en! (Oh, don't you know dat) Ba-by-lon is fall-en! An' we's a-gwine to oc-cu-py de land.

2. Don't you see de lightnin'
Flashin' in de canebrake,
Like as if we's gwine to hab a storm?
No! You is mistaken,
'Tis de darkies' bay'nets,
An' de buttons on dar uniform.   (Chorus)

3. Way up in de cornfield,
Whar you hear de tunder,
Dat is our ole forty-pounder gun;
When de shells are missin',
Den we load wid punkins,
All de same to make de cowards run.   (Chorus)

4. Massa was de Kernel
In de Rebel army,
Eber sence he went an' run away;
But his lubly darkies,
Dey has been a-watchin',
An' dey take him pris'ner tudder day.   (Chorus)

5. We will be de Massa,
He will be de sarvant,
Try him how he like it for a spell;
So we crack de Butt'nuts,
So we take de Kernel,
So de cannon carry back de shell.   (Chorus)

De Day ob Liberty's Comin'

Words and music by George F. Root

MINSTREL AND COMIC SONGS

Loud! loud! dar voic - es ring, Good news de

Lord he bring, "Now let My peo - ple go." ____

Chorus

Just you look and see___ dat___ light! De day ob lib-er-ty's com-in', com-in',

Al -most gone de gloom - y __ night, De day ob lib-er-ty's com-in'.

323

2. De Union folks dey wait so long,
   We tink dey neber was comin', comin',
   And Secesh he get so strong,
   We tink dey neber was comin'.
   Now Uncle Abe he say,
   Come massa while you may,
   And for de slabe we'll pay,
   For we must let him go.   (Chorus)

3. White folks let us help ye trou,
   De day ob liberty's comin', comin',
   We can fight and die for you,
   De day ob liberty's comin'.
   Yes! yes! we'll shout and sing,
   Loud! loud! our voices ring,
   Soon! soon! de mighty King
   Will let His people go.   (Chorus)

4. O de Lord will bring it right,
   De day ob liberty's comin', comin',
   From dis drefful bloody fight,
   De day ob liberty's comin'.
   Shout! darkeys, shout and sing,
   Loud let your voices ring,
   Soon! soon! de mighty King,
   Will let His people go.   (Chorus)

I Goes to Fight mit Sigel

Words by F. Poole
Music: "The Girl I Left Behind Me"

MINSTREL AND COMIC SONGS

fights mit Eng - land long a - go, To _ save der Yan - kee Ea - gle; Und _

now I gets my sol - dier clothes, I goes to fight mit Si - gel.

2. Ven I comes from der Deutsche Countree,
   I vorks somedimes at baking;
   Den I keeps a lager beer saloon,
   Und den I goes shoe-making;
   But now I vas a sojer been
   To save der Yankee Eagle,
   To schlauch dem tam secession volks,
   I goes to fight mit Sigel.

3. I gets ein tam big rifle guns,
   Und puts him to mine shoulder,
   Den march so bold like a big jackhorse,
   Und may been someding bolder;
   I goes off mit de volunteers
   To save der Yankee Eagle;
   To give dem Rebel vellers fits,
   I goes to fight mit Sigel.

4. Dem Deutschen mens mit Sigel's band
   At fighting have no rival;
   Und ven Cheff Davis mens ve meet,
   Ve schlauch em like de tuyvil.
   Dere's only von ting vot I fear,
   Ven pattling for der Eagle,
   I vont get not no lager beer,
   Ven I goes to fight mit Sigel.

5. For rations dey gives salty pork,
   I dinks dat vas a great sell;
   I petter likes de sauerkraut,
   Der Schvitzer-kase und bretzel.
   If Fighting Joe will give us dem,
   Ve'll save der Yankee Eagle,
   Und I'll put mine vrou in breech-a-loons,
   To go and fight mit Sigel.

The Girl I Left Behind Me

Words: anonymous (adapted from Samuel Lover)
Music: traditional

1. The hour was sad I left the maid,
   A ling'ring farewell taking;
   Her sighs and tears my steps delayed,
   I thought her heart was breaking;
   In hurried words her name I blessed,
   I breath'd the vows that bind me,
   And to my heart in anguish pressed
   The girl I left behind me.

2. Then to the South we bore away,
   To win a name in story,
   And there where dawns the sun of day,
   There dawned our sun of glory;
   Both blazed in noon on Freedom's height,
   Where in the post assigned me,
   I shared the glory of that fight,
   Sweet girl I left behind me.

3. Full many a name our banners bore,
   Of former deeds of daring,
   But they were days of Seventy-Six,
   In which we had no sharing;
   But now *our* laurels freshly won,
   With the old ones shall entwined be,
   Still worthy of our sires each son,
   Sweet girl I left behind me.

4. The hope of final victory,
   Within my bosom burning,
   Is mingling with sweet thoughts of thee,
   And of my fond returning;
   But should I ne'er return again,
   Still worth thy love thou'lt find me,
   Dishonor's breath shall never stain
   The name I'll leave behind me.

327

Sambo's Right to Be Kilt

Words by "Private" Miles O'Reilly
Music by S. Lover

Some tell me 'tis a burn - in' shame To make the nay - gers

fight, And that the trade of be - in' kilt Be-

longs but to the white. But as for me, up-

on my soul! So lib-'ral are we here, I'll

let Sam-bo be shot in-stead of my-self— On ev-'ry day in the

year. On ——— ev-'ry day in the year, boys, And in

ev-'ry hour in the day, The — right to be kilt I'll di-

vide — wid him, And — dev - il a word I'll say.

2. In battles wild commotion,
   I shouldn't at all object,
   If Sambo's body should stop a ball
   That's comin' for me direct;
   And the prod of a Southern bagnet*
   So ginerous are we here,
   I'll resign and let Sambo take it
   On every day in the year.
     On ev'ry day in the year, boys,
     And wid none 'iv your nasty pride,
     All my rights in a Southern bagnet prod,
     Wid Sambo I'll divide.

3. The men who object to Sambo
   Should take his place and fight;
   And it's better to have a nayger's hue
   Than a liver that's wake and white.
   Though Sambo's black as the ace of spades,
   His fingers a trigger can pull,
   And his eye runs straight on the barrel sight,
   From under the thatch of wool.
     On ev'ry day in the year, boys,
     Don't think that I'm tippin' you chaff,
     The right to be kilt we'll divide with him, boys,
     And give him the largest half.

* Bayonet

Richmond Is a Hard Road to Travel

Words: anonymous
Music by Daniel D. Emmett ("Jordan Is a Hard Road to Travel")

MINSTREL AND COMIC SONGS

slips,   And the   ver - y   lat - est   burst - ing   of the   bub - ble?
shore,   That   Rich - mond   was a   hard   road to   trav - el.

Chorus

Then   pull off   your   coat   and   roll __ up your sleeve,   For

Rich - mond   is a   hard   road to   trav - el;   Then

pull   off   your   coat   and   roll __   up   your sleeve,   For

Rich - mond is a hard road to trav - el, I be - lieve!

2. First, McDowell, bold and gay, set forth the shortest way,
   By Manassas in the pleasant summer weather,
   But unfortunately ran on a Stonewall, foolish man,
   And had a "rocky journey" altogether;
   And he found it rather hard to ride o'er Beauregard,
   And Johnston proved a deuce of a bother,
   And 'twas clear beyond a doubt that he didn't like the route,
   And a second time would have to try another.
      Then pull off your coat and roll up your sleeve,
      For Manassas is a hard road to travel;
      Manassas gave us fits, and Bull Run made us grieve,
      For Richmond is a hard road to travel, I believe!

3. Next came the Wooly-Horse,* with an overwhelming force,
   To march down to Richmond by the Valley,
   But he couldn't find the road, and his "onward movement" showed
   His campaigning was a mere shilly-shally.
   Then Commissary Banks, with his motley foreign ranks,
   Kicking up a great noise, fuss, and flurry,
   Lost the whole of his supplies, and with tears in his eyes,
   From the Stonewall ran away in a hurry.
      Then pull off your coat and roll up your sleeve,
      For the Valley is a hard road to travel;
      The Valley wouldn't do and we all had to leave,
      For Richmond is a hard road to travel, I believe!

4. Then the great Galena came, with her portholes all aflame,
   And the Monitor that famous naval wonder,
   But the guns at Drury's Bluff gave them speedily enough,
   The loudest sort of reg'lar Rebel thunder.
   The Galena was astonished and the Monitor admonished,
   Our patent shot and shell were mocked at,
   While the dreadful Naugatuck, by the hardest kind of luck,
   Was knocked into an ugly cocked hat.
      Then pull off your coat and roll up your sleeve,
      For James River is a hard road to travel;
      The gun-boats gave it up in terror and despair,
      For Richmond is a hard road to travel, I declare!

* General Fremont

5. Then McClellan followed soon, both with spade and balloon,
   To try the Peninsular approaches,
   But one and all agreed that his best rate of speed
   Was no faster than the slowest of "slow coaches."
   Instead of easy ground, at Williamsburg he found
   A *Longstreet* indeed, and nothing shorter,
   And it put him in the dumps, that spades wasn't trumps,
   And the *Hills* he couldn't level "as he orter."
   > Then pull off your coat and roll up your sleeve,
   > For *Longstreet* is a hard road to travel;
   > Lay down the shovel, and throw away the spade,
   > For Richmond is a hard road to travel, I'm afraid!

6. Then said Lincoln unto Pope, "You can make the trip, I hope—
   I will save the Universal Yankee nation,
   To make sure of no defeat, I'll leave no lines of retreat,
   And issue a famous proclamation."
   But that same dreaded Jackson, this fellow laid his whacks on,
   And made him, by compulsion, a *seceder,*†
   And Pope took rapid flight from Manassas' second fight,
   'Twas his very last appearance as a leader.
   > Then pull off your coat and roll up your sleeve,
   > For *Stonewall* is a hard road to travel;
   > Pope did his very best, but was evidently sold,
   > For Richmond is a hard road to travel, I am told!

7. Last of all the *brave* Burnside, with his pontoon bridges, tried
   A road no one had thought of before him,
   With two hundred thousand men for the Rebel slaughter pen,
   And the blessed Union flag waving o'er him;
   But he met a fire like hell, of canister and shell,
   That mowed his men down with great slaughter,
   'Twas a shocking sight to view, that second Waterloo,
   And the river ran with more blood than water.
   > Then pull off your coat and roll up your sleeve,
   > Rappahannock is a hard road to travel;
   > Burnside got in a trap, which caused him for to grieve,
   > For Richmond is a hard road to travel, I believe!

8. We are very much perplexed to know who is the next
   To command the new Richmond expedition,
   For the Capital must blaze, and that in ninety days,
   And Jeff and his men be sent to perdition.
   We'll take the cursed town, and then we'll burn it down,
   And plunder and hang up each cursed Rebel;
   Yet the contraband was right when he told us they would fight,
   "Oh, yes, massa, they fight like the devil!"
   > Then pull off your coat and roll up your sleeve,
   > For Richmond is a hard road to travel;
   > Then pull off your coat and roll up your sleeve,
   > For Richmond is a hard road to travel, I believe!

† The Battle of Cedar Run

Overtures from Richmond

Words by Francis J. Child
Music: "Lilliburlero"

MINSTREL AND COMIC SONGS

2. "So, Uncle Sam, just lay down your arms,"
   Lilliburlero, old Uncle Sam,
   "Then you shall hear my reas'nable terms,"
   Lilliburlero, old Uncle Sam.
   "Lero, lero, I'd like to hear-o
   I'd like to hear," says old Uncle Sam,
   "Lero, lero, filibuster-o,
   I'd like to hear," says old Uncle Sam.

3. "First you must own I've beat you in fight,"
   Lilliburlero, old Uncle Sam,
   "Then that I always have been in the right,"
   Lilliburlero, old Uncle Sam.
   "Lero, lero, rather severe-o
   Rather severe," says old Uncle Sam,
   "Lero, lero, filibuster-o,
   Rather severe," says old Uncle Sam.

4. "Then you must pay my national debts,"
  Lilliburlero, old Uncle Sam,
  "No questions asked about my assets,"
  Lilliburlero, old Uncle Sam.
  "Lero, lero, that's very dear-o
  That's very dear," says old Uncle Sam,
  "Lero, lero, filibuster-o,
  That's very dear," says old Uncle Sam.

5. "Also some few IOU's and bets,"
  Lilliburlero, old Uncle Sam,
  "Mine, and Bob Toombs', and Sidell's and
    Rhett's,"
  Lilliburlero, old Uncle Sam.
  "Lero, lero, that leaves me zero,
  That leaves me zero," says Uncle Sam,
  "Lero, lero, filibuster-o,
  That leaves me zero," says Uncle Sam.

6. "And by the way, one little thing more,"
  Lilliburlero, old Uncle Sam,
  "You're to refund the costs of the war,"
  Lilliburlero, old Uncle Sam.
  "Lero, lero, just what I fear-o,
  Just what I fear," says old Uncle Sam,
  "Lero, lero, filibuster-o,
  Just what I fear," says old Uncle Sam.

7. "Next, you must own our Cavalier blood!"
  Lilliburlero, old Uncle Sam,
  "And that your Puritans sprang from the mud!"
  Lilliburlero, old Uncle Sam.
  "Lero, lero, that mud is clear-o,
  That mud is clear," says old Uncle Sam,
  "Lero, lero, filibuster-o,
  That mud is clear," says old Uncle Sam.

8. "Slavery's, of course, the chief corner-stone,"
  Lilliburlero, old Uncle Sam,
  "Of our new civ-il-i-za-tion!"
  Lilliburlero, old Uncle Sam.
  "Lero, lero, that's quite sincere-o,
  That's quite sincere," says old Uncle Sam,
  "Lero, lero, filibuster-o,
  That's quite sincere," says old Uncle Sam.

9. "You'll understand, my recreant tool,"
  Lilliburlero, old Uncle Sam,
  "You're to submit, and we are to rule,"
  Lilliburlero, old Uncle Sam.
  "Lero, lero, aren't you a hero!
  Aren't you a hero," says Uncle Sam,
  "Lero, lero, filibuster-o,
  Aren't you a hero," says Uncle Sam.

10. "If to these terms you fully consent,"
  Lilliburlero, old Uncle Sam,
  "I'll be Perpetual King-President,"
  Lilliburlero, old Uncle Sam.
  "Lero, lero, take your sombrero,
  Off to your swamps," says old Uncle Sam,
  "Lero, lero, filibuster-o,
  Cut, double quick!" says old Uncle Sam.

High-Toned Southern Gentleman

Words: anonymous
Music: "Fine Old English Gentleman" (traditional)

MINSTREL AND COMIC SONGS

fre-quent-ly con-demns his eyes un - to an aw-ful fate, A

Quite slow ♪ = 96

high - toned South - ern gen - tle -man, one of the pres -ent time.

2. He always wears a full dress coat, pre-Adamite in cut,
   With waistcoat of the broadest style, through which his ruffles jut;
   Six breastpins deck his horrid front, and on his fingers shine
   Whole invoices of diamond rings, *which would hardly pass muster with the "Original
   Jacobs" in Chatham Street* for jewels genuine;
   This "high-toned Southern gentleman," one of the present time.

3. He takes to euchre kindly, too, and plays an awful hand,
   Especially when those he tricks his style don't understand,
   And if he wins, why then he stops to pocket all the stakes,
   But if he loses, then he says *to the unfortunate stranger who had chanced to win, "It's my
   opinion you are a cursed Abolitionist, and if you don't leave South Carolina in an hour,
   you'll be hung like a dog!" but no offer* to pay his losses makes;
   This "high-toned Southern gentleman," one of the present time.

4. Of course, he's all the time in debt to those who credit give,
   Yet manages upon the best the market yields to live;
   But if a Northern creditor asks him his bill to heed,
   This honorable gentleman *instantly draws his bowie knife and pistols, dons a blue cockade,
   and declares that, in consequence of the repeated aggressions of the North and its gross
   violations of the Constitution, he feels that it would utterly degrade him to pay any debt
   whatever, and in fact that he has at last* determined to SECEDE!
   This "high-toned Southern gentleman," one of the present time.

Note: Italicized words should be chanted in a monotone at an increasing tempo.

Hard Times in Dixie

Words by M. K.
Music by Eugarps

MINSTREL AND COMIC SONGS

And the bur-den of their song Is hard up in Dix-ie!

Chorus

Ra-tions up and funds so low, Foe-men come and nig-gers go,

Worst of all the Yank-ees know, We're hard up in Dix-ie.

2. Grant is close upon their track,
   It's hard times in Dixie!
   Southern fire won't turn him back,
   Hard times in Dixie.
      With his Heroes tested well,
      What cares he for shot or shell,
      Southern brag or Southern swell—
      They're hard up in Dixie!   (Chorus)

3. Uncle Abe don't flinch a bit
   For hard times in Dixie!
   Tough as any rail he's split,
   Hard up in Dixie;
      Holding out his honest hands,
      Welcoming all *loyal* bands,
      Abraham well understands
      They're hard up in Dixie!   (Chorus)

4. Butler, with his soldiers true,
   Makes hard times in Dixie!
   When he came the Rebels knew
   Hard times in Dixie!
   Johnny Rebs don't see the fun,
   Want begins and credit's done,
   White man works and darkey runs,
   They're hard up in Dixie!   (Chorus)

5. Beat the drum and toll the bell,
   For hard times in Dixie!
   Chant Rebellion's funeral knell—
   Hard times in Dixie!
   And while over land and sea,
   Floats the banner of the free,
   Traitors shall forever be
   Hard up in Dixie!   (Chorus)

Jeff in Petticoats

Words by Henry Tucker
Music by George Cooper

Sprightly ♩ = 126

Jeff – Da - vis was a he - ro bold, You've heard of him, I know, He

tried to make him - self a King Where south - ern breez - es blow; But

"Un - cle Sam," he laid the youth A - cross his might - y knee, And

343

MINSTREL AND COMIC SONGS

spanked him well, and that's the end Of brave old Jef - fy D.

Chorus

Oh! Jef - fy D.! You "flow'r of chiv - al - ree," Oh roy - al Jef - fy D.! _____ Your _ em - pire's but a tin - clad skirt, Oh, charm - ing Jef - fy D.

2. This Davis, he was always full
   Of bluster and of brag,
   He swore, on all our Northern walls,
   He'd plant his Rebel rag;
   But when to battle he did go,
   He said, "I'm not so green,
   To dodge the bullets, I will wear
   My tin-clad crinoline."   (Chorus)

3. Now when he saw the game was up,
   He started for the woods,
   His bandbox hung upon his arm
   Quite full of fancy goods;
   Said Jeff, "They'll never take me now,
   I'm sure I'll not be seen.
   They'd never think to look for me
   Beneath my crinoline."   (Chorus)

4. Jeff took with him, the people say,
   A mine of golden coin,
   Which he, from banks and other places,
   Managed to purloin;
   But while he ran, like every thief,
   He had to drop the spoons,
   And maybe that's the reason why
   He dropped his pantaloons.   (Chorus)

5. Our Union boys were on his track
   For many nights and days,
   His palpitating heart it beat,
   Enough to burst his stays;
   Oh! what a dash he must have cut
   With form so tall and lean;
   Just fancy now the "What is it?"
   Dressed up in crinoline!   (Chorus)

6. The ditch that Jeff was hunting for,
   He found was very near;
   He tried to "shift" his base again,
   His neck felt rather queer;
   Just on the out-"skirts" of a wood
   His dainty shape was seen,
   His boots stuck out, and now they'll hang
   Old Jeff in crinoline.   (Chorus)

The Blue and the Gray

POST-WAR SONGS AND SONGS INSPIRED BY THE CIVIL WAR

Under the sod and the dew,
Waiting the Judgement Day,
Love and tears for the Blue,
Tears and love for the Gray.

Oh come, brothers all,
'Tis Columbia's earnest call,
To make her people one again.
. . .
Come then, oh North and South united,
Come then, oh East and West as one;
Rejoice in the light
Which has chased away the night,
And heralds now the rising sun.

With Lee's surrender at Appomattox and the collapse of the Confederacy, a great wave of relief swept across a war-weary nation; the stirring martial songs of wartime gave way to hymns of peace and reconciliation as a triumphant Union rejoiced in victory and an embittered South resigned itself to defeat. George F. Root, whose battle songs had been second to none, summed up the national sentiment:

Now that the battle rage is over,
Now that the minute guns are cold,
Oh haste, knit again,
What the sword has cleft in twain,
Be friends and brothers, as of old.

But there were other songs of the post-war era. "Unreconstructed Rebels" continued to chant their defiance of the Union, although the sullen response which these songs evoked was but a faint shadow of the Rebel surge of 1861 when all the world, it seemed, was singing "Dixie."

So far as the music of the Negro was concerned, the Civil War marked the end of an era. Freedom seems to have brought to a close the period in which the traditional spirituals were created. The post-war religious songs of the Negro are less concerned with secular matters. The great "freedom" spirituals—"Go Down Moses," "Joshua Fit the Battle of Jericho," "Didn't My Lord Deliver Daniel," etc.—had all been created. Other Negro musical forms began to develop, and when the Negro again found the need for songs which held one meaning for the white man and many meanings for himself, he turned to the blues and, eventually, to jazz.

The post-war era also saw the rise of veterans' songs, songs of reunion and reminiscence, songs of sorrowful memory and renewed dedication. At veterans' conventions for the next few decades, the "old boys" sang:

Don't you hear the bugle calling, comrades, today?
Echoing still in memory of the days passed away!
Rally 'round the campfire from near and from far,
We were comrades together in the days of the war.

And Miles O'Reilly, who pleaded so vigorously for "Sambo's Right to Be Kilt," recalled in a glow of romantic reminiscence:

We've shared our blankets and tent together,
And marched and fought in all kinds of weather,
And hungry and full we've been,
Had days of battle and days of rest,
But this memory I cling to and love the best,
We have drunk from the same canteen.

With the passage of the years, the memories of wartime comradeship took on an even more sentimental hue:

We are the boys, the gay old boys,
Who marched in Sixty-One;
We'll ne'er forget old times, my boys,
When you and I were young.

In memory of fallen comrades, other songs became popular, songs like "The Flag They Loved So Well," "Sleep, Sacred Dust," "A Tear for the Comrade That's Gone," and "Sleeping in the Battlefield,"

Sleeping in the battlefield,
Lies our soldier boy,
Far from home and loved ones,
Rests our soldier boy;
Sweetest of roses bedeck his lonely grave,
But sweeter blooms his memory brave.

But the musical postscript to the Civil War is not yet complete. Songs inspired by or dealing with America's greatest conflict continue to be written. I have included two examples of such songs in this section.

The Civil War was, of course, never completely concluded. The dramatic struggle taking place in the South today is a constant reminder of the unfinished task which still remains for American

349

democracy. And from that struggle, too, new songs are coming—defiant songs of white supremacy and states rights, determined songs of equal rights and human dignity.

THE BLUE AND THE GRAY. While outward expressions of reconciliation dominated the Northern scene, a defeated and embittered South was slower and more reluctant to accept a brotherhood based on conquest. For that reason, an incident of early 1867 in Columbus, Mississippi, was greeted throughout the nation as a heartening reflection of a new spirit in the air. Let the following news item from the New York *Tribune* tell the story:

The women of Columbus, Mississippi, animated by nobler sentiments than many of their sisters, have shown themselves impartial in their offerings made to the memory of the dead. They strewed flowers alike on the graves of the Confederate and of the National Soldiers.

It is hard to imagine today the electric effect this incident had upon the country, and part of the impact must be credited to the tender and moving poem written by Francis Miles Finch, in later years an Associate Justice of the New York State Court of Appeals. The poem appeared in the *Atlantic Monthly* for September, 1867, with the above news item attached. A number of musical settings soon appeared, including one by George H. Briggs and another by John Hutchinson of the singing family. One of the most popular was this melody by Felix Schelling.

OH, I'M A GOOD OLD REBEL. For that portion of the conquered South which viewed Reconstruction and all its accoutrements with bitter resentment, this Rebel song of defiance was a last rallying cry flung in the face of history. The song was written by a cultivated Southerner of letters, Major Innes Randolph of the C.S.A., who won a minor reputation as a Southern poet. Its attempt to convey its sentiment in the words and style of a backwoods, semiliterate "unreconstructed Rebel" was so successful, however, that the song became a part of oral tradition throughout the rural South.

In later years, the Prince of Wales listened to an uncensored rendition performed by the Duchess of Manchester, and, so the story goes, the Prince insisted on a repeat performance of "that fine American song with the cuss words in it."

Folk versions have retained a remarkable resemblance to the original, with practically no changes of substance in the text recorded. John Lomax, however, turned up a completely new verse in Texas, this one presumably an addition to the original by an unknown Rebel rhymester:

I won't be reconstructed! I'm better now than them;
And for a carpetbagger, I don't give a damn;
So I'm off for the frontier, soon as I can go,
I'll prepare me a weapon and start for Mexico.

Many Southerners poured their resentment at the Union triumph into song. An anonymous North Carolina poet parodied the Irish "Wearing of the Green" to keep alive the dying hopes of the Confederacy:

Then since the color we must wear
Is of the hateful blue,
The children of the sunny South
Must be to memory true.
. . .
Nor even in the dying hour,
While passing calm away,
Can we forget or e'er regret
The wearin' of the gray!

In "The Conquered Banner," a Catholic priest of Tennessee urged the South to "furl that banner, for 'tis weary," only to have a pro-Confederate Englishman reply:

Keep it, widowed, sonless mothers,
Keep it, sisters, mourning brothers,
Furl it with an iron will;
Furl it now, but—keep it still,
Think not that its work is done.

Another song struck a note of sorrowful pride:

We know that we were Rebels,
We don't deny the name,
We speak of that which we have done
With grief, but not with shame!
And we never will acknowledge
That the blood the South has spilt
Was shed defending what we deemed
A cause of wrong and guilt.

But no song had the defiant venom and unconquerable bitterness of "Good Old Rebel," which, appropriately enough, was ironically dedicated to that most ardent advocate of a "tough" peace, Thaddeus Stevens.

HOLD THE FORT. During the Georgia campaign of October, 1864, shortly before Sherman's historic march to the sea, a battle took place at Altoona Pass, not many miles from Atlanta, which served as the inspiration for this song. A brigade of some 1,500 Union troops under the command of General Corse was defending an extremely important fort at the Pass when they were attacked by 6,000 Confederate troops under the command of General French. French's forces surrounded the fort and demanded its surrender, but Corse refused, and the Southern artillery unleashed a murderous hail of fire, a barrage which took the life of the Union commander.

At the peak of the battle, when the Union position seemed completely hopeless, a Northern officer caught sight of a white signal flag some fifteen miles distant. The signal was acknowledged and soon the following message was relayed across the mountains:

HOLD THE FORT   I AM COMING   W T SHERMAN.

Their sinking morale buoyed by Sherman's message, the Union soldiers returned to the task of defending their position with renewed vigor. For more than three hours General French's men tried to take the fort, but every assault was repulsed. Finally, the Confederates were forced to abandon their attack in order to escape before Sherman's reinforcements arrived.

Years later, an otherwise unidentified Major Whittle was engaged in a speaking tour which brought him to a Sunday school meeting in the little town of Rockford, Illinois. In the course of the meeting, Major Whittle related the incident recounted above. One of those in the audience was a Sunday school teacher and song writer by the name of Philip Paul Bliss. Bliss was so moved by the narrative that he immediately wrote a gospel hymn based on the story.

The hymn, "Hold the Fort," was an instantaneous success, and has remained to this day one of the most popular gospel songs ever written. At the time of Bliss's untimely death in 1876, in a train wreck, the Chicago *Inter-Ocean* (a newspaper) commented that the song

was written on the impulse of the moment and it has traveled the world over. It has been translated into not only nearly all the European languages, but into Chinese and the native languages of India. It is not too much to say that it is popular beyond any other Sabbath School song of the age.

In subsequent years, numerous parodies were written to the song.*

The special memorial edition of "Hold the Fort," published in 1877, bears the following inscription:

To William Tecumseh Sherman, General of the Army of the United States, from whom the song derived its inspiration, this volume is respectfully inscribed.

DANCE ME A JIG. Out of the dark byways of history and the hidden tracks of the Underground Railroad have come stories and legends of escape and bravery, of cruelty and ingenuity, songs and anecdotes lighting a backward trail which lives in the transcribed memories of those long gone.

Of all the conductors on the secret trains of the Underground Railroad, none was as determined or successful as the dark-skinned woman who returned again and again into the heart of slavery in pursuit of her personal war against the South—Harriet Tubman. With Dixie in turmoil during the Civil War, Harriet Tubman's missions to the South became more frequent and the courageous Negro woman was employed by the Union Army in the official capacity of scout. On one mission, so the legend goes, Harriet Tubman led a raid on a South Carolina plantation and helped free a large group of slaves. As the Negroes marched off through the woods, burdened down with all their worldly possessions and as much of the master's movable property as they could carry, Harriet Tubman spotted a slave woman struggling with her grandchildren, a huge basket of clothing, and a pair of newly liberated recalcitrant pigs.

As she noticed Miss Tubman's look of concern over the delay, the old woman yanked violently at the ropes holding the two poor creatures and exclaimed: "Come along, Jeff Davis! Get on Beauregard!" Seeing that the woman had two such important prisoners-of-war, Harriet Tubman

* Suffragettes, Populists, Prohibitionists, Socialists, etc., penned new words to the stirring melody. In England, British transport workers adapted Bliss's hymn to create one of the best-known labor songs of the English-speaking world:

> Hold the fort for we are coming,
> Union men be strong;
> Side by side, we battle onward,
> Victory will come.

had no choice but to have the party keep closer to the old woman's pace.

From such fragile material come songs. Almost a century later, a popular song writer, Al Wood, himself of Negro background, fashioned this anecdote into a ballad of wry humor and fetching rhythm.

TWO BROTHERS. The historical memory which is the Civil War lives on in the consciousness of another age. Our heritage from that era is marked in photograph and legend, in volumes of fact and volumes of fiction, in the searing imprint of courage and fear and dedication with which the arsenals of both armies were fully stocked. This heritage is still alive in the songs of the Civil War, the old songs, the marching songs, the sentimental songs, the songs of haunting long-dead laughter. It lives, too, in songs of today inspired by the Civil War and the men and women who fought it.

Here is such an echo of the past, written only a few years ago, bringing to life again not the giants but the ordinary men and women who strode the blood-soaked earth of America one hundred years ago.

The Blue and the Gray

Words by M. F. Finch
Music by Felix Schelling

By the flow of the in-land _ riv-er, Where the fleet of _ i-ron has fled, Where the blades of the grave grass quiv-er, A-sleep are the ranks of the dead. Un-der the sod and the

POST-WAR SONGS

dew   Wait - ing the Judge - ment   Day,

Un - der the one the Blue,   Un - der the oth-er   the Gray.

Chorus

Un - der the sod and the dew,   Wait - ing the Judge-ment Day,

Un - der the one the Blue,   Un - der the oth·er   the Gray.

2. Those in the robings of glory,
   Those in the gloom of defeat;
   All with the battle blood gory,
   In the dusk of Eternity meet.
   Under the sod and the dew,
   Waiting the Judgement Day,
   Under the laurel, the Blue,
   Under the willow, the Gray.

3. From the silence of sorrowful hours,
   The desolate mourners go,
   Lovingly laden with flowers,
   Alike for the friends and the foe.
   Under the sod and the dew,
   Waiting the Judgement Day,
   Under the roses, the Blue,
   Under the lilies, the Gray.

4. So, with an equal splendor,
   The morning sunrays fall,
   With a touch impartially tender,
   On the blossoms blooming for all.
   Under the sod and the dew,
   Waiting the Judgement Day,
   Broidered with gold, the Blue,
   Mellowed with gold, the Gray.

5. So, when the summer calleth,
   On forest and field of grain,
   With an equal murmur falleth,
   The cooling drip of the rain.
   Under the sod and the dew,
   Waiting the Judgement Day,
   Wet with the rain, the Blue,
   Wet with the rain, the Gray.

6. Sadly, but not with upbraiding,
   The generous deed was done,
   In the storm of the years that are fading,
   No braver battle was won.
   Under the sod and the dew,
   Waiting the Judgement Day,
   Under the blossoms, the Blue,
   Under the garlands, the Gray.

7. No more shall the war cry sever,
   Or the winding rivers be red;
   They banish our anger forever,
   When they laurel the graves of our dead.
   Under the sod and the dew,
   Waiting the Judgement Day,
   Love and tears for the Blue,
   Tears and love for the Gray.

Oh, I'm a Good Old Rebel

Words ascribed to Major Innes Randolph, C.S.A.
Music: "Joe Bowers"

Oh, I'm a good old Reb - el, Now that's just what I am, For this "Fair Land of Free - dom" I do not give a damn! I'm glad I fit a - gainst it, I on - ly wish we'd won, And

POST-WAR SONGS

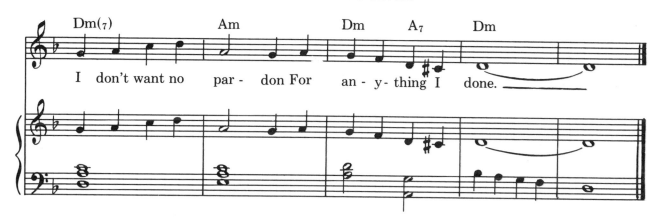

2. I hates the Constitution,
   This Great Republic, too,
   I hates the Freedman's Buro,
   In uniforms of blue;
   I hates the nasty eagle,
   With all his brag and fuss,
   The lyin', thievin' Yankees,
   I hates 'em wuss and wuss.

3. I hates the Yankee nation
   And everything they do,
   I hates the Declaration
   Of Independence, too;
   I hates the "glorious Union,"
   'Tis dripping with our blood,
   I hates their striped banner,
   I fit it all I could.

4. I followed old Marse Robert
   For four year, near about,
   Got wounded in three places
   And starved at P'int Lookout;
   I cotch the "roomatism,"
   A-campin' in the snow,
   But I killed a chance o' Yankees,
   I'd like to kill some mo'.

5. Three hundred thousand Yankees
   Is stiff in Southern dust;
   We got three hundred thousand
   Before they conquered us;
   They died of Southern fever
   And Southern steel and shot,
   I wish they was three million
   Instead of what we got.

6. I can't take up my musket
   And fight 'em now no more,
   But I ain't a-going to love 'em,
   Now that is sarten sure;
   And I don't want no pardon
   For what I was and am,
   I won't be reconstructed
   And I don't care a damn!

Hold the Fort

Words and music by Philip Paul Bliss

POST-WAR SONGS

2. See the mighty host advancing,
   Satan leading on,
   Mighty men around us falling,
   Courage almost gone.   (Chorus)

3. See the glorious banner waving,
   Hear the bugle blow,
   In our Leader's name we'll triumph
   Over every foe.   (Chorus)

4. Fierce and long the battle rages,
   But our Help is near,
   Onward comes our great Commander,
   Cheer, my comrades, cheer.   (Chorus)

Dance Me a Jig

Words and music by Al Wood

close His eyes. While I dance me a jig, and I dance me a jog, 'Cause I got me a pig and I got me a hog; Ain't no one gon-na take 'em from me. Get a-long, Jeff Da-vis, Come on Gen-er-al Lee!

Verses 1–4

Verse 5

* Guitarists: You may play any random combination of notes in place of E♭7.

2. When my two sons escaped early last year,
   Master like to tore out all his hair;
   When he misses me I'm gonna laugh till I cry,
   'Cause that poor fool will probably stretch out and die.   (Chorus)

3. I didn't want no posses a-chasing after me,
   So I took all the livestock and set 'em free;
   Now master's so mad that he's liable to bust,
   'Cause he's gotta catch 'em all while I'm kicking up dust.   (Chorus)

4. If you pigs are wondering how you got your name,
   Well, you and them two rascals are just the same;
   And if you don't stop acting like your two namesakes,
   I'll have roast pork in the morning and tasty ham steaks.   (Chorus)

5. I am an old lady, but I'd like to bet,
   That I'm one woman old master won't forget;
   The look on his face will be something to see,
   When he finds the pigs are gone—and I am free!   (Chorus)

Two Brothers

Words and music by Irving Gordon

POST-WAR SONGS

One wore blue and one wore gray; As they marched a-

long their way, A fife and drum be-gan to play, There on a beau-ti-ful morn-ing.

2. One was gentle, one was kind,
   One was gentle, one was kind,
   One came home, one stayed behind;
   A cannon ball don't pay no mind,
   A cannon ball don't pay no mind,
   Though you're gentle or you're kind,
   It don't think of the folks behind,
   There on a beautiful morning.

3. Two girls waitin' by the railroad track,
   Two girls waitin' by the railroad track,
   For their darlin's to come back;
   One wore blue and one wore black,
   One wore blue and one wore black,
   Waitin' by the railroad track,
   For their darlin's to come back,
   There on a beautiful morning.

Sources

Note: The first reference after each song title refers to the particular source for the version published in this collection. Subsequent references are for variant versions, parodies, additional background, or similar songs as cited in the introductory notes, the numbers referring to the sources listed in the bibliography.

THE UNION FOREVER

Battle Cry of Freedom (Rallying Song): Sheet music, pub. by Root & Cady, Chicago, 1862; see also 109, 193*d*, 144 (Vol. X), 218, 220, 223.

Battle Cry of Freedom, II (Battle Song): Sheet music, pub. by Root & Cady, Chicago, 1863, 1864; see also 130.

Southern "Battle Cry of Freedom": 36; see also sheet music (Barnes-Schreiner), pub. by J. C. Schreiner, Macon, Ga., 1864.

Battle Hymn of the Republic: Sheet music, pub. by Oliver Ditson & Co., Boston, 1862; see also 23, 57, 18, 213, 220, 223.

John Brown's Body: Sheet music, pub. by Oliver Ditson & Co., Boston, 1861; see also 193*g*, 209, 145 (Vol. IV).

John Brown's Body, II: Sheet music, pub. by Root & Cady, Chicago, 1862.

The President's Proclamation: 90.

Marching Song of the First Arkansas: Broadside pub. by the Supervisory Committee for Recruiting Colored Regiments, n.d.; see also 93.

For the Dear Old Flag I Die: Sheet music, pub. by E. A. Daggett, New York, 1863; see also 63.

Marching Along: Sheet music pub. by Firth Pond & Co., New York, 1862; see also 2, 158, 145 (Vol. III), 220.

The Army of The Free: 93; see also 149.

Tramp! Tramp! Tramp!: Sheet music, pub. by Root & Cady, Chicago, 1863; "On, On, On" and "Starved in Prison" also from sheet music, pub. by Root & Cady, Chicago, 1865; see also 102 (Vol. II), 126, 42, 220, 223.

Tramp! Tramp! Tramp!, II (Southern Version): 121.

Nine Miles to the Junction: Sheet music, pub. by H. B. Dodworth, New York, date unclear; see also 134.

The Why and Wherefore: 23.

Marching Through Georgia: Sheet music, pub. by Root & Cady, Chicago, 1865; see also General William T. Sherman, "The Grand Strategy of the Last Year of the War," in 201 (Vol. IV); also 200 (pp. 663–80); 208 (Vol. III), 223.

IN DIXIE LAND

Dixie's Land: Sheet music, pub. by Firth, Pond, & Co., New York, 1860; see also 58 (pp. 41–52), 75, 49, 193*f*, 144 (Vol. VII), 145 (Vol. III), 221.

Dixie: Sheet music, pub. by Werlein & Halsey, New Orleans, 1861; see also 91, 202; "Dixie War Song" (Stanton) from sheet music, pub. by A. E. Blackmar, New Orleans, 1861.

The Officers of Dixie: 49; see also 179.

Union Dixie: Collated text from two broadside sheets numbered, respectively, "Dixie's Land No. 5" and "Dixie's Land No. 6," but otherwise unidentified as to publisher or date of printing.

The Bonnie Blue Flag: Sheet music, pub. by A. E. Blackmar, New Orleans, 1861; see also 193*e*, 17 (Vol. III), 7, 49, 46, 59, 144 (Vol. X), 213, 218, 220, 221; "Our Country's Flag," sheet music, pub. by A. E. Blackmar, New Orleans, 1867; "Flag with Thirty-Four Stars," from broadside, pub. by Charles Magnu, New York, n.d.; "Stars and Stripes" from 93.

The Homespun Dress: 162; see also sheet music, pub. by A. E. Blackmar, New Orleans, 1865; see also 59, 94, 102 (Vol. II), 7, 17 (Vol. III), 134, 218.

The Bonnie White Flag: 49.

Maryland, My Maryland: Sheet music, pub. by A. E. Blackmar, New Orleans, 1862; see also 181, 125, 91, 18, 58, 145 (Vol. IV), 220; also James Ryder Randall, *The Poems of James Ryder Randall.*

Answer to "My Maryland": 90; the various parodies quoted come from different pieces of sheet music by many publishers.

Kentucky! O Kentucky!: 88.

We Conquer or Die: Sheet music, pub. by P. P. Werlein & Halsey, New Orleans, 1861; see also 162.

The Yellow Rose of Texas: Sheet music, pub. by Firth, Pond, & Co., New York, 1858; see also 49, 59, 27, 144 (Vol. III), 221; "Arkansas Kate" and "Belle ob Tenisee" from *White's New Illustrated Melodeon.*

Stonewall Jackson's Way: Sheet music, pub. by George Zwillig, Baltimore, 1862; see also 58 (pp. 75–77), 4, 192, 220.

Riding a Raid: Sheet music, pub. by J. W. Randolph, Richmond, n.d.; see also 49.

The Young Volunteer: Sheet music, pub. by J. C. Schreiner & Son, Macon & Savannah, Ga., 1863; see also 60, 58 (pp. 26–40).

OLD ABE LINCOLN CAME OUT OF THE WILDERNESS

Old Abe Lincoln Came Out of the Wilderness: 111; see also 122, 194*g*, 144 (Vol. IV).

Lincoln and Liberty: 161; see also 175, 213.

The Liberty Ball: 177; see also 175, 155, 128, 29, Brown, William, *The Anti-Slavery Harp.*

Abraham's Daughter: Sheet music, pub. by Septimus

Winner, Philadelphia, 1861; see also 149, 164 (pp. 26, 43, 50), 28.

We Are Coming Father Abr'am: 130; see also 18, 193*a*, 191, 206, 220. "How Are You Greenbacks?" from broadside pub. by H. De Marsan, New York, n.d.

We'll Fight for Uncle Abe: Sheet music, pub. by Oliver Ditson & Co., Boston, 1863. See also 144 (Vol. XIII).

Booth Killed Lincoln: 216.

WEEPING SAD AND LONELY

Weeping Sad and Lonely: Sheet music, pub. by Sawyer & Thompson, Brooklyn, N. Y., 1863; see also 46, 191, 162, 153, 58, 59, 17 (Vol. III), 7, 147, 144 (Vol. X), 213, 220.

Down in Charleston Jail: 213, 212; see also 42.

All Quiet Along the Potomac Tonight: Sheet music, pub. by Lee & Walker, Philadelphia, 1862; see also 68, 206, 125, 213, 220, 221.

Do They Miss Me at Home? Sheet music, pub. by Oliver Ditson & Co., Boston, 1852; see also 86, 179.

Do They Miss Me in the Trenches? 49; see also 42.

Lorena: Sheet music, pub. by J. C. Schreiner, Macon, Ga., n.d.; see also 42, 102 (Vol. IV), 125, 213, 220, 221.

The Vacant Chair: Sheet music, pub. by Root & Cady, Chicago, 1861; see also 16, 144 (Vol. XII), 220, 223.

The Drummer Boy of Shiloh: Sheet music, pub. by D. P. Faulds, Louisville, 1862; see also 211 (p. 297), 122 (pp. 158–59).

Home, Sweet Home: Sheet music, pub. by George Bacon, Philadelphia, 1823; see also 122 (pp. 55–58), 203 (p. 178).

Somebody's Darling: Sheet music, pub. by J. C. Schreiner & Son, Macon and Savannah, Ga., 1864; see also 119, 58, 77, 221.

The Southern Soldier Boy: Sheet music, pub. by George Dunn & Co., Julian A. Selby, Richmond and Columbia, S.C., 1863; see also 49, 102 (Vol. II), 112 (Vol. II, p. 274).

Just Before the Battle, Mother: Sheet music, pub. by Root & Cady, Chicago, 1862; see also 31, 125, 144 (Vol. XII), 220, 223, *The Singing Streets* (Folkways Records, Album FW8501).

Farewell, Mother: 36; see also 42.

Just After the Battle: Sheet music, pub. by Root & Cady, Chicago, 1863; see also 220.

Who Will Care for Mother Now? Sheet music, pub. by Sawyer and Thompson, Brooklyn, N.Y., 1863; see also 144 (Vol. X), 220; various replies from published sheet music and broadsides, many publishers.

Who Will Care for Micky Now? Broadside, pub. by Charles Magnus, New York, n.d.

The Faded Coat of Blue: Sheet music, pub. by J. H. McNaughton, Caledonia, N.Y., 1865; see also 64, 220.

TENTING ON THE OLD CAMP GROUND

Tenting on the Old Camp Ground: Sheet music, pub. by Oliver Ditson Co., Boston, 1864; see also 15 (pp. 214–19), 71, 18 (pp. 198–201), 220, 223.

Tenting on the Old Camp Ground, II (Southern Version): 121.

Goober Peas: Sheet music, pub. by A. E. Blackmar, New Orleans, 1866; see also 5, 59, 213, 220.

The New York Volunteer: 149.

Drink It Down: 149; see also (for background) 211 (Vol. I, pp. 247–62, Vol. II, pp. 36–58).

Farewell to Grog: Book of Navy Songs (Trident Society).

Wait for the Wagon: Sheet music, pub. by Lee & Walker, Philadelphia, 1851; see also 68, 52 (p. 26), 128 (p. 151), 71 (p. 241), 106, 144 (Vol. I); Lincoln campaign song from broadside, pub. by John D. Gay, Philadelphia, 1864.

The Old Union Wagon: Sheet music, pub. by Lee & Walker, Philadelphia, 1863; see also 180 (p. 32), 157 (p. 34), 4 (p. 120), 145 (Vol. I).

The Southern Wagon: Composite based on versions appearing in 131, 88, 91, 49, 4; "Stonewall Jackson" parody from 181 (pp. 66–67); Union reply from 7 (p. 397).

The Brass-Mounted Army: 138; see also 102 (Vol. II).

The Valiant Conscript: 134; "The Bugler" from 49; "The Soldier's Fare" from 5; "The Soldier's Amen" from 138; "Would You Be a Soldier, Laddy?" from 23.

Confederate Yankee Doodle: 91; see also 36 (p. 29), 88 (p. 414).

I'll Be a Sergeant: 23; see also 157 (p. 9).

There Was an Old Soldier: 213; see also 214, 111, 14.

Johnny Is My Darling: Broadside, pub. anonymously 1863, from the Library of Congress; for Scottish song, see Richard Dyer-Bennet, Vol. III (phonograph record, Dyer-Bennet Records), and Max Dunbar, *Songs and Ballads of the Scottish Wars* (phonograph record, Folkways FW3006).

When Johnny Comes Marching Home: Sheet music, pub. by Henry Tolman & Co., Boston, 1863; see also 35, 77, 113, 122 (p. 154), 146, 213, 220, 223.

For Bales: Sheet music, pub. by Blackmar & Co., New Orleans, 1864; "Johnny Fill Up the Bowl" from sheet music, pub. by John J. Daly, New York, 1863; "Copperhead" parody from broadside, pub. by J. H. Johnson, Philadelphia, n.d.; "We Are the Boys, etc.," from 42; see also 142, 185, 221.

The Rebel Soldier: Cecil J. Sharp, *English Folksongs from the Southern Appalachians,* Vol. II, p. 213, "B" version, used with the kind permission of Oxford Univ. Press; see also 31 (p. 279), 102 (Vol. II, p. 317), 138 (p. 80), 7 (p. 374), 80 (p. 170).

The Southern Soldier: 216.

Pat Murphy of the Irish Brigade: 219 (learned by Miss Stekert from Ezra "Fuzzy" Barhight of Cohocton, New York; based on a Civil War broadside, "Pat Murphy of Meagher's Brigade," pub. by H. Wrigley, New York); for "No Irish Need Apply," see 114, 170; for various songs quoted in introduction, see 163, 164, 218, 49, 7.

Here's Your Mule: Sheet music, pub. by C. D. Benson, Louisville, 1862; see also 59, 220.

How Are You, John Morgan? Sheet music, pub. by C. D. Benson, Nashville, 1864; "Three Cheers for Our Jack Morgan" from sheet music, words by Eugene Raymond (pseudonym for John H. Hewitt) to a Dan Emmett

SOURCES

melody, pub. by Blackmar & Bros., Augusta, Ga., 1864.

I Can Whip the Scoundrel: 213; see also 88 (p. 251), 212, 201, 94 (p. 28), 17 (Vol. II, p. 658).

Cumberland Gap: 54; see also 80, 213, 17 (Vol. III).

IT'S ALL ABOUT THAT TERRIBLE FIGHT

Flight of Doodles: 91; see "Root Hog or Die," sheet music pub. by Oliver Ditson Co., Boston, 1856; also sheet music pub. by E. A. Daggett, New York, 1856; see also 162, 144 (Vol. I).

Root Hog or Die (Southern Version): 181; see also 162 (p. 35), 149 (p. 17), 138 (p. 35), 90; also broadsides (Nos. 1–5) pub. by H. DeMarsan, New York, New York Public Library.

The Battle of Shiloh: As sung by Mr. Philander Fitzgerald of Nash, Virginia, 1918, and published in Cecil J. Sharp, *English Folksongs from the Southern Appalachians,* used here with the kind permission of Oxford Univ. Press.

The Battle of Shiloh Hill: 138; see also 102 (Vol. II, p. 220), 17 (Vol. II, p. 535), 64 (p. 260).

Cairo: 180; see also 145 (Vol. I), 201 (Vol. I, pp. 278–81); for background information on Cairo, I am indebted to Miss Virginia B. Herbert of the Cairo Historical Assn., Cairo, Ill.

Brother Green: from the singing of Mrs. Emma L. Dusenberry of Mena, Ark., recorded by Waldemar Hille; see also 102 (Vol. II), 14, 7, 45, 17 (Vol. III, p. 468), 31.

Roll, Alabama, Roll: 213 (Hermes Nye tells me that this is his own free adaptation of printed versions); see also 212, 41 (pp. 32–37), 30 (p. 65), 88 (pp. 87–91), 46 (p. 167).

Virginia's Bloody Soil: 218.

The Cumberland and The Merrimac: 219; see also 17 (Vol. II, pp. 530–33); Cowell, Sidney Robertson, *Wolf River Songs* (Folkways Records FM4001), as sung by Warde Ford; for other literary material see 88 (pp. 106, 371).

The Cumberland Crew: 199 (Vol. IV, No. 1); see also 127, 216, 41, 21, 213.

When Sherman Marched Down to the Sea: Sheet music, pub. by Lee & Walker, Philadelphia, 1865; see also 42, 130, 46 (Vol. II).

The Fall of Charleston: Broadside, pub. by Charles Magnus, New York, n.d., presumably 1865; see also "Whack Row De-Dow," sheet music, pub. by Firth, Son, & Co., New York, 1861; 134 (pp. 56–58), 164 (p. 25).

LET MY PEOPLE GO

Go Down Moses: A composite from the following sources: sheet music, "The Song of the Contrabands," pub. by Horace Waters, New York, 1861; and 100, 69 (Vol. I), 137, 38.

Follow the Drinking Gourd: 114 (this version based principally on the song as sung by Lee Hays and The Weavers); for detailed historical background, see 40.

Steal Away to Jesus: 100; see also 38 (p. 111 and p. vii, Appendix); 50 (p. 66).

Clear the Track: 65; see also 199 (Vol. VI, No. 3), 71, 15.

We Wait Beneath the Furnace Blast: Sheet music, "The Furnace Blast or Prohibited Song as Sung by the Hutchinson Family," pub. by Firth & Pond, New York, 1862; see also 24 (p. 8), 15 (pp. 203–12), 88 (pp. 148, 437), 208 (Vol. I, p. 561); for "Uncle Sam, What Ails You?" see sheet music, pub. by Sawyer & Thompson, Brooklyn, N.Y., 1862.

My Father, How Long? 2.

The Gold Band: 2; see also 112 (under title "Sinner Man").

Oh Freedom: 61; see also 194a, 82 (pp. 341, 370), 38.

Give Us a Flag: 93; see also 207; "Hoist Up the Flag" from the sheet music, pub. by Septimus Winner, Philadelphia, 1863.

Many Thousand Gone: 2; see also 100.

Free at Last: 136; see also 69 (Vol. II).

Slavery Chain Done Broke at Last: 38.

GRAFTED INTO THE ARMY

Grafted into the Army: Sheet music, pub. by Root & Cady, Chicago, 1862; various songs cited are excerpted from sheet music and broadsides of different publishers; see also 220.

Billy Barlow: Broadside, pub. by H. De Marsan, New York, n.d.; see also sheet music pub. by George Endicott, New York, 1836; also 189, 7, 199 (Vol. IV, No. 1, and Vol. VI, No. 1).

Kingdom Coming: Sheet music, pub. by Root & Cady, Chicago, 1862; see also 135, 124, 102 (Vol. II), 17 (Vol. II), 5, 145 (Vol. IV), 196a,b, 223.

Babylon Is Fallen: Sheet music, pub. by Root & Cady, Chicago, 1863; 102 (Vol. II), 144 (Vol. XII).

De Day ob Liberty's Comin': Sheet music, pub. by Root & Cady, Chicago, 1862.

I Goes to Fight mit Sigel: Broadside, pub. by H. De Marsan, New York, n.d.; see also 151, 166, 202, 144 (Vol. XII); for "Corporal Schnapps" see sheet music pub. by Root & Cady, Chicago, 1864, and 42; for "Dutch Volunteer" see 49.

The Girl I Left Behind Me: 157; see also 68, 51, 80, 144 (Vol. III).

Sambo's Right to Be Kilt: Sheet music, pub. by William Hall & Son, New York, 1864; see also 88 (p. 269), 202.

Richmond Is a Hard Road to Travel: Sheet music, pub. by A. E. Blackmar, Augusta, Ga., 1863; see also 25, 124, 58, 65, 27, 105, 175, 144 (Vol. III).

Overtures from Richmond: 23; see also 51 (pp. 204–7), 53 (p. 286).

High-Toned Southern Gentleman: 23; see also 93, 68, 124, 176, 91, 138, 144 (Vol. III).

Hard Times in Dixie: Sheet music, pub. by W. W. Whitney, Toledo, Ohio, 1864.

Jeff in Petticoats: Sheet music, pub. by William Pond, New York, 1865; see also 79, 142; for historical background, see "The Capture of Jefferson Davis," by David Rankin Barbee, *Tyler's Quarterly Historical and Genealogical Magazine,* Vol. XXIX, No. 1, July, 1947.

367

SOURCES

THE BLUE AND THE GRAY

The Blue and the Gray: Sheet music, pub. by Reed Meyer, Philadelphia, 1869; see also 6.

Oh, I'm a Good Old Rebel: Sheet music, pub. anonymously, n.d., ascribed by Dichter and Shapiro (39) to A. E. Blackmar, New Orleans, 1866; see also 80, 17 (Vol. III), 102 (Vol. II), 31, 213, 218; for other songs quoted, see 49 (pp. 356, 364, 373, 375).

Hold the Fort: Sheet music, pub. by S. Brainard's Sons, Cleveland, 1870; see also 8.

Dance Me a Jig: 199 (Vol. III, No. 6, copyright 1952, used by permission); see also 205.

Two Brothers: Sheet music, pub. by Shapiro, Bernstein, & Co., New York, copyright 1951, used by permission.

368

References

I. MUSIC ANTHOLOGIES AND BIBLIOGRAPHICAL SOURCES ON MUSIC AND COMPOSERS

1. Kurt Adler. *Songs of Many Wars.* New York, Howell, Soskin Pub., 1943.
2. William Francis Allen, with Charles Pickard Ware and Lucy McKim Garrison. *Slave Songs of the United States.* Original pub. 1867; reprinted by Peter Smith, New York, 1951. (Dover, 1995.)
3. *The American Collection of Vocal and Instrumental War Music.* Chicago and New York, National Music Co., 1898.
4. *American War Songs.* Published under the supervision of the National Committee for the Preservation of Existing Records of the National Society of the Colonial Dames of America. Privately printed. Philadelphia, 1925.
5. Byron Arnold. *Folksongs of Alabama.* Birmingham, Univ. of Alabama Press, 1950.
6. Louis Albert Banks. *Immortal Songs of Camp and Field.* Cleveland, Burrows Bros. Co., 1899.
7. H. M. Belden. *Ballads and Songs of Missouri.* Collected by the Missouri Folklore Society. Columbia, Missouri, Univ. of Missouri Studies, 1940, 1955.
8. Philip Paul Bliss. *Hold the Fort.* Memorial ed. Boston, William F. Gill & Co., 1877.
9. Margaret Bradford Boni. *Fireside Book of Favorite American Songs.* New York, Simon & Schuster, 1952.
10. Margaret Bradford Boni. *Fireside Book of Folksongs.* New York, Simon & Schuster, 1947.
11. B. A. Botkin. *A Treasury of Southern Folklore.* New York, Crown, 1949.
12. William B. Bradbury. *Bradbury's Golden Chain of Sabbath School Melodies.* New York, Ivison. Phinney & Co., 1861.
13. Oscar Brand. *Singing Holidays.* New York, Alfred A. Knopf, 1957.
14. Paul G. Brewster. *Ballads and Songs of Indiana.* Bloomington, Ind., Indiana Univ. Publications, 1940. Folklore Series No. 1.
15. Carol Brink. *Harps in the Wind: The Story of the Singing Hutchinsons.* New York, Macmillan, 1947.
16. Howard Futhey Brinton. *Patriotic Songs of the American People.* New Haven, Tuttle, Morehouse, Taylor & Co., 1900.
17. Frank C. Brown. *The Frank C. Brown Collection of North Carolina Folklore.* Newman Ivey White, general editor. 5 vols. Durham, N.C., Duke Univ. Press, 1952.
18. C. A. Browne. *The Story of Our National Ballads.* New York, Thomas Y. Crowell Co., 1919.
19. Henry Brownell. *Lyrics of a Day.* New York, Carleton Pub., 1864.
20. A. R. Carrington. *Concert War Songs.* Arranged and adapted by the famous "Drummer Boy of Shiloh." Cleveland and Chicago, S. Brainard's & Sons, 1888.
21. Norman Cazden. *The Abelard Folk Song Book.* New York, Abelard-Schuman, 1958.
22. Gilbert Chase. *America's Music: From the Pilgrims to the Present.* New York, McGraw-Hill, 1955.
23. Francis James Child. *War Songs for Freemen.* Boston, Ticknor & Fields, 1863.
24. *Chimes of Freedom and Union: A Collection of Poems for the Times by Various Authors.* Boston, Benjamin B. Russell, 1861.
25. E. P. Christy. *Christy and White's Ethiopian Melodies.* Philadelphia, T. B. Peterson & Bros., 1854.
26. E. P. Christy. *Christy's Minstrels' Song Book.* 2 vols. London, Boosey & Sons, n.d.
27. E. P. Christy. *Christy's Plantation Melodies.* 3 vols. New York, Fisher & Bros., 1851, 1853.
28. Charles Eugene Claghorn. *The Mocking Bird: The Life and Diary of its Author, Septimus Winner.* Philadelphia, The Magee Press, 1937.
29. George W. Clark. *The Liberty Minstrel.* New York, Saxton & Miles and Myron Finch, 1845.
30. Joanna C. Colcord. *Songs of American Sailormen.* New York, W. W. Norton & Co., 1938.
31. John Harrington Cox. *Folk Songs of the South.* Cambridge, Harvard Univ. Press, 1925.
32. J. W. Dadman and Arthur B. Fuller. *Army and Navy Melodies.* Boston, J. P. Magee, 1862.
33. Francis Colgate Dale. *The Seventh Regiment Song Book.* New York, Hinds, Noble, and Eldredge, 1914.
34. Lizzie C. Daniel. *Confederate Scrap Book.* Richmond, J. L. Hill Printing Co., 1893.
35. Marwood Darlington. *Irish Orpheus: The Life of Patrick S. Gilmore, Bandmaster Extraordinary.* Philadelphia, Olivier-Maney-Klein Co., 1950.
36. Nora Fontaine M. Davidson. *Cullings from the Confederacy.* Washington, D.C., Rufus H. Derby Printing Co., 1903.
37. T. C. De Leon. *South Songs: From the Lays of Later Days.* New York, Blelock & Co., 1866.
38. R. Nathaniel Dett. *Religious Folk Songs of the Negro: As Sung at Hampton Institute.* Hampton, Va., Hampton Institute Press, 1874. (A number of editions have been published since 1874.)
39. Harry Dichter and Elliot Shapiro. *Early American*

REFERENCES

Sheet Music: Its Lure and Its Lore, 1768–1899. New York, R. R. Bowker Co., 1941.

40. J. Frank Dobie. *Follow the Drinkin' Gou'd.* Austin, Texas, 1928. Publications of the Texas Folk Lore Society, No. VII.

41. William Doerflinger. *Shantymen and Shantyboys.* New York, Macmillan, 1951.

42. Edward Arthur Dolph. *"Sound Off!"* New York, Cosmopolitan Book Corp., 1929.

43. Lester Douglas. *Songs Between the States.* Washington, D.C., Judd & Detweiler, Inc., 1946.

44. *The Drum Beat.* New York, T. S. Gordon, 1865.

45. Mary O. Eddy. *Ballads and Songs from Ohio.* New York, J. J. Augustin, 1939.

46. George Cary Eggleston. *American War Ballads and Lyrics.* 2 vols. New York, G. P. Putnam's Sons, 1889.

47. David Ewen. *Panorama of American Popular Music.* New York, Prentice-Hall, 1957.

48. David Ewen. *Songs of America.* Chicago, Ziff-Davis Pub., 1947.

49. W. L. Fagan. *Southern War Songs: Camp-Fire, Patriotic and Sentimental.* New York, M. T. Richardson & Co., 1890.

50. Miles Mark Fisher. *Negro Slave Songs in the United States.* Ithaca, N.Y., Cornell Univ. Press, 1953.

51. S. J. Adair Fitzgerald. *Stories of Famous Songs.* London, John C. Nimmo, 1898.

52. *The Freemen's Glee Book.* A collection of songs, odes, glees, and ballads, with music, original and selected, harmonized, and arranged for each, publised under the auspices of the Central Fremont and Dayton Glee Club of the City of New York. New York and Auburn, Miller, Orton, & Mulligan, 1856.

53. Albert B. Friedman. *The Viking Book of Folk Ballads of the English-Speaking World.* New York, Viking Press, 1956.

54. Harvey H. Fuson. *Ballads of the Kentucky Highlands.* London, The Mitre Press, 1931.

55. Robert W. Gordon. *Folksongs of America.* National Service Bureau, Federal Theater Project, Works Progress Administration, 1938.

56. *The Grayjackets—and How They Fought and Died for Dixie, with Incidents and Sketchs of Life in the Confederacy by a Confederate.* Richmond and Atlanta, Jones Bros. & Co., 1867.

57. Florence Howe Hall. *The Story of the Battle Hymn of the Republic.* New York, Harper & Bros., 1916.

58. Richard B. Harwell. *Confederate Music.* Chapel Hill, Univ. of North Carolina Press, 1950.

59. Richard B. Harwell. *Songs of the Confederacy.* New York, Broadcast Music, Inc., 1951.

60. John H. Hewitt. *Shadows on the Wall—or Glimpses of the Past.* Baltimore, Turnbull Bros., 1877.

61. Waldemar Hille. *The People's Songbook.* New York, Boni & Gaer, 1948.

62. *History of the Battle of Atlanta.* Also containing Confederate songs and poems. Knoxville, Ga., C. B. H. Moncrief, 1940.

63. John Tasker Howard. *A Treasury of Stephen Foster.* New York, Random House, 1946.

64. Arthur Palmer Hudson. *Folksongs of Mississippi and Their Background.* Chapel Hill, Univ. of North Carolina Press, 1936.

65. Hutchinson (family). *Hutchinson Family's Book of Poetry.* Containing 67 of their most popular songs. Boston, S. Chism-Franklin Printing House, 1858.

66. Burl Ives. *The Burl Ives Songbook.* New York, Ballantine Books, 1953.

67. George Stuyvesant Jackson. *Early Songs of Uncle Sam.* Boston, Bruce Humphries, 1933.

68. Helen Kendrick Johnson. *Our Familiar Songs, and Those Who Made Them.* New York, Henry Holt & Co., 1881, 1909.

69. James Weldon Johnson and J. Rosamond Johnson. *The Books of American Negro Spirituals.* New York, Viking Press, 1925.

70. S. B. Jones. *Twenty Favorite Songs of the Grand Army of the Republic.* Omaha, Republican Publishing and Printing House, 1882.

71. Philip D. Jordan. *Singin' Yankees.* Minneapolis, Univ. of Minnesota Press, 1946.

72. Philip D. Jordan. *Songs of Yesterday.* Garden City, N.Y., Doubleday Doran & Co., 1941.

73. Charles O'Brien Kennedy. *A Treasury of American Ballads.* New York, McBride Co., 1954.

74. Frazar Kirkland. *The Pictorial Book of Anecdotes and Incidents of the War of the Rebellion.* Hartford, Conn., Hartford Pub. Co., 1866.

75. John Lair. *Songs Lincoln Loved.* New York, Duell, Sloan, & Pearce, 1954.

76. MacEdward Leach. *The Ballad Book.* New York, Harper & Bros., 1955.

77. John C. Linehan, "The Music and Songs of the War," Chapter 38 of Lieutenant Charles N. Kent, *History of the 17th Regiment New Hampshire Volunteer Infantry, 1862–1863.* Concord, N.H., Seventeenth New Hampshire Veterans Assn., 1898.

78. E. W. Locke. *Three Years in Camp and Hospital.* Boston, George D. Russell & Co., 1870.

79. Arthur Loesser. *Humor in American Song.* New York, Howell, Soskin, & Co., 1942.

80. John A. Lomax and Alan Lomax. *American Ballads and Folksongs.* New York, Macmillan, 1934. (Dover, 1994.)

81. John A. Lomax and Alan Lomax. *Cowboy Songs,* rev. ed. New York, Macmillan, 1957.

82. John A. Lomax and Alan Lomax. *Folksong, U.S.A.* New York, Duell, Sloan, & Pearce, 1947.

83. S. Ward Loper. "The Life of Henry Clay Work." Unpublished manuscript written for the Middlesex County Historical Society, 1907. Photostatic copy on deposit in the New York Public Library.

84. Samuel Lover. *Book of Irish Songs.* Philadelphia, A. Winch, 1860.

85. Frank Luther. *Americans and Their Songs.* New York, Harper & Bros. 1942.

86. Caroline A. Mason (nee Briggs). *Utterance, or Private Voices to the Public Heart: A Collection of Home Poems.* Boston, Phillips, Sampson, & Co., 1852.

87. A. L. Mitchell. *Songs of the Confederacy and Plan-*

tation Melodies. Cincinnati, George B. Jennings Co., 1901.

88. Frank Moore. *The Civil War in Song and Story.* New York, P. F. Collier, 1892.

89. Frank Moore. *Lyrics of Loyalty.* New York, George P. Putnam, 1864.

90. Frank Moore. *Personal and Political Ballads.* New York, George P. Putnam, 1864.

91. Frank Moore. *Rebel Rhymes and Rhapsodies.* New York, George P. Putnam, 1864.

92. Frank Moore. *Songs and Ballads of the Southern People.* New York, D. Appleton & Co., 1886.

93. Frank Moore. *Songs of the Soldiers.* New York, George P. Putnam, 1864.

94. Alton C. Morris. *Folksongs of Florida.* Gainesville, Fla., Univ. of Florida Press, 1950.

95. George Clinton Densmore Odell. *Annals of the New York Stage.* Vol. VI, 1850–57; Vol. VII, 1857–65. New York, Columbia Univ. Press, 1931.

96. *Our National War Songs.* Chicago and Cleveland, S. Brainard's Sons, 1884, 1892.

97. *The Patriotic Glee Book.* Chicago, H. M. Higgins Co., 1863.

98. *The Patriotic Song Book,* new and enlarged edition. 96 pages of songs, duets, and choruses, both sacred and secular, including fourteen pages of prayers for sick and dying soldiers. New York, Horace Waters, 1862.

99. *Picket Line and Campfire Stories.* A collection of war anecdotes both brave and gay, illustrative of the trials and triumphs of soldier life; with a thousand and one humorous stories told of and by Abraham Lincoln, together with a full collection of Northern and Southern songs. By a member of the GAR. New York, Hurst & Co., [188?].

100. G. D. Pike. *The Jubilee Singers, and Their Campaign for Twenty Thousand Dollars.* Boston and New York, Lee & Shepard, 1873.

101. Louise Pound. *American Ballads and Songs.* New York, Charles Scribner's Sons, 1922.

102. Vance Randolph. *Ozark Folksongs.* 4 vols. Columbia, Mo., State Historical Society of Missouri, 1948.

103. Frank Rauscher. *Music on the March.* Philadelphia, William Field & Co., 1892.

104. Harry Reynolds. *Minstrel Memories:* The Story of Burnt Cork Minstrelsy in Great Britain from 1836 to 1927. London, Alston Rivers Ltd., 1928.

105. Dan Rice. *Dan Rice's Great American Humorist Song Book.* 1863.

106. Leroy Rice. *Monarchs of Minstrelsy.* New York, Kenny Pub. Co., 1911.

107. George F. Root. *The Bugle Call.* Cincinnati, John Church & Co., 1863, 1886.

108. George F. Root. *The Silver Lute.* Chicago, Root & Cady, 1865.

109. George F. Root. *The Story of a Musical Life.* Cincinnati, John Church Co., 1891.

110. E. L. Rudolph. *Confederate Broadside Verse.* New Braunfels, Texas, The Book Farm, 1950. Heartman's Historical Series, No. 76.

111. Carl Sandburg. *The American Songbag.* New York, Harcourt, Brace, & Co., 1927.

112. Cecil J. Sharp. *English Folk Songs from the Southern Appalachians.* Edited by Maud Karpeles. 2 vols. London, Oxford Univ. Press, 1932.

113. Elie Siegmeister and Olin Downes. *A Treasury of American Song.* New York, Howell, Soskin, & Co., 1940.

114. Irwin Silber. *Lift Every Voice.* New York, People's Artists, Inc., 1953.

115. William Gilmore Simms. *War Poetry of the South.* New York, Richardson & Co., 1867.

116. W. G. Smith. *Grand Army War Songs.* Cleveland and Chicago, S. Brainard's Sons, 1886.

117. *Soldiers and Sailors Patriotic Songs.* New York, Loyal Publication Society, 1864.

118. *Songs for War-Time.* German airs with English words. Boston, Gould & Lincoln, 1863.

119. *Songs of Dixie.* New York and Chicago, S. Brainard's Sons, 1890.

120. *Southern War Poetry of the Civil War.* Philadelphia, Hershey Press, 1918.

121. *Southern War Songs.* A collection of war songs of the South by the Ladies of the Marietta Memorial Assn., for the benefit of the Confederate Cemetery at Marietta, Georgia. Atlanta, The Franklin Printing & Pub. Co., 1895.

122. Sigmund Spaeth. *A History of Popular Music in America.* New York, Random House, 1948.

123. Sigmund Spaeth. *Read 'Em and Weep.* New York, Doubleday, Page, & Co., 1925.

124. Sigmund Spaeth and Dailey Paskman. *Gentlemen, Be Seated!:* A Parade of the Old-Time Minstrels. Garden City, N.Y., Doubleday Doran & Co., 1928.

125. Kate E. Staton. *Old Southern Songs of the Period of the Confederacy.* New York, Samuel French, 1926. The Dixie Trophy Collection.

126. Jean Thomas. *Ballad Makin' in the Mountains of Kentucky.* New York, Henry Holt Co., 1939.

127. Harold W. Thompson. *Body, Boots and Britches.* Philadelphia, J. B. Lippincott Co., 1940.

128. Harold W. Thompson. *A Pioneer Songster.* Texts from the Stevens-Douglass Manuscript of Western New York, 1841–1856. Ithaca, N.Y., Cornell Univ. Press, 1958.

129. *The Trumpet of Freedom.* New York, W. A. Pond & Co., 1864.

130. *War Songs,* 1st and 2d ed. Boston, Oliver Ditson Co., 1883, 1906.

131. *War Songs of the Blue and the Gray.* New York, Hurst & Co., 1905.

132. Richard Grant White. *National Hymns: How They Are Written and How They Are Not Written.* New York, Rudd & Carleton, 1861.

133. Albert E. Wier. *Songs of the Sunny South.* New York, D. Appleton & Co., 1929.

134. Alfred M. Williams. *Studies in Folk Song and Popular Poetry.* London, Elliot Stock, 1895.

135. Carl Wittke. *Tambo and Bones: A History of the American Minstrel Stage.* Durham, N.C., Duke Univ. Press, 1930.

REFERENCES

136. Bertram G. Work. *Songs of Henry Clay Work.* New York, J. J. Little & Ives Co., 1920.

137. John W. Work. *American Negro Songs.* New York, Howell, Soskin, & Co., 1940.

II. SONGSTERS OF THE CIVIL WAR AND MID-NINETEENTH CENTURY

138. *Allan's Lone Star Ballads.* Written during Confederate Times. A collection of Southern patriotic songs compiled by Francis D. Allan. Galveston, Texas, J. D. Sawyer, 1874.

139. *American Anthems on the Triumph of Liberty and Union over Slavery and Treason.* Edited by Henry O'Reilly. New York American News Co., 1865.

140. *Angelo's Original Comic Songs.* Philadelphia, A. Winch, 1862.

141. *The Arkansas Traveler's Songster.* New York, Dick & Fitzgerald, 1863.

142. *The Banner Songster.* New York, American News Co., 1865.

143. *Beadle's Dime Military Song Book and Songs for the War.* New York, Beadle & Co., 1860.

144. *Beadle's Dime Song Books.* 15 vols. New York, Beadle & Co., 1858–64.

145. *Beadle's Dime Union Song Books.* 4 vols. New York, Beadle & Co., 1861–65.

146. *Ben Cotton's Own Songster,* No. 2. San Francisco, D. E. Appleton & Co., 1864.

147. *Billy Morris' Songs.* As sung at Morris Brothers, Pell and Trowbridge's Opera House. Boston, G. D. Russell & Co., 1864.

148. *The Campfire Companion.* A choice collection of songs for the soldier. Philadelphia, King & Baird, 1861.

149. *The Campfire Songster.* New York, Dick & Fitzgerald, 1862.

150. *Camp Songs.* Boston, Oliver Ditson Co., 1862.

151. *The Double Quick Comic Songster.* New York, Dick & Fitzgerald, 1862.

152. *The Flag of Our Union Songster.* A collection of patriotic Union and naval songs, original and selected, from the best authors, and adapted to the times. New York, T. W. Strong, 1861.

153. *Frank Brower's Black Diamond Songster.* New York, Dick & Fitzgerald, 1863.

154. *Fred May's Comic Irish Songster.* Containing all the most popular Irish comic songs as sung by Fred May & J. H. Ogden. New York, Dick & Fitzgerald, 1862.

155. *The Granite Songster.* Songs of the Hutchinson Family—without the music. Boston, A. B. Hutchinson, 1847.

156. *The Guiding Star Songster.* New York, American News Co., 1865.

157. *Gus Williams' Old Fashioned GAR Camp-Fire Songster.* New York, Frank Tousey, n.d.

158. *Harrison's Comic Songster.* New York, Dick & Fitzgerald, 1862.

159. *Hopkins' New Orleans 5-Cent Songbook.* New Orleans, John Hopkins, 1861.

160. *Hutchinson Family Book of Words.* Boston, J. S. Potter & Co., 1855.

161. *Hutchinson's Republican Songster for the Campaign of 1860.* New York, O. Hutchinson, 1860.

162. *The Jack Morgan Songster.* Compiled by a captain in General Lee's Army. Raleigh, N.C., Bronson & Farrar, 1864.

163. *Joe English's Irish and Comic Songster.* New York, Dick & Fitzgerald, 1864.

164. *John Brown and the Union Right or Wrong Songster.* San Francisco, D. Appleton & Co., 1863.

165. *Johnson's New Comic Songs,* No. 2. San Francisco, D. Appleton & Co., 1863.

166. *Lanigan's Ball Comic Songster.* Containing a choice collection of Irish songs, Dutch songs, burlesque speeches, scarps of fun, and popular comic songs. New York, Dick & Fitzgerald, 1863.

167. *The Little Mac Songster.* New York, Dick & Fitzgerald, 1862.

168. *McClellan Campaign Melodist.* A collection of patriotic campaign songs in favor of The Constitution and the Union, the election of General McClellan, the restoration of the Federal Authority, and the speedy extermination of treason. Edited by Sidney Herbert. New York, B. W. Hitchcock, 1864.

169. *The Negro Melodist.* Containing a great variety of the most popular airs, songs, and melodies, comic, humorous, sentimental, and patriotic. Cincinnati, C. P. James, [186?].

170. *Paddy Is the Boy Songster.* New York, Dick & Fitzgerald, [186?].

171. *Psalms of Freedom for the American Patriot.* New York, George Leach, 1861.

172. *Red, White and Blue Songster.* New York, J. J. Feeks, 1861.

173. *Red, White and Blue Songster,* No. 1. National patriotic songs written to popular airs. Indianapolis, C. O. Perrine, 1861.

174. *The Republican Campaign Songster.* A collection of lyrics, original and selected, specifically prepared for the friends of freedom in the campaign of 'Fifty-Six. New York and Auburn, N.Y. Miller, Orton, & Mulligan, 1856.

175. *The Republican Campaign Songster for 1860.* Compiled by William H. Burleigh. New York, H. Dayton, 1860.

176. *The Rough and Ready Songster.* By an American Officer. New York, Nafis & Cornish, [184?].

177. *Songs for the Great Campaign of 1860.* Compiled by C. W. Civis. New York, New York *Tribune,* 1860.

178. *Songs for the Union.* A collection of patriotic, national, original and selected songs, several of which have been written to suit the times. Philadelphia, A. Winch, 1861.

179. *Songs of Love and Liberty.* Compiled by a North Carolina lady. Raleigh, N. C., Branson & Farrar, 1864.

REFERENCES

180. *Songs of the Nation for 1861.* New York, Minard W. Wilson, 1861.
181. *Songs of the South.* Richmond, J. W. Randolph, 1862.
182. *The Southern Monthly.* Collection of patriotic songs and heroic poems. Memphis, Tenn., Hutton & Freligh, 1862.
183. *Tent and Forecastle Songster.* New York, Dick & Fitzgerald, 1862.
184. *Tony Pastor's Comic Songster.* New York, 1864.
185. *Tony Pastor's "444" Combination Songster.* Embracing all the new comic and Irish lyrics, as sung by that celebrated vocalist and comedian. New York, Dick & Fitzgerald, 1864.

186. *Touch the Elbow Songster.* New York, Dick & Fitzgerald, 1862.
187. *War Songs of the American Union.* Applicable to the present issue and to the right side of that issue. Boston, William V. Spencer, 1861.
188. *War Songs of the South.* Edited by "Bohemian," correspondent for *The Richmond Dispatch.* Richmond, West & Johnson, 1862.
189. *Yankee Doodle Songster.* Philadelphia, A. Winch, 1861.
190. *The Young Volunteer Campaign Melodist.* Compiled by Sidney Herbert. Boston, 1864.

III. PERIODICALS

191. *The Abraham Lincoln Quarterly.* Published by Abraham Lincoln Assn., Springfield, Ill.
     Philip D. Jordan, "Some Lincoln and Civil War Songs." Sept., 1942.
192. *The Century Magazine.*
     Brander Matthews, "The Songs of the War," August, 1887.
193. *Civil War History.* Published by State Univ. of Iowa, Iowa City. Vol. IV, No. 3, of this quarterly is devoted to Civil War Music, and contains, among others, the following articles:
     a. Kenneth A. Bernard, "Lincoln and the Music of the Civil War."
     b. Fred Blum, "Music During the Civil War: A Preliminary Survey."
     c. Gilbert Chase, "A Note on Negro Spirituals."
     d. Dena J. Epstein, "The Battle Cry of Freedom."
     e. Richard B. Harwell, "The Star of the Bonnie Blue Flag."
     f. Hans Nathan, "Emmett's Walk-Arounds."
     g. Boyd B. Stutler, "John Brown's Body."
194. *Journal of American Folklore.*
     a. E. M. Backus—Cradle Songs of Negroes in North Carolina; Vol. 7, 1894.
     b. Arthur Palmer Hudson—Ballads and Songs from Mississippi; Vol. 39, 1926.
     c. G. L. Kittredge—Ballads and Songs; Vol. 30, 1912.
     d. Henry E. Mellinger—Still More Ballads and Folk Songs from the Southern Highlands; Vol. 45, 1932.

     e. Ruth Ann Musick—The Old Album of William A. Larkin; Vol. 60, 1947.
     f. Bess Alice Owens—Songs of the Cumberlands; Vol. 49, 1936.
     g. Edwin F. Piper—Some Play-Party Games of the Middle West; Vol. 28, 1915.
195. *Maryland Historical Magazine.*
     Ralph Semmes, "Civil War Song Sheets." Vol. XXXVIII, No. 3 (Sept. 1943).
196. *Notes* (Music Library Assn.).
     a. Dena J. Epstein, "Music Publishing in Chicago Before 1871": Chap. III, "Root and Cady Prior to the Civil War"; Chap. IV, "The Civil War Period." Second Series, Vol. 2, No. 1 (Dec., 1944) and No. 2 (March, 1945).
     b. Richard S. Hill, "The Mysterious Chord of Henry Clay Work" (in two parts). Second Series, Vol. 10, No. 2 (March, 1953) and No. 3 (June, 1953).
197. *The Palimpsest* (State Historical Society of Iowa).
     Pauline Grahame, "Some Songs of Long Ago." March, 1929.
198. *The People's Songs Bulletin.*
     Monthly magazine of People's Songs, Inc., published in New York, 1946–49, containing songs and articles on folk song and topical song.
199. *Sing Out!*
     Quarterly magazine of folksong, published by Sing Out, Inc., New York, beginning 1950, containing numerous articles and songs pertinent to the subject of this collection.

IV. BIBLIOGRAPHICAL SOURCES ON GENERAL HISTORY

200. James Truslow Adams. *Album of American History,* Vol. III, 1853–1893. New York, Scribner's Sons, 1946.
201. *Battles and Leaders of the Civil War.* 4 vols. New ed. pub. by Thomas Yoseloff, Inc., New York, 1956.
202. Mark M. Boatner, III. *The Civil War Dictionary.* New York, David McKay Co., 1959.
203. Bruce Catton. *Mr. Lincoln's Army.* New York, Doubleday & Co., 1951.

204. *The Civil War.* 2 vols. New York, Grosset & Dunlap, 1956.
     a. Otto Eisenschiml and Ralph Newman. *The American Iliad.*
     b. Ralph Newman and E. B. Long. *The Picture Chronicle.*
205. Earl Conrad. *Harriet Tubman.* Washington, D.C., Associated Publishers Inc., 1943.
206. Rossiter Johnson. *Campfires and Battlefields:* A

REFERENCES

Pictorial Narrative of the Civil War. New York, The Blue and the Gray Press, 1958.

207. Benjamin Quarles. *The Negro in the Civil War.* Boston, Little, Brown & Co., 1953.

208. Carl Sandburg. *Abraham Lincoln: The War Years.* 4 vols. New York, Harcourt, Brace, & Co., 1939.

209. O. G. Villard. *John Brown.* Boston, Houghton, Mifflin Co., 1910.

210. Irving Werstein. *July, 1863.* New York, Julian Messner Inc., 1957.

211. Bell Irvin Wiley. *The Common Soldier in the Civil War.* Originally in two volumes as *The Life of Billy Yank* and *The Life of Johnny Reb.* New York, Grosset & Dunlap, 1951.

V. DISCOGRAPHY

212. Moses Asch. *Ballads of the Civil War.* Separate accompanying text to Ref. 213 containing song lyrics and extensive historical background. New York, Folkways Records, FH5004.

213. *Ballads of the Civil War.* Sung by Hermes Nye. 2 records. New York, Folkways Records. FH5004.

214. *Bay State Ballads.* Sung by Paul Clayton. New York, Folkways Records, FA2106.

215. *Cumberland Mountain Folksongs.* Sung by Paul Clayton. New York, Folkways Records, FA2007.

216. *Folk Music of the United States: Songs and Ballads of American History and of the Assassination of Presidents.* Archive of American Folk Song, Library of Congress, Music Division, Washington, D.C., AAFS L29.

217. *Ohio State Ballads.* Sung by Anne Grimes. New York, Folkways Records, FH5217.

218. *Songs and Ballads of America's Wars.* Sung by Frank Warner. New York, Elektra Records, EKL13.

219. *Songs of a New York Lumberjack.* Sung by Ellen Stekert. New York, Folkways Records, FA2354.

220. *Songs of the North and South.* Sung by Frank Luther and Zora Layman with the Century Quartet. New York, Decca Records, DL8093.

221. *The Confederacy.* Richard Bales conducting the National Gallery Orchestra and the *Cantata Choir of the Lutheran Church of the Reformation.* New York, Columbia Records, DL220.

222. *Wolf River Songs.* Recorded by Sidney Robertson Cowell. New York, Folkways Records, FM4001.

223. *The Union.* Richard Bales conducting the National Gallery Orchestra and the Cantata Choir of the Lutheran Church of the Reformation. New York, Columbia Records, DL244.

I. Index to Titles

INDEX TO TITLES

II. Index to First Lines

III. General Index

GENERAL INDEX